CW00554308

PENGUIN

THE MOTHER-IN-LAW

Veena Venugopal is the editor of *BLink*, the Saturday edition of the *Hindu Business Line*. She is the author of *Would You Like Some Bread with That Book?*

The
Mother-in-Law

The other woman in your marriage

VEENA VENUGOPAL

PENGUIN BOOKS

PENGUIN BOOKS
Published by the Penguin Group
Penguin Books India Pvt. Ltd, 11 Community Centre, Panchsheel Park,
New Delhi 110 017, India
Penguin Group (USA) Inc., 375 Hudson Street, New York, New York 10014, USA
Penguin Group (Canada), 90 Eglinton Avenue East, Suite 700, Toronto, Ontario,
M4P 2Y3, Canada (a division of Pearson Penguin Canada Inc.)
Penguin Books Ltd, 80 Strand, London WC2R 0RL, England
Penguin Ireland, 25 St Stephen's Green, Dublin 2, Ireland (a division of
Penguin Books Ltd)
Penguin Group (Australia), 707 Collins Street, Melbourne, Victoria 3008, Australia
(a division of Pearson Australia Group Pty Ltd)
Penguin Group (NZ), 67 Apollo Drive, Rosedale, Auckland 0632, New Zealand
(a division of Pearson New Zealand Ltd)
Penguin Group (South Africa) (Pty) Ltd, Block D, Rosebank Office Park,
181 Jan Smuts Avenue, Parktown North, Johannesburg 2193, South Africa

Penguin Books Ltd, Registered Offices: 80 Strand, London WC2R 0RL, England

First published by Penguin Books India 2014

Copyright © Veena Venugopal 2014

ISBN 9780143419877

Typeset in Adobe Caslon Pro by R. Ajith Kumar, New Delhi
Printed at Yash Printographics, Noida

Contents

Introduction

I got married at twenty-three for reasons related to real estate. My boyfriend and I graduated from business school to discover that we didn't make enough money to pay auto fares between his place and mine to see each other every day. We were forced to live together, there was no choice. In Mumbai in the late 1990s, you had to pretend you were married if you wanted to rent a house. So I bought a black, beaded mangalsutra from a store outside the railway station, boyfriend negotiated a house with a low deposit and we were in the business of false matrimony and authentic cohabitation.

We were very happy. For a few weeks, that is. One evening, boyfriend came home from work and asked that I pack up all my stuff, including 'the three dozen tiny bottles of indeterminate purpose in the bathroom'.

'Why?' I asked, incredulous.

'My father has filed a suit against someone in the Mumbai High Court, he is coming tomorrow and staying until Tuesday. Mummy is coming with him, just to meet me.'

I spent all evening packing and hating at first the man who

bounced a cheque and forced my boyfriend's father to file a case. As the minutes ticked past, I managed to transfer all that anger to my boyfriend's father and, for good measure, his mother. I moved out and stayed with a friend and, on Tuesday evening, arrived bag and baggage to resume my life. This carried on. Every couple of months, there was a hearing in the court, or a meeting with a lawyer or some other, what I thought as inconsequential activity but which absolutely required that my boyfriend's parents visit Mumbai.

By the end of that year, I knew we had only two choices. Either he rent an apartment he could move into while his parents visited or we get married and live legitimately in this one. The first option was financially unviable and so, just like that, even before I had time to think about 'other opportunities', real estate forced my hand into marriage.

Once we decided, though, I was determined to forgive my soon-to-be in-laws' frequent jaunts to Mumbai. Friends asked me how I planned to 'deal' with my mother-in-law. Other than as a reason to get married, I hadn't really thought about her. When I did, I was certain that I didn't want my relationship with my mother-in-law to be reduced to a cliché. I did not want to be the sort of person who began all conversations with 'you won't believe what a bitch my mother-in-law is'. I told myself we would be cordial and pleasant. Yet, even then, flushed at the prospect of matrimony at twenty-three, I was sensible enough not to answer, 'Why, she'll be like my own mum of course!'

After the wedding, Mummy and I settled down to a comfortable indifference. We didn't live in the same city, so we met rarely. Since I was legitimately married by then, I saw no sense in wearing a mangalsutra. She raised this matter a couple of times, but in a defeated, I-don't-want-to-make-an-issue-out-of-it kind of way. 'My own daughter does not wear one, how can I ask you to,' was her standard strategy. I suppose a better daughter-in-law would have immediately slapped the mangalsutra on and demonstrated how she was better than the daughter, but despite the fact that I had three of them (one their way, one our way and one fake) I just smiled and agreed with her that she couldn't ask me if her daughter wasn't wearing one.

We didn't speak the same language, although she does speak reasonably good English, and I used that as an excuse not to take on the responsibility of calling and checking on her. I did remind the husband every once in a while that he was supposed to call his mother, though. For the first five years of my marriage, to be honest, Mummy was a benign presence with potential for trouble far away somewhere, like the threat of an asteroid collision or nuclear warfare.

When I was about to have a baby, Mummy became a more prominent player in my life. Since my gynaecologist had said she would have to induce labour, it gave enough time for two sets of grandparents to assemble in our tiny apartment in Mumbai. As things turned out, the baby, when she was born, weighed precariously little, and was moved to the neonatal intensive care unit for about ten days. By the time, we came back home, I was already a guilt-ridden, harried mum.

Then started the grandmothers' regimen. There were some forty must-dos and never-don'ts in my mother's list and some hundred things in mother-in-law's list. Between the two of them and a frail baby who had to be fed every three hours by the clock, I was a mess. That was when trouble began. My mother, I could yell at. If she rebuked me for not eating the boiled root of an itchy tuber that was supposed to help snap my uterus back into shape, I could ask her to shut up. She was my mother, it was my right.

But when Mummy wheeled out her instructions, I had only two choices. I could follow them or I could pretend to follow them. I chose the latter but after the first week realized I didn't even have the energy for duplicity. So she instructed, I ignored and resentment built up rapidly on both sides. Every time the baby cried or didn't poop or threw up, Mummy told her son the list of things I had neglected. I complained to him about her endless harassment. Husband did the only thing he knows to do well, he dived for his BlackBerry and buried his nose in it.

Eventually, some five months after the baby was born, Mummy left. By this point, we were barely talking to each other. Despite myself, I realized, we had become the cliché. I found it hard to muster the courtesy required to even say goodbye. And when I had friends over that evening, after we'd opened the beers and cheered loudly, it felt different. I felt a lot freer, like an actual physical weight had been lifted off my shoulder. I couldn't pretend to be sad, not even a little bit. I was being a bitch, I realized, but then so was she.

Over the next few months, our relationship improved. She would often call to inquire about the baby, and I managed to revert to an earlier time when there was more respect and dignity in our conversations. She was careful not to nag me with instructions and I was careful not to let her feel like she wasn't a part of her granddaughter's life.

Two years later, when the baby was a toddler, we moved to Delhi. Well, the husband moved first, when he took up a new job. I had a work-from-home gig, which wouldn't be valid in Delhi, and more importantly had managed to lure the best nanny in the neighbourhood. Safely ensconced in these two hope-affirming life conditions, I refused to move. The husband pleaded, he was missing the child and it was getting too expensive for him to visit every weekend. By then I was smart enough to know that in a toss-up between being with the husband and retaining a good nanny, the latter is the wiser choice.

So I declined the prospect of wider roads and ice creams at India Gate. Eventually, after months of heavily dropping hints, the nanny said that she was ready to move with us to Delhi. Once the nanny blessed the deal, I began the process of negotiating for a transfer. The transfer came through and we quickly got our stuff packed and were ready to move. With three days to go, the nanny had a change of heart. The place was too far, she said, and her family wasn't ready to let her go. I cajoled her for a bit and then cried. But there was no moving the nanny. I did the only sensible thing I could think of: I got the husband to call his mother.

'But you swore you'd never live with her,' he pointed out, helpfully.

'I also swore we'd have sex every night. Things change, now dial the number,' I snapped.

So it was, that when I landed in Delhi it was with Mummy in tow. In a few weeks, we settled into a better rhythm. Setting up the house, finding a play school, not to mention hiring an army of domestic help were team activities and we managed to negotiate these well. I went to work, she supervised the house. It was all rather pleasant. On Fridays, without fail, she instructed the housekeeper to keep the beers in the fridge. If I stopped by to shop on my way back from work, I always made sure I picked something up for her.

In the early months, Mummy was the epitome of cool. One night our friends upstairs threw a massive party. The man was turning forty and the wife, as modern wives are expected to, hired the services of a professional belly dancer for the evening. When I went up at ten for the party, the wife pulled me aside and asked if it was OK if the belly dancer changed into her costume at my house. Of course, I said, that shouldn't be a problem. At eleven, the wife told me the belly dancer had arrived. At eleven forty, worried about what the hell was going on at home, I went downstairs to check.

In the flat, I noticed that my bedroom was locked. The belly dancer was either going through my stuff or getting into hers. When I peeped into the family room, I was struck by the strangest sight. Mummy and a much-muscled man, with a bald head and a baseball bat, were calmly seated and watching Telugu television. 'This is the bouncer,' Mummy introduced us and I didn't know whether to laugh or kiss her. The next morning, I thought she would have a list of complaints about our bad behaviour and rowdy friends. When husband emerged from the room, all she asked him was if the belly dancer was still inside the bedroom. He said no. She had no further questions.

So we were equable, in that sense, Mummy and I. Still, we were careful around each other. Overall, I would say that at least for a few months we managed to be the anti-cliché.

Then the small irritants began. I hated the fact that mother-in-law was a fan of deep-frying everything. First, I provided feedback. Then I took to chanting the health implications of fried food at each mealtime. When that wasn't heeded, I began serving myself minuscule portions. When she, encouraged by my opposition, deep-fried curd, I simply stopped eating anything other than the basic chapatti and dal. In return, mother-in-law boycotted the Sunday treat I cooked—pastas, grilled fish, stews and salads, which she had relished earlier.

Mummy began to talk more and more about how casual we were. It took me a few weeks to realize that when she said casual, she meant careless. I had lent a music player to a friend. Two weeks later, the friend called and apologized for not returning it before we asked for it. 'Who asked for it?' I was bewildered. 'Your mother-in-law,' she said. I went home and told her she should stay out of my transactions just like I stayed out of hers. So that became an issue. One year passed and then the next. And our annoyances with each other began to grow. We went through phases of snapping at each other. Then we went through weeks when we wouldn't speak to each other. The husband stayed out of much of this. If I complained to him about his mother, he would either nod his head in absent-minded agreement or annoyingly ask me to 'take a chill pill.'

The one meal that the family ate together was dinner. Mummy pulled her endgame for this. She began to converse with husband in Telugu. The toddler, who was by then almost five, and I, had no idea what was going on. The toddler asked for explanations, I refused to let on that I cared. They may have been talking about the weather or what was on TV. But I was certain it was about me and that they weren't being complimentary. My simmering tensions with mother-in-law spread to husband too. I asked him why they were speaking in a language I couldn't follow. 'Arre, we were just talking about nothing, certainly nothing about you,' he would say. But I was convinced it was a conspiracy.

Finally, late one night, there was a rare occurrence of marital passion. The dog, which usually liked to be a semi-passive observer of his guardians' sex life, was locked out of the room. Since he knew something was up and was reluctant to miss any of the action, he began to bark. It was a yelp a minute at first. But soon he worked himself into a frenzy of noise and spit. And right there, while we were in flagrante and trying to wrap up our business, mother-in-law opened the door to let the dog in. There was nothing we could say to one another after that. I resigned myself to a life of never making eye contact with her. Ever. Nor would I ever be able to have any kind of nocturnal excitement without eternally worrying about how many locks on the door were engaged. Mummy had won.

In the last year, I spoke to scores of women about their mothers-in-law. The stories I heard were so insane and so weird that my own account of Mummy seemed like fluff. Most of the time, my story merely ended up annoying the listener, like when thin people say they don't diet and are just genetically disposed to be skinny.

From Kolkata to Mumbai and Delhi to Chennai, I met women who occupied some point of the cliché scale with their mothers-in-law. No matter whom you talk to—new brides, old wives, Hindu, Christian, Muslim, Anglo-Indian—just about every married Indian woman is engaged in close combat with her mother-in-law.

Their stories just needed the slightest prod to bubble up to the surface. Get a bunch of married women together, any bunch, and simply say, 'Goodness, you won't believe my mother-in-law.'

Then, shut up and listen. Out come stories of control, betrayal and harassment. After the first few meetings, I stopped being surprised by the fact that everyone seemed to have a dispute with their mothers-in-law. But what continued to shock me was how intensely damaged most of these relationships were. Most daughters-in-law, it seemed to me, were huddled at the extreme end of the cliché scale.

Within minutes (*minutes!*) of posting a Facebook request asking if someone knew anyone who had had a typical arranged marriage (yes, that was the only qualifier I published, since I did not want to reveal the reason why I was asking) not only did I find someone who had taken the matrimonial ad, horoscope route to marriage, but one who had a mother-in-law so rotten, just listening about her gave me a migraine. 'It can't be,' I kept hearing myself, 'it just cannot be so easy!' But it was.

And I'm sure if I had cast my net a little wider, I would have heard stories that would have given me not just a migraine, but a whole brain tumour. It's true, a monster mother-in-law is a national affliction. Even women who told me they were lucky to have a decent mother-in-law often proceeded to recount a really bad story about their Mummyji. That's how bad the situation is.

Mother-in-law maladies are neither new nor are they restricted to India. In the West, the mother-in-law is an endless subject of jokes. But in South Asia, even in popular culture, the mother-in-law has traditionally been a source of much angst and villainy. Yet, the more people I talked to, the more it seemed to me that in India the mother-in-law dynamic has worsened over the years.

We now live in a society that was unimaginable twenty years ago. There is no doubt that our lives have improved since 1991. We don't have to suffer *Krishi Darshan*, Campa Cola or multi-year wait lists to buy really badly made cars.

Economic liberalization brought with it social liberalization, too. We have a surfeit of options and ample liberty in choosing what we wear, the kind of degrees we want to pursue and the kind of places we would like to visit. We are far more open, liberated and in control of all aspects of our lives.

The only exception, to me, seems to be our relationship with our mothers-in-law. In the last twenty years, there has been an utter breakdown in the Mummyji–daughter-in-law dynamic. In urban India, pretty much all daughters-in-law, across all demographics, are more educated than they were twenty years ago. The middle-class daughter has been raised with the notion that she is capable of doing everything her brother is. They have been educated with a career in mind. And when they graduate, a large majority of women seek employment. If they work in fields like IT, it is more likely than not that they travel abroad on projects. So when they are ready to get married—at twenty-four on an average, or twenty-five—they have lived a bit, formed their opinions and decided on their choices.

Mummyji, however, is stuck at *Mughal-e-Azam*. She has raised her daughter to be independent and liberal, because that was the cue she got from others around her. She thinks of the freedom she allows her daughter as a short vacation. She constantly tells her daughter that she shouldn't expect to be allowed to behave in a 'modern' fashion once she gets married and goes to her husband's home. And she hasn't thought about how liberated her daughter-in-law should be.

She assumes the husband's home is the place where cultural control is maintained. So even compared to her own daughter, she tends to have stricter rules for the daughter-in-law. That right there is the reason why this is the worst generation for Mummyji conflicts. Daughters-in-law who expect to live modern, post-liberalized lives are finding themselves stuck with pre-liberalized Mummyjis. Expectations are asymmetric. It is a mismatch made in hell. This is the reason we were watching *Yeh Jo Hai Zindagi* on TV in 1989 and we are watching one or the other descendant of *Kyunki Saas Bhi Kabhi Bahu Thi* now.

Lalitha, a sixty-year-old daughter-in-law I met in Bangalore, dealt with her mother-in-law's taunts as a young wife by simply tuning her out. She neither confronted nor argued with her. 'I would let this in from one ear and let it out through the other,' she told me. But Payal, a thirty-four-year-old daughter-in-law in Mumbai, wasn't going to let her mother-in-law's accusations go unchallenged. She took her on, confident that her own parents were supporting her in this battle, and eventually changed her living situation to one that was favourable to her.

Supportive parents are a running theme. When urban, educated daughters complain to their parents about the unfairness of their in-laws, they aren't sent back with the refrain that they must compromise and just live with the situation. Most modern and indulgent parents tell their daughters not to go back until things are permanently and favourably resolved. This gives rise to a whole other set of problems. Most daughters-in-law who have been yelled at by their mothers-in-law tell me that the first abuse that is hurled at them is about their own parents. 'What kind of an upbringing have you had?' is a line I consistently ran into.

The very construct of the mother-in-law relationship is lopsided. It is built to be awkward. This can be gleaned from just the nomenclature. In north India mothers-in-law are often called Mummyji. If mother-in-law were Mummy, it would imply that the daughter-in-law could interact with her with the intimacy and honesty that a relationship with Mummy implies. The 'ji' in Mummyji forces respect, decorum and a definite imbalance in the power structure of the relationship. Perhaps, daughters-in-law are much better off addressing Mummyji as Auntyji. That way they aren't forcing the baggage of unconditional maternal love. At best, you expect Auntyji to be polite and friendly. At worst, you expect her to be distant and indifferent. With Mummy, you expect tolerance and affection. Then the 'ji' gets stuck on, and all you get is unmitigated authority and unadulterated bitchiness.

The following chapters showcase several nasty Mummyjis, through stories told by their daughters-in-law. These women are urban, educated and raised to make something of their own lives. Yet the minute they married, the cliché came alive in their lives. You may identify with some of their stories—these may be events and incidents that happened to you or someone you know. Some stories are so nasty, you'd be glad you weren't a part of it. All accounts are true, only the names of women and some identifying traits have been altered. This is merely a small sample of the madness of Mummyji. Beyond the cities and the demographic of the financially secure, the stories only get worse.

At the heart of the mother-in-law–daughter-in-law conflict lies control. The sheer number of things the mother-in-law tries to control took me by surprise. First up, she wants to control the decision of who becomes her daughter-in-law. There is often a long list of qualifying criteria that puts an admission form for Harvard University to shame. If the daughter-in-law qualifies on all these fronts, it is still wrong to assume that Mummyji has found the perfect girl. It merely means that she has found her perfect moulding clay. She has seen potential. Mummyji is smart enough to know that a flawless daughter-in-law is the one she has made herself, like her son's favourite besan ka laddoo; no one else can do it right.

Rachna Sethi was spotted at a wedding by her future mother-in-law. And through their long and intense courtship, her future mother-in-law systematically changed everything about her. From picking out her outfits to making appointments with her personal trainer and skin specialist, Mummyji was on the job 24×7. The modern Indian marriage follows the ancient Greek script of Pygmalion. The daughter-in-law has to be made to fit to 'our way'. If she has her way, well, God knows what that could lead to!

Forget her way, even in 2013 in urban India, a large number of families don't want the daughter-in-law to even bring her own name into the marriage. While the rest of the world is wondering how to deal with the last name after the marriage—with the current trend pointing to a double-barrelled hers and his—Indian families still change their daughters-in-law's first names. In many communities, especially in north India, changing the name of the daughter-in-law is part of the wedding custom. This wipes her clean of the past and gives her a whole new identity, that of merely being a wife. Even in families where this is not a custom, it is employed as a convenience. When Keisha got married, her husband's family decided she should be called Kamla. Not only was it disorienting for her to be addressed by a name that did not belong to her, she was appalled that even in the wedding invitation, her name was printed as Kamla. The stated excuse was that her name was unpronounceable. Surely, if you can say Asha, you can say Keisha. Arti, who had a proper arranged marriage, was shocked that her mother-in-law picked a new name for her, even though it wasn't the done thing among Kashmiris. Michelle, whose mother-in-law calls her Meena, is a lot more unfazed. She waited four years for her Mummyji to approve of the wedding, she wasn't going to let a small thing like a moniker come in the way of her marriage.

Once the name is sorted, mother-in-law moves her attention to the areas of dress and appearance. There is no fashion police stricter than the Indian mother-in-law. I am surprised it is not yet a show on television. All Mummyjis assume they are in charge of their daughter-in-law's wardrobe. The daughter-in-law contributes to this in a way. Here's a tip: if you are looking to buy shares in a company that is guaranteed to grow, invest your money in a salwar kurta manufacturer. Across the length and breadth of the country, daughters-in-law decide on a salwar kurta as the appropriate attire for that first meeting with Mummyji. Why, even Carla who is from Austria picked a red 'suit' for her first meeting with Mummyji. I must confess, I did too. It seemed like an ideal middle path—traditional enough to be acceptable and not overtly traditional like a sari. Once that original salwar kameez is approved, Mummyji takes over. Most Indian marriages begin with a list of dos and don'ts in the wardrobe department.

Dos
- Must wear mangalsutra, sindoor and all other symbols of being married.
- Salwar kameez must have dupatta.
- Saris are mandatory for all religious and social events.
- Blouses must have sleeves.
- Blouses must have backs that begin at the nape of the neck.
- Blouses must be buttoned down from the first rib.

Don'ts
- No pants
- No jeans
- No skirts
- No capris
- No T-shirts
- No tops
- Nothing that vaguely outlines critical body parts like thighs, breasts, armpits or butt.

When the rules are first laid down, the daughter-in-law agrees to everything. Well, without that, there is often no wedding. In most cases, early on, the girls think these minor sacrifices are worth the man they marry. Slowly, as boyfriend becomes fiancé, husband and then just 'man', the daughter-in-law realizes that she would rather go out looking smashing in that sleeveless crop top and tight jeans than yards of dreary fabric. From then on, it is a savage game of hide-and-seek with Mummyji.

Most urban Indian women are now adept dressers in the car. If you have been reading about layering in the fashion pages of magazines and wondering why in heaven's name women living in a warm, humid tropical country would wear layers, you haven't understood the easiest route to violating the mother-in-law's strictly enforced dress code. Layer at home, de-layer in the car. Good daughter-in-law in a full-sleeved long tunic and salwar leaves the house. Once in the car, in seconds, the tunic is unbuttoned to reveal a thigh-high clingy dress and the salwar comes off to display super smooth waxed legs. The tunic and salwar are folded properly and re-worn when the car is parked at 2 a.m. Only the stupid and the short-sighted would think of walking in, in their party clothes even at that hour. The smart and the intelligent know that Mummyji will be awake and waiting to catch the unsuspecting daughter-in-law for a nocturnal wardrobe violation.

Then there is the other kind of mother-in-law. The one who is focused on presenting a modern, hip bahu to the world. While this Mummyji is more liberal about the kind of clothes the daughter-in-law wears, she has to make absolutely sure that she can carry it off like a supermodel. So she will gift a gym membership to the daughter-in-law and point out to everyone within hearing distance that she has also added on the services of a personal trainer. Then Mummyji will keep an alarm and wake the daughter-in-law up at 5 a.m. so she won't miss her workout. After a while, she adds on other treatments. Some skin-whitening, maybe laser hair treatment, botox, chin-tightening, and other nips and tucks she considers necessary.

The daughter-in-law might be initially delighted with all the attention. But eventually, it fades. She may want to sleep in once in a while or she isn't happy with being zapped, snipped or stretched. But that's not an option since it would delay the daughter-in-law's supermodel debut. While liberal, this Mummyji also is as much a control freak as the no-capri, no-sleeveless Mummyji. Anshika Dewani knew her mother-in-law desired a fair, thin bahu. And while, to the naked eye, she seems both thin and fair, Mummy saw otherwise. For the last five years, Mummy has not only gifted her gym memberships every six months but also hasn't let ten minutes pass without observing how fat Anshika has gotten. Yep, that's every ten minutes. Apparently that's how long it takes for significant cellular growth to be visible.

If appearance is the biggest area of conflict between the modern-day Mummyji and her daughter-in-law, the second is work. Even before they agree to the wedding, most mothers-in-law categorically state that the daughter-in-law should quit her job. It is no wonder at all that even when measured against other culturally similar Asian countries, India has the largest 'leaking pipeline'. This is research-speak for the number of women who quit their jobs between junior and middle levels. In India, about 50 per cent of women employees quit their jobs before they get into middle management roles.

Know why? Because Mummyji is worried that her employed daughter-in-law is having random sex with all kinds of arbitrary men at work. I don't know what mothers-in-law think when they hear the terms 'target', 'performance report' and 'appraisal', but it certainly does not involve sitting across a boardroom table discussing things written on paper. When Nikita's boyfriend, Arun, told his mother that he was keen on marrying his colleague, she put her foot down purely based on the fact that she would not accept a daughter-in-law who worked. Months later, when she was still to bless the union, Nikita told her she was prepared to quit her job. But Mama was not to be moved. 'She has worked in an office once,' she told her son, 'she is tainted for life.'

Deepa's mother-in-law, Neeta Aunty, was even more obtuse. Although she herself had worked right through her marriage, she refused to allow Deepa to. 'If you don't spend a few years getting to know your husband, your marriage will never work,' she told Deepa. Ironically, Neeta Aunty's own marriage apparently never suffered from this lack of 'quantity time'. She was too busy hopping across countries in her job as an air hostess in an international airline. She was also having too much fun lounging around swimming pools in her bikini to worry about getting to know her husband. But Deepa herself wouldn't be allowed any of this.

So if the daughter-in-law isn't allowed to go to work, what is she supposed to do? Why, there is enough work around the house! Yes, she is expected to be a housemaid. Cook, clean, wash, make babies. My Austrian friend, Carla, was aghast at the fact that while her Mummyji insisted she take her turn doing all the chores of the house, she wouldn't for a minute entertain the notion that her son help. When, after months of Carla telling him that the housework was a shared affair, her husband Ankit went to the kitchen to do the dishes, his mother mocked him and chased him out of there. 'What's next?' she asked her son. 'Do you want to wear a sari and some bangles too?'

In a survey of men in Brazil, Croatia, Rwanda, Mexico, Chile and India, only 16 per cent of Indian men said they considered it their responsibility to share the household chores more or less equally. Eighty-six per cent of Indian men said the responsibilities of changing diapers and looking after the children were entirely their wives'. In Brazil, only 10 per cent of men thought so. In Croatia that number was 29 per cent and in Mexico 26 per cent. Yet 81 per cent Indian men concurred that the final decision of anything in their homes was theirs. The poor wife is run off her feet, where does she have the time? What the study illustrates is the importance of laying an example. These men themselves say that if they had seen their fathers help their mothers around the house, they would have been likely to do it themselves. But of course Carla's mother-in-law would never take that risk. A boy. In the kitchen. Ha!

In both the issues of dress code and work, the north Indian Mummyji takes a much stronger stance than the south Indian Amma. While in the north, a strict list of what is acceptable to wear is defined and maintained, the south Indian mother-in-law is usually vague and generic. They expected daughters-in-law to dress 'decently', especially when male members of the family were present. Lalitha, who is both a daughter-in-law and mother-in-law, wears saris herself, but is OK with Michelle dressing as she pleases when she is in New York or Delhi. When Michelle visits her in Bangalore though, she expects her to be 'decent'. She also expects that Michelle wear her mangalsutra all the time. She suspects she does not. But it's not a deal-breaker for Lalitha. At least, not any more. She is also much more comfortable with the fact that Michelle has a career of her own. It didn't occur to her even once to ask her to quit. Even Seema, who was engaged in a multi-year battle with her Tamil Brahmin mother-in-law over a nine-yard sari, never had trouble convincing her mother-in-law of her need for a career. That issue never came up. Not before the wedding, in fact, not even after she had a baby.

Like most trends, Mummyji's need to control all that goes on around her has crossed over from the alarming to the comical. Companies are cashing in on this. If you are ever missing Mummyji and are at a loss as to how to decide what you should do, you can buy a set of mother-in-law dice. Sold by a company called Happily Unmarried, the mother-in-law dice come in sets of four. Each of them has options, such as Sex, Headache, Curry, Chinese, Always, Don't Know, etched on each side. Throw the dice and simply follow the instructions. 'The mother-in-law dice helps you in deciding everything from what to do on weekends to who gets what in case of a fight. A set of four dice for maximum decision making,' is how the company advertises it. It is particularly interesting that the mother-in-law dice also give you an option for a 'headache'.

In a couple of areas, Indian mothers-in-law surprised me positively. The first was about differences in religion or caste. Many of the women I spoke to had chosen their own spouses. Religion and caste didn't seem to be big issues in their Mummyjis' decision of accepting these daughters-in-law. When Supriya married Robert, there was never any conversation about her converting to Christianity. Religion popped its divisive head much later in her marriage. Similarly, even though Deepa's was an arranged marriage, the issue of caste never came up. Their parents decided that the families' outlooks matched and that was good enough for them.

On the other hand, Anshika's mother-in-law wasn't happy that she was marrying her son, even though she was from not just the same caste, but even the same sub-caste. To me it seemed like caste was usually just an excuse for opposition in middle-class urban homes. Mummyji's reluctance with love marriages came from the sense of betrayal that her son had gone ahead and decided whom he wanted to marry, on his own. If the caste or religion was different, then she picked on it as a seemingly credible ground for opposition. If the daughter-in-law was from the same caste, then she merely found something else to criticize.

The other misconception I had was that the Mummyji situation had an economic demographic; that most conflicts between the mother-in-law and the daughter-in-law took place in lower-middle-class and poorer homes. There isn't a more laughable assumption. Payal walked out of her home twice because of her mother-in-law. And her home is in Mumbai's tony neighbourhood, Worli. Keisha, who works in a multinational company in Kolkata, was routinely raped by her husband until a year ago. Not only did her Mataji (who was in the next room and privy to the screams and sounds) not think it a cause worthy enough for her to intervene and put an end to, when Keisha complained to her about it, she told her that, as her husband, it was Ashwin's right to do to her as he pleased. Arti, who isn't even allowed to sit on the sofa in her husband's house, or accidentally step into the air-conditioned room, was traumatized not just by her mother-in-law, but also by her husband's sisters. Her three sisters-in-law are all postgraduates—one is a PhD in fact—and employed in high positions in prestigious organizations. The reality is that the Mummyji torment cuts through class and caste. And in a fight, the language used quickly deteriorates into the abusive and trashy, no matter how rich the family or how educated its members.

The most curious aspect of the sordid mother-in-law saga is the man at the centre of it. The son/husband is the epicentre of the troubles. Yet, he himself remains rather unruffled through them. Recently, I watched an episode of *The Big Bang Theory*. One of the characters, Howard—an astrophysicist—is in space. His new bride, Bernadette, convinces him that it would be best if they lived by themselves when he comes back to earth and not with his loud, annoying mother. Howard agrees. He's too scared to take ownership of the decision, so he pitches it to his mother like it was his wife's idea. The mother yells so loud, she barely needs any equipment to be heard in space. Howard dutifully tells her that he will convince Bernadette and they'll live with her. When Bernadette calls, he doesn't have the, er, balls, to tell her the truth either. So he tells her all is well with the move. His counterpart, a Russian astronaut, cannot believe his country lost the Cold War to wusses like Howard. When he asks him what he plans to do, Howard has only one option. He'll stay in space. Earth is where there are problems between his wife and mother. He's safe in space. He's not the only one. The world is full of conflicted husbands wishing they could be in space and away from the fights between their mothers and wives.

Even though the son/husband is the link between Mummyji and the daughter-in-law, his favourite strategy is to pretend that these tensions don't exist. Most husbands of the women I spoke to were really nice people. They were gentle and loving and most of them made good fathers. When their mothers complained to them about their wives, their way of dealing with it was to agree with them and then forget about it. When their wives complained about their mothers, they did the same. Their role is to be a wall of Zen between the two. As long as they keep the two women away from each other's throats, they think they are doing their job. When the two do meet and things blow up, they dive for their phones or the TV remote to shut the noise away.

Despite this, overall, homes where the husband sees through his mother's deviousness are relatively happier. The first time she met her mother-in-law, Payal felt that they didn't vibe well. She told Parag that the meeting didn't go well. 'It doesn't matter what my mother thinks of you, I love you,' is what he said. The two of them have held on to that through their troubles.

Mummyji did not raise her son to take a stance. And if you expect that as a husband it is his job to take one, well you've only yourself to blame. As characters in their lives, the husbands are important. As participants in the reality show of Living with the Mother-in-Law, the husbands are useless.

'My husband is the person my mother-in-law loves the most in this world. She would rather die than see him hurt,' was another consistent statement that daughters-in-law across the country made to me. Indian mothers do have an obsessive love for their sons. The whole notion of preference for the boy child feeds into this obsession. As an exercise, pick any newspaper in any part of the country and read the crime stories. From robbery to murder to death, the one person any convict has on his side is his mother. 'My son is not capable of a crime like this,' is a standard Indian-mother-of-the-culprit quote. If the son is found standing with the smoking gun and blood on his clothes, his mother will find a way to blame a friend for making her son wayward. No Indian Mummyji would ever believe that her son is capable of any ill-doing. Her faith, like her love, is blind. When this can't-do-any-wrong son gets married, Mummyji is filled with a mix of fear and disappointment. She takes up cudgels on his behalf, even when there is no need to. If a quarrel does not exist for her to prove how fierce her loyalties are, well, Mummyji will make sure she creates one.

Drowned as I was deeply in stories of many Mummyjis and their villainy, it took me entirely by surprise to run into a forum that actually seeks to protect them. 'All India Mother-in-Law Protection Forum is the first ever social forum created to protect the rights and interests of the mother-in-law. It is a non-funded non-profit organization which will create awareness about the problems faced by mothers-in-law and also fight against the de-facto villainous projection in the socio-legal arena,' claims its website.

One mellow Thursday morning, I call the helpline listed on the site. A lady who introduces herself as Mrs Manjeet Puri answers the phone. Mrs Puri does not have much patience with rogue daughters-in-law. She gets three or four calls every day, she tells me, from harassed mothers-in-law. Most of them are accused of violence against their daughters-in-law. In India, this falls under Section 498 of the penal code and is not an immediately bailable offence. But what worries Mrs Puri now is the number of calls she receives from abroad. Countries like the USA, UK and Australia are teeming with scared desi mothers-in-law worried about being imprisoned in a strange land on the sheer basis of a phone call that their daughter-in-law makes to the police.

'The daughter-in-law just has to say that my mother-in-law is making me do odd jobs around the house and not letting me take up a job in an office. That's all that's required. The cops haul the poor mother-in-law off to jail,' she tells me. But because they are so far away and governed by the laws of another country, concerned and sympathetic as she is, Mrs Puri is unable to help them.

In India, it is pertinent that Section 498 is prone to misuse. But the existence of the law itself is testimony to the fact that daughters-in-law need protection. Mrs Puri herself is a harassed mother-in-law, she tells me, her son was married twice and both his wives were only interested in appropriating their house and other property.

I ask her about the boundaries of control that are acceptable to Mummyjis. 'Should they have a say in how the daughter-in-law dresses, for example?' I ask.

Jeans and T-shirts are common enough now and mothers-in-law should get over that objection, she tells me. 'But sometimes these daughters-in-law wear clothes that expose everything. The neckline is so low, you can literally see right in. Then of course, the mother-in-law has a right to ask her to change, you know, because the family's name is at stake,' she tells me.

Next I quiz her about the daughters-in-law having a career. I get the same kind of 'it's OK, but not quite' response. 'Jobs are OK,' she says, 'but then lots of girls go ahead and have affairs with their bosses, no?' And so our conversation bumps along, between a confused reality and a harsh ideal. Mrs Puri's commitment to mothers-in-law like herself is absolute and commendable, but in her own muddled views lies the entire spectrum of society's Mummyji tribulations.

Over my year of research, a lot of people told me that I was paying excessive attention to a non-problem. That this whole Mummyji myth was a media creation. These people were usually Mummyjis themselves. Or men. Or people who have never read newspapers. Truth is, the Mummyji issue is so big in this country that it took the biggest court to drill some sense. In May 2013, the Supreme Court had to use its super serious powers to give Mummyjis a special instruction. The crux of its statement was, and I quote, 'A daughter-in-law is to be treated as a family member, not a housemaid.' What kind of a non-problem requires advice from the Supreme Court? For the moment, let's keep aside what this implies the court thinks of housemaids. 'A daughter-in-law should be treated with warmth and affection and not as a stranger with respectable and ignoble indifference.' It is a pity that the court did not define warmth and affection. It will only take a smart lawyer to point out that, technically speaking, bride-burning is an activity that generates warmth (after all, heat is just warmth in higher degrees). In the same judgement, the court also observed that marriage and life with in-laws leave many daughters-in-law with 'no desire to live'. No desire to live! So not only are Mummyjis cold and nasty, they are an active life-destroying force. Like a cyclone. Or a volcanic explosion. That's how bad it is. Don't take my word for it. Ask the Supreme Court.

1

How I Met My Mother-in-Law

Name	Age (in 2013)	Husband	Married
Rachna	30	Gaurav	2013

If you have reached the stage of potentially having a mother-in-law, you are perhaps under the illusion that it is because your romance with her son is going well. You probably had a perfect first meeting—part serendipity and part destiny; your friends can't stop saying how good you look together; he remembers your birthday and Valentine's Day and celebrates your monthly 'anniversary' with flowers and wine. It's everything you've always wanted it to be. Yet, in the larger scheme of life, all of this is merely the equivalent of skiing on the nursery slopes. The real romance is when you meet your mother-in-law.

You probably already have a vision of the perfect Mummyji. You imagine her as your mum plus plus version: that is, she would be everything you think your mother should have been. She'll be hip and with it. She'll be your best friend. She'll laugh at all your jokes. And she'll never be the kind to yell at you for fidgeting with your hair or biting your nails. You know exactly how your first meeting with her should turn out. It will be in a well-dusted home, over a plate of fat-free samosas. Or in a restaurant where she will order the perfect mother-in-law meal while being very polite with the waiter and looking at you over the flame of the candle and winking when he turns his back. That is the dream, the perfect mother-in-law romance.

For Rachna Sethi and her mother-in-law, it was love at first sight. Rachna's mother-in-law decided she was the one, the minute she clapped eyes on her. It's an awkward narrative, but not an uncommon one, that Rachna met her mother-in-law before she met her husband. Wait, I should add to-be. Rachna met her mother-in-law-to-be even before she met her husband-to-be. Big deal, you may shrug, you've heard about a thousand arranged marriages that started like this. What is unusual about Rachna's story is that she fell in love with her mother-in-law (to-be) even before she met her husband (to-be).

Rachna tells the story of that first meeting in a much-practised and perfectly choreographed manner. She begins with what she was wearing. An 'onion pink' lehenga. Almost original Manish Malhotra, which means an expensively tailored knock-off, perfectly acceptable by south Delhi standards, nothing to be ashamed of. She had had it made for a cousin's wedding and had worn it in Dehradun where her family lives. So when a former colleague and current friend invited her for her sangeet, she decided the crowd was so different, it was safe to give the lehenga a second airing. She matched it with a necklace and a pair of earrings studded with emeralds, 'almost real'.

The friend wasn't her best friend and so she didn't have much of a role to play. She wasn't in any of the dances where the bride's friends teased the groom or told the story of how they met and fell in love. 'To be honest, I only went for the wedding because it gave me a chance to wear my dress,' she says. So she stood by, with a few other non-best friends. All she had to do was look pretty and laugh a lot, until the dance floor was thrown open. She had had a tooth extracted earlier in the week and was on the last day of a course of antibiotics. So when she went to the bar, she asked for a glass of orange juice. 'With vodka?' the harried barman asked her. 'Without, thanks,' she said.

The lady next to her said, 'It's very rare to find a young girl who doesn't want vodka in her orange juice these days.' That was the moment Rachna first saw her mother-in-law. 'Don't you drink?' was the first question she was asked. Since Rachna's rule is never to admit to anything until she is caught and trapped beyond escape, she said, 'Of course not.' The well-dressed aunty in a 'full ruby choker' engaged her in conversation. 'Most of it was about random stuff, I don't even remember what she asked. But she called me beta a lot, which I liked,' she says. She asked for Rachna's number which the young woman gave to her enthusiastically—insisting that aunty call it right then in order to make sure she wrote it correctly though she also remembers finding it a bit strange that this nice older lady seemed so keen on her. 'But then she shook my chin and said, "You look divine, beta, like an angel." So I put my discomfort away. There are some people who are immediately warm and aunty was one of them,' she says.

Rachna lives in Malviya Nagar, in a three-bedroom apartment that she shares with two other girls. One of her flatmates, Anuja, is a former colleague of mine. When I mentioned to her that I was looking to talk to women who had interesting stories about their mothers-in-law, Anuja insisted that I meet Rachna. 'You will not meet a daughter-in-law more in love with her mother-in-law. And vice versa,' she told me.

I am meeting Rachna at home, in her very tidy room. She has offered me beer and we have settled in for a chat. She sits on the bed, her legs tucked under her and her laptop open in front, her hair piled up in a ponytail, wisps framing her fair face. Hers is one of the tidiest rooms I've ever seen. Everything is in its place.

Rachna is steadfast about her appearance, she is always

perfectly turned out. She is like a machine, Anuja tells me, and obsessed about organizing things down to their minutest detail. 'Even for changing from her summer wardrobe to her winter one, she makes an excel sheet and adds reminders on her phone. She is a freak!'

There is something very trusting about Rachna, I feel, something fragile. She is the sort of person whose safety you might worry about, if you saw her standing alone on a Delhi street. The young woman grew up in Dehradun, she tells me, and has lived in Delhi for seven years. There was hardly any resistance to her moving to a big city and living by herself, since opportunities were slim in Dehradun and her parents had raised her to be independent and career-minded. She worked in a call centre for a year and then got a job in a public relations firm.

'So that's how we met,' she continues with her story and smiles, 'at a friend's wedding, over a glass of orange juice, no vodka.' Nothing happened for a few days. A week must have gone by and suddenly Rachna got a call from her. She introduced herself as the 'friend' she had made at the sangeet. The conversation was general—cheerful how-are-yous punctuated with awkward silences. Then aunty called the following day and the day after and so on. In another week, she had become Auntyji. She called every evening, asking her about her day, her family, her school life, where she went to college, why she had picked the subjects she did. The conversations lasted half an hour, sometimes longer.

Soon Auntyji knew everything about her day, which clients she was meeting, the trouble she was having with her boss, what she had for lunch and what she was planning to wear to work the next day. 'I told you it's bizarre,' Anuja tells me, rolling her eyes. Rachna merely smiles. She may even have blushed a little. Anuja and their other flatmate, Radhika, teased Rachna endlessly about Auntyji. They were all hoping for some romance in their lives, but none of them guessed that it would come in the form of an Auntyji.

Anuja and Radhika were highly suspicious of the older woman's enthusiasm. Rachna defended her, although at times she too wondered why Auntyji was making such a lot of effort with her. 'I mean if it was a guy I'd met at the wedding and he behaved like this, I would have thought what a chipku he is,' Rachna admits. The turning point came one evening a few weeks later. Rachna had mentioned to Auntyji that she had ordered dinner from the restaurant down the road. It was the second time in the week and Auntyji remarked about what an unhealthy lifestyle this was. The flatmates were having trouble finding a cook, the last one had gone back to the village and none of them was around during the day to interview prospects or show a new recruit around.

The next evening, the three of them were squabbling about what they should order and from where, when the doorbell rang. Anuja opened it. A man stood outside and asked for Rachna. When she went to the door, he introduced himself as Auntyji's driver and handed over a massive dabba. 'It was one of those five-tier things and each tier was filled to the brim with super delicious home-cooked food,' Anuja tells me. The three of them had been away from their families for so long that they nearly cried while eating it. Rachna kept going, 'Gosh, Auntyji is too good, gosh, she is so amazing.' She called her as soon as the meal was over and thanked her so much that it is entirely possible that she ended the call saying, 'I love you.'

With the five-tiered dabba, Auntyji moved from being a subject of dinner-time conversation to an actual presence on their dinner plates. The driver brought them phulkas, dal and curries every day, Anuja says. 'Not every day,' Rachna blushes, 'it's more like every other day. Come on.' It is a struggle to remind myself that we are still talking about the mother-in-law. I write an instruction to myself in bold—DON'T Laugh—and underline it several times on all the pages of my notes during this meeting. Rachna talks about her mother-in-law with all the earnest enthusiasm that other people reserve for the retelling of how they met Shah Rukh Khan. Or their husbands. Usually the former.

Once the dabba system was established, Auntyji began a new tradition. She called on a Saturday morning and asked if Rachna was free. There was this handbag she had seen in a store window during the week and wanted a second opinion on it, before buying. She wanted Rachna to go with her and see the bag, after which, if she had the time, they could stop for a spot of lunch. Rachna said yes, of course. Over the course of three weekends, that became their 'thing'. Shopping or a movie on Saturday mornings, followed by lunch.

Auntyji insisted on paying for the tickets and the meal. If there was something that Rachna liked but found too expensive, Auntyji would ask her what she was prepared to pay and offer to make good the difference. Rachna often declined, but she did pick up a couple of dresses and a pair of boots she wouldn't otherwise have. 'It's their daytime date,' Anuja says, before dissolving in a judging, giggling heap. Rachna shakes her head gamely, but goes on. 'Listen, it's like having a friend. Also, she is much younger than her age, you know. It's not like hanging around with your mother, it's like hanging around with a fun aunt.' And so the friendship flowered, settling into a rhythm of phulkas during the week and PVR on weekends.

'Tell her about your birthday,' Anuja prompts. It was Rachna's birthday in April, four months or so after her daily chats with Auntyji had begun. The three housemates decided they would throw a party, invite all their friends from their respective offices and make it an easy affair, where people could come and leave as they pleased. It would be a birthday-plus-we-haven't-thrown-a-party-in-the-house party. The girls would buy some booze and snacks and guests would be encouraged to bring their own. Over Auntyji's dabba at dinner, they made a guest list, wrote down the things they needed to buy, and spoke to an agency to clean the house before and after the party. The Sunday before the event, the three of them even went and bought new outfits. Rachna's was a gift from the other two.

Auntyji brought up her birthday on their Saturday date. She asked her what her plans were. Since Rachna did not want to mention the drinking and the anticipation of a wild night, she told her she had no fixed plans. Over the next couple of days, when asked, she told Auntyji it was low-key and that she might go for brunch with her flatmates on Sunday. On Friday, Auntyji asked her again what she was doing and she said nothing. On Saturday, she met Auntyji for lunch as usual, leaving the other two to get things organized. 'I didn't want to make her feel suspicious,' she says. Auntyji wished her warmly but brought no gift. After lunch, they walked around the mall and Rachna was a little surprised she didn't buy her anything. Eventually, they shared a cupcake and said their goodbyes.

Around eight that evening, the guests began to arrive. In an hour the apartment was crowded and people had stopped bothering with introductions. The music was loud and the booze was flowing. A couple of glasses were already broken. Around nine-thirty someone told Rachna that her aunt was looking for her. She went and found Auntyji at the door, a huge red box in one hand. She looked a bit startled and pale, but came over and kissed her on both cheeks and gave her the present. 'My flatmates threw me a surprise party,' Rachna said. 'How lovely!' Auntyji said and walked in. She stayed till midnight, monopolizing Rachna and making conversation with her.

When her friends dragged her to dance, Auntyji encouraged her to go, and sat alone in a corner, watching Rachna dance and nodding her head in encouragement. For one song, Auntyji joined her on the floor and danced rather vigorously for a minute but then felt too shy and sat down. Rachna worried that Auntyji was getting bored. If she stepped away from her to talk to someone or get something, she insisted that Anuja or Radhika sit with Auntyji.

They hissed at Rachna asking her how long her aunt was planning to stay at the party. She was bringing the mood of the party down. Rachna had long abandoned her glass and picked up one that was only Coke, no rum. Everyone felt forced to behave properly, since an adult was in the room. 'I mean we are all adults, but a mom type adult, you know,' Anuja tells me.

Rachna concedes that it was uncomfortable having Auntyji there. She also felt like she was caught lying to her. 'I mean of course it was my fault she turned up at that awkward time, but maybe she should have left after ten minutes.' But Rachna was very happy with the gift. The box had about half a dozen things she had pointed out while at the mall, including a pair of shoes for Rs 8,000 that they had both agreed wasn't worth the money.

A couple of months after the birthday, Auntyji began to bring up the matter of her son. The first thing she said about Gaurav was that he was voted the most handsome boy in his class when he was in the tenth standard. He had finished his MBA from London Business School two years ago and was working for a financial services company there. But now, he had taken up an offer from a venture capital firm that was setting up its office in India, and was moving back to Delhi. Auntyji showed her photographs of Gaurav on her phone. 'Of course, even earlier she had mentioned her son. But when Gaurav got this job and decided to move, that was all Auntyji could talk about,' she says.

When Gaurav had applied for his MBA, Auntyji told Rachna, he had been accepted by both Harvard Business School and London Business School. He deferred the decision to her and she picked London since it was closer to Delhi. 'Sure, it's not how I would have decided, but hey, he's the only son—the only child, actually—and I think it's nice of him to listen to his mother's wishes,' Rachna shrugs.

Auntyji insisted that Rachna and Gaurav would get along well, that they were perfect for each other. At times, she even teased

Rachna about Gaurav, like friends do. Or did, in the 1980s. Rachna couldn't wait to meet Gaurav.

The week he arrived, Auntyji was in a frenzy of cooking and cleaning. Well, getting stuff cooked and getting things cleaned. But she called Rachna that Friday, three days after Gaurav's much celebrated homecoming. 'I have spoken to Gaurav. He is very excited about meeting you. How about tomorrow evening at 7? I suggested 1911 at The Imperial. Classy and quiet. Is that OK with you, beta?' she asked. Rachna was so happy, her eyes welled up. Nobody had ever been so kind to her or cared so much about her. She realized she was quite in love with Auntyji.

She spent the next morning in the beauty salon and then sat on her bed in a mess of confusion and chaos as her two flatmates went through her wardrobe to find a suitable 'meet Gaurav' dress. They finally agreed on a pair of jeans and a top from Zara. At 4 p.m., Rachna closed the door, set the alarm and decided on an hour's nap. At 4.30, there was a knock on the door. When she opened it, there stood Auntyji. In her hand was a black dress; knee-length with polka dots and a white lace collar. 'I brought you what you should wear tonight,' Auntyji said, 'this would suit you perfectly.'

Rachna was a bit shocked. 'But in a happy way,' she says, 'who would know her son's taste better than his mother? I loved the fact that she was going out of her way to look out for me.' Auntyji had even picked out earrings and a bracelet to go with the dress. 'Wear black heels,' she said, as she waited for Rachna to change and show her the fit.

Rachna liked the dress. It wasn't something she would have ever bought for herself, but it was pretty and suited her. 'She looked like a secretary from *Mad Men*,' Anuja whispers in my ear.

Auntyji drove with her to the hotel, to make sure that she got there comfortably. Rachna was happy she didn't have to take an autorickshaw and mess her hair up. But once the car pulled up to the porch of the hotel, Auntyji got out saying, 'I may as well wait and go back with Gaurav.'

They walked in together. Gaurav was already there. Auntyji introduced Rachna to him and said she would give them some privacy and moved away. Rachna's heart sank when she saw where she had decided to wait. *Right at the next table!*

'It was awkward that she was there, directly in my line of sight. I had to turn and look at the garden on the right, because if I looked at Gaurav, she would appear in my peripheral vision and then she would smile or wave or shudder with joy,' Rachna says. 'But I couldn't really blame her; she had been excited about this meeting for weeks.'

Gaurav turned out to be nice. He was as handsome as his mother had promised. 'My mother is very interested in you,' were his first words to her. The conversation was stilted. Rachna was nervous and Gaurav may have been too. He asked her a little bit about her work and education. She answered him as humorously as she could, having decided that she would focus on being the funny one. But Auntyji's presence within earshot left both of them edgy and out of sorts.

'I couldn't wait for my cold coffee to arrive so I could gulp it down and run,' Rachna says, 'and the service was so slow, I nearly craned my neck from trying to catch the waiter's eye.' Eventually, after what seemed like a long time and a conversation that had more silence than an art film, they said their goodbyes. 'We should catch up again, soon,' Gaurav said and she said she would love to.

They met the following week and it went pretty much the same way. Auntyji picked the place and her outfit and insisted on waiting at the next table. Gaurav and Rachna attempted another open and honest conversation, but failed. 'We spent more time looking at our phones,' she says.

The third time Auntyji dragged Uncleji too along and the four of them went for brunch on a Sunday to Olive. 'I worried that people around us would think we were a family and Gaurav my brother. There was no conversation at all at the table. Well, there was. Auntyji talked and we all listened. After a while, Gaurav started playing Angry Birds on his phone. And Uncleji, who is anyway in his own world, said he had some calls to make and stepped out. It was just the two of us and we chatted like friends. But it was awkward. I felt stretched in different directions,' she says.

Auntyji insisted Rachna should ask her parents to come to Delhi. It was time to make things official, she told her. Rachna worried about how little she knew Gaurav. Both Anuja and Radhika told her she ought to get to know him better before committing. 'You can't marry the son because you are in love with his mother, no?' Anuja says. Rachna concedes it is a valid argument. And then makes a fact sheet for herself.

Age—28

Number of boyfriends, so far—3

Number of serious and want-to-get-married type boyfriends—0

Number of interesting marriageable men she had met in the last two years—0

Possibility that she would have to settle for an arranged marriage—99.9 per cent.

'Therefore,' she explains to me, 'what I should compare this with is not a relationship but an arranged marriage. In an arranged marriage scenario, I would have spent only as little time with my potential husband as I did with Gaurav, before saying yes. And here at least I know Auntyji well,' she says.

So Rachna briefed her parents about the developments in her life. They came from Dehradun. Auntyji invited them home for lunch on a Sunday. That morning, the driver arrived with a package for her. It was an onion-pink-coloured salwar kurta which was embroidered with golden thread. 'Our lucky colour,' Auntyji had written on the note attached to the dress. It was the shade of the outfit she was wearing when they first met at that sangeet.

'Rachna, they love you so much already,' her mother remarked when she saw the outfit. 'These days it is even more important to get along with the mother-in-law.'

That was the first time Rachna felt a little unsure about this whole business with Auntyji. But her parents were here and everyone seemed so happy and excited that she didn't want to say anything. Lunch was fabulous. Auntyji was an accomplished hostess and she knitted the conversations together. Afterwards, Rachna went upstairs and hung out with Gaurav in his room. He showed her his yearbooks and school photographs. They talked about music and movies. It was the first time she was spending so much time with him without Auntyji peering at them from the corner of her eye. 'At one point, I leaned in thinking we could kiss, but Gaurav said he was worried his mother would come up. And that was that,' she says.

Rachna's parents were thrilled. The family seemed nice, they had a big house, Gaurav obviously had a bright future and there was no talk about any dowry. Auntyji had told Rachna's mother several times that she only cared about finding a 'good girl' for her son, it did not matter at all what kind of financial background she came from. 'By Delhi standards, it was all very progressive.'

In the meantime, Rachna's niggling worry about her mother-in-law was getting stronger. Gaurav and she got no time to themselves at all. When Gaurav arrived to pick her up for a movie date after the big lunch, Auntyji was firmly positioned in the front seat of the car. 'I was so busy arranging the lunch for your parents last weekend, that I missed talking to you. Gaurav was at the door when I asked him where he was going and, when he said he was meeting you, I told him I *had* to come along,' she said when Rachna boarded the car.

At the movie hall, Rachna sat in between mother and son. But Gaurav wouldn't even hold her hand because his mum was there. 'You should have simply held Auntyji's hand,' Anuja says, 'since she is the one who is in a relationship with you.'

I met Rachna in August 2012. The wedding was fixed for November. Thus far, Auntyji had picked the venue, the outfits for the mehendi, pheras and sangeet, as well as finalized the DJ.

In July they had a small engagement party. Auntyji ran around making all the arrangements. Rachna tried telling her what she wanted, but Auntyji shot down all her ideas. In the end, it was entirely about Auntyji. 'It was like a party for her friends, where Gaurav and I were like the ice sculpture or something. People came and admired us, but the only person they wanted to hang out with was Auntyji,' she says.

I ask her if she did not raise this issue with Gaurav. She did, she tells me, but after a lot of agonizing. Auntyji is her first friend, so she felt she was betraying her by criticizing her to Gaurav. Still, she expected sympathy and solutions from her fiancé. Instead Gaurav just shrugged and told her she was being ungrateful for all the work his mother was doing.

'That's mom yaar,' he said. 'She likes doing these things and she loves you. Sometimes I think she loves you more than she loves me,' he told her. Rachna says that is not a possibility. Gaurav is an only child, well, an only son, and there is no way Auntyji could love anyone more than him. Irrespective, she concedes that as far as future mothers-in-law go, hers was incredibly fond of her.

I met Rachna again a couple of months later. She postponed several appointments and eventually I left her with no choice when I turned up at their home late one evening, under the pretext of meeting Anuja.

'Sorry, I'm really tied for time,' Rachna said as soon as she saw me.

With the wedding date fast approaching, Auntyji had signed her up for gym and yoga. Five days a week she did cardio in the morning and kapalbhathi in the evening. She had to be in perfect shape for the big day. That wasn't all. Auntyji had also paid for a laser hair removal treatment. So Rachna spent six painful weekends being zapped by a laser on her upper lips and under arms. Then there was the run-up to the wedding day salon package—papaya facials and dark circle removers. Part by part, Rachna was getting squeezed, shrunk and zapped in preparation for the wedding.

'Are you OK with all of this?' I asked her.

Rachna simply shook her head and shrugged her shoulders. I noticed she had a vacant expression about her. Between the workout and the beauty treatments and her job, she was exhausted. 'Auntyji feels since you only get married once, it's important to do it right. Maybe she is right,' she said. Then after a long pause, she added, 'Maybe she isn't. Who knows? Who cares? Only Auntyji. Auntyji. Auntyjiiiiiiiiiiiiiiiiiiiiii!'

Then she slumped back on the sofa, closed her eyes and didn't speak to me for the rest of the evening. When I was leaving, I popped into her room to say goodbye. She was sitting on her bed, the laptop was open in front of her.

'Show her the engagement photos no yaar,' Anuja said and Rachna invited me in. She opened the Facebook tab where, of course, she and Auntyji were 'friends'. There were about 650 photos in the album and Auntyji was in almost all of them. Gaurav and Rachna looked very well suited. He was tall, fair and clean-shaven with a runner's body. Rachna was glowing next to him. But Auntyji was unmistakably the major presence. She was dressed in a blue and red sari. Large sapphires glittered from her earlobes, neck and her fingers. She had even worn a sapphire piece in the parting of her hair. Her hair was up in an elaborate coiffure. She looked classy and bossy.

Rachna was clicking rapidly through the photos, but paused at one. Only she and Auntyji were in the frame. Auntyji was tucking an errant strand of hair behind Rachna's ear. You could see her shrinking away from the touch, her face was in a tight grimace.

She looked at that picture for a long time. 'My God, she will soon be Mummyji,' she gasped. Then she looked closely at that photograph again. In a loud whisper, she said, 'She is going to run my life, isn't she? Telling me what to wear, how to cook, when to go to the loo . . . Oh my God, I am handing my life over to a class A bitch!!!!' She looked again at that photo. 'You bitch!' she spat and slammed the screen shut. Anuja laughed and told her she had warned her about this all the while. I legged it out of there.

On my way home, I wondered about Auntyji's fairly quick fall from angeldom to bitchhood. And although I didn't tell her, I felt certain that Rachna was marrying Gaurav for the wrong reasons.

It was October and I hadn't received an invitation for the wedding. Anuja was on a holiday in South Africa and so I casually pinged Rachna to find out what was going on. She was fine, she told me, busy with work. We spent several minutes talking about Anuja's envy-inducing itinerary in South Africa. Finally, when I couldn't hold out any more, I asked her how the preparations for the wedding were going.

'Actually, we've decided to postpone it,' she typed.

'Why? Is everything OK?' I asked.

'Yeah, well, Gaurav and I just thought we should spend a little more time before getting married-married. The wedding is on, just not in November,' she told me.

When Anuja returned from her holiday, I asked her out for lunch. Driving to the restaurant, on a whim, we decided to take the long route just so we could drive past Auntyji's home. It was a typical west Delhi house in a west Delhi colony. It was painted pink and brown and stood two storeys tall. Even from outside it was easy to imagine the gigantic television screen and the golden chandeliers inside. Outside four big cars were lined up. 'More money than good taste,' Anuja grumbled.

Over lunch, Anuja told me why the wedding was postponed. Rachna was feeling increasingly suffocated by Auntyji, she told me. Gaurav was also very distant. He had never made an effort to touch her or kiss her. Rachna was worried that he found her unattractive. 'I think he might be gay,' Anuja told me.

Rachna, it seems, tried to broach this with Auntyji. She told her that perhaps Gaurav didn't find her attractive. She suggested that maybe he was interested in someone else, maybe they should call the whole thing off. Auntyji was so offended, she did not speak to her for three days. Wracked with guilt, Rachna sent a text message saying sorry. A deluge of replies followed.

Auntyji wrote 150-word messages detailing her emotional distress. She couldn't believe Rachna would be so rude to her. She couldn't believe how casually Rachna seemed to be taking the relationship. She couldn't believe Rachna didn't care for her as much as she did for her. Most of all, she couldn't believe that Rachna thought Gaurav would marry someone his mother did not approve of. Wasn't she listening when she told her that Gaurav chose LBS to be closer to his mum? Didn't she hear her say that Gaurav came back to India because his mother said he should?

'Remember how it was when you were in class two and did katti with your friend? All those accusations, the emotional guilt-tripping? It was just like that. Except, neither of them was in class two,' Anuja told me.

Rachna had no choice but to apologize a million times. She bought Auntyji a gift and when she saw that the gesture moved Auntyji to tears, she couldn't help shedding a few of her own. 'It was their first fight. But there was no make-up sex,' Anuja said. Rachna used that make-up conversation to tell Auntyji that she and Gaurav weren't spending enough time together. She said it was best, for all three of them, if they waited a while.

When she related the incident to Gaurav, he assured Rachna he would talk to his mother. That evening, he told his mother things were moving too fast. They all needed some more time before the wedding. Auntyji wasn't thrilled about the idea, but she agreed reluctantly. 'She did call up my parents and cry to them. And whenever I'm with her and someone calls her to find out why the wedding is postponed, she says, "*Aaj kal ke bachche na...*" and throws these really nasty looks my way,' Rachna told Anuja.

Picking another date was the next problem. The argument was between wait and weather. Auntyji didn't want to wait too long for the wedding and Rachna didn't want to marry in any season except winter. They went back and forth on it for the next three months. Gaurav, in the meantime, seemed more and more disconnected from the entire proceedings.

Rachna and he have spent more time together since. But he seems distant and often disinterested. And from what Anuja knows, while they have kissed and fooled around for a little bit, they haven't had actual sex. 'Can you imagine in this day and age?' she asks me. 'And Rachna is more than keen to go all the way, but Gaurav keeps making up these excuses. I am sure this is just a please-his-mum wedding; he is gay,' she says.

Rachna says eventually she asked him about it. His response was a counter question. 'Are you crazy?' he asked her and did not volunteer any further information. 'He is just old-fashioned,' Rachna says, 'he knows his mum wouldn't approve and so he just wants to wait till we marry.'

As far as Rachna and Auntyji are concerned, nothing much has changed. They talk every day and they still have their Saturday dates. It's mostly fun. 'I do wish Auntyji was just a friend. Then I am OK with her. What worries me is that she is so bossy already, once I am her daughter-in-law, I'll just have to follow her orders all the time.'

Since Rachna is now the fiancée, she is invited to be part of all the functions in the extended family and their large circle of friends. Every other week, there is some event or the other. Auntyji fusses over each of them. 'Every day we have a conversation about what I will be wearing, where I am getting my hair done, things like that. I like dressing up, but once in a while. I feel this is too much, this obsession with presentation. But if I tell her something, for example, that I'll just come straight from office, she behaves like I took an actual knife and plunged it into her actual heart. Everything is high drama,' Rachna says.

Meanwhile a new wedding date has been finally fixed. It is on 3 November, a week short of a year from the earlier plan. The festivities will start on Friday, 1 November. With so much time on her hands, Auntyji has branched out from dressing up Rachna to even her immediate family. She has finalized clothes and jewellery for Rachna's mum and aunts. She has sent them photographs and price lists and kept constant pressure to get them to send the money and seal the deal. 'That was hazaar weird,' she says.

After the infamous Delhi gang rape case, Auntyji was so worried about Rachna travelling by herself that she badgered her parents into buying her a car. Then she interviewed nearly three dozen prospects and hired a driver for Rachna. 'She said it wouldn't look nice if she bought me a car before the wedding, but she pays the driver's salary,' Rachna tells me.

One morning, while on her commute to work, she called me. Had I seen the *Delhi Times* that morning, she asked. I hadn't. 'This article says that Sharmila is planning everything for the Saif–Kareena wedding,' she said, 'so I am not the only one with a mother-in-law more interested than the bride in the wedding.'

'Does that make you feel better?' I asked her.

'Well, if it can happen to her, I suppose it can happen to me. I take some comfort in that,' she said. I suppose even in the race for bitchy mothers-in-law-to-be, there is comfort to be found in a celebrity endorsement.

Increasingly, Rachna is unsure about marrying Gaurav. They have nothing in common. He is obsessed with work and not much else.

He has some friends, he plays golf all weekends. He fixes dates with her and then abandons her to his mother, while he does whatever he pleases. Auntyji has taken Rachna around everywhere and introduced her as the soon-to-be-bahu. Once Rachna asked Auntyji why Gaurav was so ambivalent. 'His nature is like that,' she told him, 'but don't worry, you have me, na?'

'But you are marrying the guy, not his mother,' Anuja points out.

'Yeah, but if I say something then she becomes so sentimental and emotional,' Rachna says.

She understands that to Auntyji she is nothing more than a doll to dress up and 'use' for amusement. Auntyji has trouble trusting her own friends and relatives. She thinks everyone is bitchy about her behind her back. Rachna is the only one whom she can control completely.

I ask Rachna what kind of a life she wanted to lead after the marriage. She wants to continue to work, she says. She loves to trek and she wants to walk and hike through all of Europe and South America. She is not sure she wants to have children.

'Does Auntyji know this?' I ask her.

In an effort to gauge Auntyji's reaction, several times Rachna has mentioned that Anuja is keen on working after marriage, going on long treks and unsure about having children.

'How did she react?'

'She flipped out. She called her stupid,' Rachna says. 'I know these are going to be issues. But if this was an arranged marriage, I would have the same issues, no?'

We sat in Rachna's room for a long time that evening. Anuja and Radhika were earnestly trying to talk 'some sense' into Rachna. This was the most bizarre arrangement they had ever heard about, they told her. Eventually, she would want a husband who cared about her, who was responsive to her needs and issues. Eventually, she would want a mother-in-law who was not in her face all the time.

Rachna agreed with them on many points. She knew she was in it for the wrong reasons. She was twenty-nine, she said, and it was possible she would never find the right person. Then she argued and debated and talked herself in circles. Eventually, she came to a single line conclusion about why she was going ahead with this—Auntyji would never agree to calling the wedding off.

'We have come such a long way. It's simply heartbreaking. I don't have the guts to break up,' she says.

'Break up with whom?' I ask

'With my mother-in-law.'

'Mother-in-law-*to-be*,' I say, emphasizing the last two words.

'To certainly be,' she shrugs.

Until late October, I hadn't received an invitation. I checked with Anuja who said the wedding was on. 'She was conflicted about inviting you,' she said. She was busy shopping for her friend's wedding; she promised me she would call me later.

On 5 November, Rachna uploaded one wedding photo. Gaurav and she were standing facing each other. Shimmering like a princess, she was looking up at Gaurav. They were both smiling. Behind them, slightly blurred, loomed Mummyji.

2

Carla Hates the Word 'Adjust'

Name	Age (in 2013)	Husband	Married
Carla	24	Ankit	2012

If 'adjust' were an Olympic sport, India would be assured of a gold medal. It's a word that is not just nationally understood but also one that can be used in a million ways. 'Adjust please' is sometimes a request, sometimes an order, sometimes a threat and sometimes a joke. But most often, it is a philosophy. 'These things happen, you have to adjust,' contains within itself everything that parents want their daughters to know, especially as they get married. To give 'adjust' its due, it is in fact the secret to the country's low divorce rate.

'Adjust' means you are making a big deal out of a small thing. That yes, there might be discomfort but it is only natural. You don't see other people whining about it, nor should you. Its more evolved cousin is 'compromise', and that word is brought out when things turn serious, when a girl begins to be described as 'stubborn'.

For someone who has been living in India for only a year, Carla is familiar with most desi idiosyncrasies—cars bearing down the wrong side of the road, fifty-degree summers, sitting down for dinner at 10.30 p.m. and fully manned automatic vending machines.

Despite this relatively quick 'Indianization', there are things that grate on her, but none more so than the standard advice for all problems—just adjust no? In the nine months that she has been married to Ankit, whenever she has turned to her Indian friends for help in trying to decode why her mother-in-law behaves the way she does, she is told, 'These things are common, just adjust no?'

Carla's detestation of 'adjust' is not the petulance of a toddler who refuses to try porridge but the weariness of the convalescent who has just had enough porridge to last a lifetime. She is twenty-four. In the last year, she has adjusted to a different country, a strange language, a new cuisine, a way of living that embraces the hyper and eschews the subtle. Though she has been told since she was fourteen that she was her own person and she could live life on her terms, she has even adjusted to the fact that her wardrobe choices are now dictated by someone else—her mother-in-law. As anyone who has sat in the Mumbai suburban train and had the seventh person squeeze into a seat meant for three knows, beyond a point, adjustment is not a choice, it is an impossibility. Short of being able to explain what an lbw is, Carla has adjusted enough as the Austrian wife of an Indian man. She doesn't want to be told to adjust any more.

I first heard from Carla in August 2012 when I emailed a Delhi-based group of expatriates asking if any of them were women married to Indian men. I was convinced that a poor, unsuspecting non–South Asian bride would have some interesting stories to tell about negotiating the cultural landmine of an Indian marriage. Carla replied, saying she wasn't yet married to an Indian man but if all went well, she would be in less than a month. I pounced on her, as much as it was electronically possible to, and insisted she meet me right away. She wasn't so sure.

The more I tried to pin her down to a time and place, the more she dawdled. Finally, she emailed me saying she was too busy with the wedding preparations and she would get in touch with me once she was back from her honeymoon. It was the non–job applicant's version of 'Don't call me, I'll call you.' I was certain I would never hear from her again.

But in October, about five weeks after my first email to her, Carla wrote to say she was back in Delhi and willing to meet. We met at a coffee shop in the crowded Safdarjang Market. Carla reached a few minutes before I did and had managed to gather around her an impressive number of gapers and gawkers. She had that half-anxious, half maniacally excited look that you find among first-time visitors in the arrival lobby of most Indian airports.

Tall and brown-haired, Carla had the casual prettiness of the young. She wore jeans and a loose-fitting T-shirt and had a scarf draped over her shoulders. She wore no make-up and looked rather serious. Once we were inside the café and had sat down at our table, she stuck her hands out and showed me the fading mehndi with a little blush and a loud giggle. When we talked, though, her expression reverted to a stony seriousness.

She wanted to talk to me, she said, because she realized how important this 'problem' of mothers-in-law in India was. Her voice had a low base and while she spoke really good English, I found her manner of speaking rather amusing. Her sentences were short, often without any articles or personal pronouns.

'(I) never thought a mother-in-law would be the source of troubles in a marriage. But here in India, (my) mother-in-law has been a problem even before my marriage. That's why (I) want to do something about it, making people aware that this is not good. Or right. In fact, this is wrong. Very wrong,' she said, explaining why she was meeting me.

Carla had come prepared with plenty of questions about the book. 'Your project' as she called it, she was understandably worried about how her identity would be protected. 'Just married,' she offered by way of an explanation of her anxieties. She remained guarded throughout the meeting and did not mention any names—

her husband's, the place she works, where she lives. Eventually, she said she would like to be a part of 'the project' but she needed some time.

She hadn't yet decided whether she should tell her brand-new husband that she was slagging his mother off to a stranger. I told her I wouldn't want to influence that decision in any way and she could take some time to think it over and let me know. As I left, I told myself I wasn't going to hear from her again. Tentatively, I told her to let me know in a fortnight. But around ten that night, my phone buzzed and it was a message from Carla saying that she had decided to talk to me and not tell her husband about it.

'Are you certain?' I asked.

'Yes. Will meet tomorrow,' she replied.

I was thrilled, but felt a bit sorry for her. Her marriage had barely begun. And already she felt forced to hide things from her husband. Her motives were clear. She had to talk about her mother-in-law just so she could stay sane. There were a lot of things about living in India that stumped her but nothing flummoxed her like her Indian mother-in-law.

But we are getting ahead of ourselves. Carla's run-in with 'adjust' began on a trip to Agra, more than a year before we met. When she was twenty-two and a recent graduate from college in Austria, Carla secured an internship with an organization that worked with orphanages in India. She left home and came to Delhi for seven weeks of what she thought would be a fun, educative and mind-broadening stint. It would be her first stop in the many adventures she hoped to have.

Carla had been in Delhi for three weeks and was keen to visit the Taj Mahal. She heard from a common friend that a bunch of people she vaguely knew was going to Agra that weekend and that there was one last seat to fill. She called the number her friend gave her. Ankit, the person who answered the phone, sounded friendly and 'safe'. There was place in the car, he said (they could adjust!) and they would pick her up early the following morning.

They chatted a bit during the journey, but overall, the trip was very much a group affair. Yet, a few hours after they returned to Delhi, Carla found a friend-request from Ankit waiting for her on Facebook. She had thought the guy was nice, so she accepted the request and wrote him something. 'Some blah blah,' she says. But as blah blahs go, this was a particularly fertile one, and quickly led to more blah blahs. Soon, in the well-trodden path through which modern-day romances progress, Facebook led to chat, which then led to Skype. At this point, the only thing Carla was adjusting was her laptop screen for optimal lighting to project a perfect facial angle.

Shortly after, another trip came up, this time to Amritsar. It was more or less the same group that had gone to Agra, a mix of young visiting interns and their local hosts. Carla and Ankit got to know each other a little better that weekend and, when they came back, the frequency of chats and Skype conversations increased significantly. At this time, Carla was writing the final report of her internship. It was boring work at a lonely desk. She looked forward to Ankit's status turning green on her computer, so they could converse. 'One evening we were talking to each other on Skype and when I looked up it was 3 a.m. (I) couldn't believe that time had passed so quickly. It was wonderful, to be able to talk to someone like that. You know, talk-talk,' she says.

Ankit was interesting and exotic. He ran his own translation company in Delhi, taking up work from around the world and commissioning his network of translators to change documents, work manuals and books from one language to another. He amused her and confused her at the same time, Carla says. A lot of their conversations were about travel. It appealed to the wanderer in Carla. 'On chat he talked a lot. We would make these plans of going to these really exotic places. And he was funny, he made me laugh all the time. And at the same time I was also impressed by how committed he was to his family,' she says. She was beginning to think of the fun life they would have together. Going to Antarctica some day, stopping at the Amazon on the way there. Carla was slowly falling in love with Ankit.

Meeting Ankit was not easy. Their acquaintanceship was still at the stage where they needed a reason to see each other. Carla's birthday allowed them the next chance. She threw a party. Ankit was invited, as were several of his friends. Amid the buzz of the various conversations at the party, her ears perked up when she heard two of Ankit's friends talking about him. One was telling the other that Ankit was getting married soon.

Not having heard of arranged marriages, Carla assumed this meant that he had a girlfriend and felt upset. But having just turned twenty-threee, she decided to shrug 'whatever' and move on. She saw Ankit answer his phone and step outside to talk. So when another of his friends inquired about him, she told him that Ankit was busy outside talking to his girlfriend. 'But he doesn't have a girlfriend,' the friend said.

'Are you sure?' she asked.

'Of course not, none of us has a girlfriend,' the friend assured her.

And being twenty-three, Carla said whatever to the previous whatever and restored his status back to 'interesting'.

In a development that will gladden the babus at India's various tourism offices, this romance continued on its 'Incredible India' theme with yet another trip. This time it was to Mussoorie. Carla decided this was her final chance to get something going. It was her last weekend in India before she returned to Austria. So in a move that was both slightly 'stupid' and significantly out of character, she texted him to ask if she could sit next to him in the car. 'He is quite shy so it was my job to do this,' she explains. He said yes.

Since her exposure to non-communicative Indian men was so limited, Carla assumed just sitting next to each other would solve everything. They would have the proximity and the relative privacy to talk about their feelings, she thought. You can't blame her for not knowing that it's easier to pull your teeth out with a Swiss army knife than get an Indian boy to 'share his feelings'.

Predictably, even though they had a good time in Mussoorie, Carla couldn't really get a fix on how exactly he felt about her. He was attentive at times, and distracted at others. Sunday evening came all too soon and a very unresolved Carla reached home. She had already tried stunts like putting her head on his shoulder, touching his elbow and clasping his hands. He wasn't really responding to any of this. At the end of it she was very frustrated and wondered, 'What the hell was this guy about anyway?'

'It was all such a stupid game,' she says. And then, once she decided it was stupid, she thought she might as well take it to its illogical conclusion. 'I decided since I have behaved like a fool anyway, I have nothing to lose by becoming a bigger fool,' she says. She took a break from the whirl of packing her stuff and sent him a message saying she had fallen in love with him. Of course, these stories—like that last drink you shouldn't have had—never end well.

Carla was horrified with what she had done. 'What if he doesn't reply?' she thought in alarm. Or worse, what if he did reply saying, 'Thanks, but I am not interested?' She was frozen, willing the phone to ring and then again willing it not to. Finally, it did buzz and it was a message from Ankit. He said he felt the same way about her. He proposed that they meet the following day. Carla packed in a whirl and went on her first date with Ankit. It was also their last date for eight months.

'Of course all this time I did not once think of his mother,' she says, apologetic that she is taking so long to come around to that aspect of her life. 'Maybe I should have.' Truth is, Carla wasn't even thinking of marriage at the time. She went back to Austria and continued to keep in touch with Ankit. But for the occasional trips and a four-hour time difference, their relationship was pretty much like it was while she was in India. She did get to know Ankit a lot better and the more she knew him, the more she liked him. Cheekily, she once even pointed to a photo of his and told her mother that was her future son-in-law.

Ankit, however, was not very forthcoming about his family. He rarely talked about them and in none of their Skype conversations did he suggest that she should say hello to anyone in his family. She knew he lived with his widowed mother, his brother, sister-in-law and niece. But beyond that she didn't know anything at all. Come Christmas, Carla decided she would rectify that situation. She wasn't sure what Ankit's mother would like, but figured she couldn't go wrong with chocolates. So she put together an enormous hamper of Christmas gifts with stuff for all of them and sent it. The package arrived in Delhi but she didn't hear anything about it. Finally, when she couldn't take the anxiety any more she asked Ankit if he got her gift. 'Yes,' he said.

'And the others? Did they like theirs?' she asked.

'Yes,' he said vaguely.

There was no other reaction. 'He didn't say it was really nice or thank you or that his family wanted to convey their wishes or anything like that. I thought it was really weird, but then thought maybe Indians show their happiness in a different way.' This was perhaps the first adjustment she imposed on herself. But she let it go.

What she didn't know of course was the havoc the hamper created. Seeing a gift 'from just a friend' come all the way from Austria, Ankit's mother hit the panic button. She knew what she had to do and she knew she had to be quick about it. Ankit had to be found a wife—not a pants-wearing, vice-filled, Austrian wife with loose morals, but a good Indian girl, one she could groom to be the perfect torchbearer of the family. With all the efficiency of a Punjabi mother, she quickly arranged a line-up of candidates.

Carla, of course, was completely unaware of the astrologers, matchmakers and assorted aunts who were suddenly employed because of the tidal wave that was set off by her Christmas gift. Ankit quietly met some of the prospective brides. Like all good Indian sons, he managed to successfully hold off the bride hunt from Carla just as well as he managed to not admit to his mother he was in a serious relationship with an Austrian girl.

In July, eight months after their first date in Delhi, Carla and Ankit met again, this time in Russia. Carla was on a project there and Ankit managed to fly out and they spent a week travelling around Moscow and St Petersburg. It was a wonderful holiday. Seeing Ankit in person reaffirmed Carla's feelings about him. She knew Ankit was the man she wanted to be with. Their conversation revolved largely around how they would break the news of their relationship to their families.

Ankit suggested a couple of times that the only way they could be together was if they got married. She wasn't sure whether he said it in jest. On her part, she knew her parents would support her in any decision she took. But they did have some concerns about her moving to another country. Having seen posters of *Pather Panchali* when it was part of a local cinema festival and the Oscar montages of *Slumdog Millionaire*, her parents assumed all Indians were bony and largely employed as rickshaw-pullers.

So Carla returned and broke the news to them and gave them a crash course in India 101. She told them India had changed, you could buy Coke in a corner store now, and that the cities had golf courses and flyovers, although she may have skipped the part where some of them collapse occasionally. Ankit on the other hand came back, and, albeit reluctantly, followed his mum's orders and met more prospective wives.

Carla found him behaving rather strangely whenever she called. He would tell her he was busy and disconnect the call. Or mumble that his family was around and he could not speak. Eventually, he confessed that his mother was anxious that he marry an Indian girl and he had 'seen' a few of them. This was the first time Carla really understood what an arranged marriage was. She was mad at Ankit. But she was even madder at his mum. 'How could his mother disapprove of me when she hadn't even met me?' she asks horrified.

The only white girls Ankit's mother had seen were 'smelly hippies' and the bikini-clad backup dancers in popular Hindi songs. Why, even during the cricket matches in the IPL, she had noticed the Indian cheerleaders were dressed in traditional attire, while the Western ones wore tight bustiers and shorts. To her a 'white girl' meant blonde hair and bikinis. She shuddered at the number of boyfriends this proposed bahu would have had. Accepting one of those into her family was out of the question.

Ankit told her he wanted to get married to her. He also told her his mother wouldn't approve of it. But then like a good Indian boy who has learned life lessons from Bollywood films, he assured her that he would get her to come around. Since Carla hadn't watched any Hindi movies, she was unsure of the sequence of this—would it be marry first and approve later or the other way round? When she heard that the wedding would most certainly have to be post-approval, she had her doubts about the whole enterprise.

Yet, she was willing to go with the plan.

Having gone so far and managed to keep their relationship alive and growing all those months, Carla wasn't ready to give up. If marriage was what it took to keep Ankit, marry was what she would do. But she knew the challenges that lay ahead. She wasn't sure if Ankit was ready to commit to her and take his mother on. She worried 'about his stamina', especially since most of their relationship was played out in front of computer monitors. She recognized, too, that she was too young to get married. Her parents insisted that she think this decision through properly before going ahead with it. But Carla was certain that she did not want her relationship with Ankit to end. And if the only way to keep her boyfriend was by marrying him before his mother found him a bride, she was willing to take that chance.

Their first step was meeting the parents—hers, that is. Ankit went to Austria. He met Carla's family, he won over her father and completely charmed her mother and grandmother. 'We all went for dinner and there was nothing awkward at all. Everyone got along great,' Carla says.

With project marriage firmly established, Carla moved to India in May for the endgame. She started working in Ankit's company as a German translator and rented a house near his. 'It was supposed to be the best time of my life, but all that we discussed was his mother. ALL THE TIME,' she says. If Carla thought maintaining a long-distance relationship via Skype was difficult, she had no idea how much more difficult maintaining a close relationship with potential Indian in-laws was. Ankit himself did not appreciate the enormity of change and adjustments she was making on his behalf. Carla was naturally missing her family, the comfort of familiar food, language, and entertainment.

Yet, Ankit was the one whining. His mother was proving to be very difficult and he didn't have the 'courage' to break the news to her. She also knew the Austrian gift-giver was down her lane, and was watching him like a hawk. He wasn't even allowed out of the house except to go to office.

For weeks, Carla and Ankit could only meet on the commute. He'd leave home for work and come and pick her up and they would drive together to office and back. Ankit would tell her he would find a way to get his mother to come around. So Carla waited. She didn't understand why his mother was obsessed about rejecting her without even meeting her, but she thought it best to see how things would unfold. 'The only thing I was thinking was what the hell is this?'

When six weeks passed with no sign of his mother thawing towards her, Carla began to panic. She started to pester Ankit about when she would meet his family. As a peace offering, Ankit brought his brother and sister-in-law to meet her. That went well. Buoyed by that success, he started wearing his mother down with requests that she 'meet' Carla and 'nothing else'. Of course, there were tears. To be let down by this favoured son was the biggest disappointment in her life, she told him.

She explained to him how difficult it would be tell their relatives that the girl is not just from a different community, but an entirely different continent. People would watch Bollywood songs of white girls frolicking in next to nothing on beaches and visualize her daughter-in-law. Imagine the horror of *that!*

Eventually, a meeting was arranged. Carla did everything but remove her skin and get into a darker one. She got a new salwar kurta tailored. She wore bangles, tied up her hair, applied make-up and made herself as Punjabi as an Austrian ancestry would allow. She took the day off and practised imaginary conversations in front of the mirror. She was told she would have to touch her mother-in-law's feet and seek her blessings. She wasn't too keen on the exercise, but of course she was willing to adjust.

So she spent the morning practising it. Do you touch the knees or the toes? Above the toes or below? What if she accidentally tipped over? Do her knees rest on the ground? Is it OK if her butt sticks up in the air? Would she be able to remember all of this and execute it with balance, grace and devotion? Several rehearsals later, she was ready and excited. Then she waited. And waited. And waited. Finally, three hours later, Ankit called her to say that his mother had changed her mind, she wasn't ready to meet Carla.

'That was a very bad beginning,' Carla says, with her characteristic dryness. Well, yes, to put it mildly. 'I thought she has never seen me. She has not met me. And she already has so many prejudices against me. Whether it was from TV or this cultural notion of Western women. And I was very angry with her. Even though I didn't know her, I started disliking her,' she says. As days passed, Carla began to wonder about her future. She felt the whole exercise would prove futile. She kept giving herself deadlines: if things didn't happen in two weeks, she would go back. Then when those two weeks passed, she would give herself another two.

It took two more months and a lot more effort by Ankit's siblings to convince their mother to meet Carla and have her home for dinner. On the big day, Carla wore her salwar kurta and her bangles again. This time though, Ankit did arrive to pick her up. As soon as Carla was introduced to her mother-in-law, she said, *'Namastey, aap kaise hain?'* ('Hello, how are you?') and touched her feet. Ankit's mother said nothing. All evening, she sat in the family living room, not speaking a word but just looking at Carla.

'She didn't speak a word?' I ask.

Carla's mouth tightens. She thinks for a bit. 'She did smile, once,' she says . . . well . . . adjustingly. When it was time for dinner, Carla helped a little with laying the table. But it was a stiff and formal affair. Carla felt as if under close scrutiny, and since her mother-in-law made no conversation at all, she felt awkward and uneasy.

'She never made me feel welcome. I felt she was staring at me like she wanted me to be scared and run from there,' she says. Despite the cold reception, Carla felt a bit relieved. Now that they had finally met, a big hurdle had been cleared, she thought. She wanted to be kind about her mother-in-law, so she told herself that it was not about her feelings, she was only worried about society. Things went on as though nothing had happened. Carla packed the salwar kameez away and waited.

For cultural comparison, I ask Carla how things would have gone had she married a fellow Austrian. She is shocked by the question and takes a while to reply. I could tell she hadn't thought to compare the two but now that she is forced, she is startled by the differences. 'Well, the marriage itself wouldn't have been an issue,' she says, by which she means that she wouldn't be forced to marry so soon and her boyfriend wouldn't have been carried by the scruff of his neck to meet potential wives. 'We may have gone out for a meal—my mother-in-law and I—and she would have asked me questions. About my job, my family, my likes and dislikes. After that, we would have had a relationship independent of my husband. If we had similar interests, we would have been like friends, else we would have behaved like polite acquaintances,' she says.

Eventually, as things turned out, Carla married Ankit, six weeks after she met his mother. There was no other meeting before the wedding. Ankit just badgered his mother until her resistance wore down and she said yes out of sheer fatigue. Carla's parents couldn't make it because of visa issues. It was a small affair. Ankit's immediate family members and some of Carla's friends came over from Austria. But it was a proper Indian wedding with a lot of dancing, singing and eating. Carla was thrilled to be Ankit's wife. She was also relieved that they had finally managed to pull it through. And for whatever it was worth, she was glad that Mummyji both approved (though grudgingly) and attended the wedding.

Shortly before Carla got married, Ankit's Ma had begun laying down the rules. She told her that in India it was not 'proper' for women, especially married women, to dress in Western wear. She was told not to wear clothes that exposed her arms or legs. She also had to help with the housework. Being eager to adjust, Carla agreed to everything. It was decided that the house was too small, so until a loan was secured and another floor constructed, Carla was allowed to stay in her apartment—which was a few doors down the road.

But this of course did not mean that the precious son would be exposed to the risk of being out of mommy's view. So in a bizarre living arrangement, Ankit now spends the night at Carla's but leaves for his mother's house the moment he wakes up. All his stuff is there and while his mother can pretend that he is sleeping in his room, she absolutely must see him brush his teeth, drink his milk and finish his parathas in the morning.

Why does Carla put up with this, you ask? I don't now. Maybe that's how Austrians atone for World War II. Carla pointed out the silver lining in this arrangement. 'This way, my husband and I have some personal space. I can have my friends over, I can wear what I like, I can cook what I like. When the house is ready I will have to move. THAT will be a bad arrangement.' Carla herself is now exempt from going over to the family home in the mornings, but she has to go every evening, after work.

Over the next few months, some of the rules slackened. Carla wears jeans and, though it has her mother-in-law's disapproval, she does not speak out against it. But capris are not allowed, and don't even mention the word skirt. The loan for the construction of the first floor has been approved and the work has begun. In a few months, Carla will have to move in there.

'Not looking forward to that at all. It is going to be very difficult to adjust. And it's very difficult because (I) won't have any privacy. She will be my boss all the time. I can't even imagine how much more I'll have to adjust there.' She thinks about it for a while and then shakes her head, slowly, sadly, for a long time. Here is a girl, young and adventurous, who could make her place in any part of the world, brought to heel by an Indian mother-in-law. If our country had any sense, they would recruit mothers-in-law like Carla's and use their skills in the external affairs ministry.

Carla's relationship with her mother-in-law has not improved substantially since the wedding. Ma has only told her what she's expected to do. That is all the conversation they have had. She has never sat Carla down and asked her about any aspect of her life. Not one thing. 'Most of the time when I'm there she only sits there and looks at me. It's very uncomfortable. I'm always thinking is this T-shirt OK, have I made a mistake, why can't she smile once?' Carla says.

She also discovered that Ankit's mother had tried to talk Ankit out of the marriage even after approving the wedding. 'That pissed me off. Because she showed a nice face towards me and behind my back she was still trying to separate her son from me. She pretended to like me and yet she did not,' she says. Like a second-generation Mother Teresa, Carla had decided to forgive her mother-in-law all her faults as soon as she agreed to the wedding. Of course, being a normal human being who was yet to reach the Punjabi-mother-of-a-son level of insanity, she assumed it was the case with Ankit's mother too. So when she discovered the MI6 level of underhanded scheming her mother-in-law was involved in, Carla began to realize the enormity of the craftiness she would have to be prepared for.

Ankit told her that the sum and substance of his mother's dislike for her is where she is from. She worries that Carla will lead Ankit astray. She worries that since divorce is so rampant in the West, Carla will walk out of the marriage easily. She especially worries that Carla will 'attract other men'. It would be simple if she talked to Carla about these fears. But she does not. Ankit has to provide a via media. Some things he shares with Carla, most he just keeps to himself.

This lack of communication also increases Carla's sense of insecurity. She has no clue what the conversations around her are. Her mother-in-law makes no attempt to speak in English when Carla is in the room. Often, she looks straight at her and talks 'very sharply' with Ankit. Carla is constantly second-guessing what the conversation is about. She gets unduly suspicious that Ma is saying something nasty about her. 'Isn't it basic decency to include a person in the room in the conversation? She never does that. The only things she tells me is something to do in the kitchen!' she says.

Throughout that first meeting, I couldn't help notice how stoically calm Carla was. She talked about 'the situation' as though she expected it to change rather quickly. She had barely touched her coffee or sandwich and while I let her finally eat—after all, this was supposed to be a meeting over lunch—I casually asked her whom she talked to about her mother-in-law troubles. 'No one,' she mumbled.

'Wouldn't it help if you talked to some friends about it?' I asked.

She shook her head while she chewed her sandwich. 'My friends in Austria can't understand it. For them all of this is so alien and unreal.'

'And your friends here? They can help, can't they?'

At this, Carla pushed her plate away, slapped the napkin down and said, 'They tell me I should adjust.' That is the only advice she has got from her friends.

'I ask how can my mother-in-law decide anyone Indian is better than me? I have to adjust. How can my mother-in-law tell me what I can wear and what I can't? I have to adjust. How can my mother-in-law tell me I should come back from office and do the housework? I have to adjust. Adjust. Adjust. How much adjust? How much?!!'

She turned red, her rage was now making her shake. Through gritted teeth she said, 'I.hate.the.word.adjust.' She thumped the table, one thump for each word.

I did not say anything. After a long pause—over ten minutes long, which is pretty long for a pause in a café that did not even have a TV on mute—she spoke again. After a sip of her coffee, she pulled the edges of her lips down and in a squeaky voice and a funny Indian accent said, 'These things happen, you have to adjust no?'

At the end of that first meeting, I worried about Carla's marriage. Left to themselves, Ankit and she may have made an adventure out of it. They would have cooked paneer makhni and eaten that with sauerkraut. He might have taught her Hindi and she would have taught him German. They might have spent Diwali with his family and Christmas with hers.

But burdened under the weight of his family's tradition, culture and rules for its women, and her mother-in-law playing a determining role in how Carla should live every day, it seemed to me to be too big a sacrifice to make. It would be for anyone, but especially so for a twenty-four-year-old who is adventurous enough to have travelled to half a dozen countries and, let's face it, chosen to live in Delhi. I felt certain that after a few years of submitting herself to the demands of her mother-in-law, Carla would be all adjusted out. She was eventually going to figure out that her marriage wasn't worth this complete makeover that was required of her.

Over the next few months, I heard sporadically from Carla. She texted me a few times asking when we would meet again. We spoke on the phone a bit. 'Things are the same,' she said, 'not much change.' Her sister-in-law ran a chocolate business. All through Diwali she was busy helping her with it. 'I stay late at their house helping in wrapping the boxes and all that,' she reported. 'I should help. But it's too much. Too much things to do. Always too much things.'

If Carla says she doesn't want to go one evening, her mother-in-law's first reaction is to look at Ankit and say, 'Didn't I tell you that a foreign girl has no sense of family and would not want to help us?' So Carla goes, for Ankit's sake.

There was still no communication at all between Carla and Ma. Over the months, Carla has tried to sit with her and talk. But her mother-in-law has expressed no interest in her life at all. 'I have asked her so many things—about how she lived when she was a child, how she grew up, came to Delhi, all of it. She hasn't asked me a single question about myself. Not even how was your day,' she says.

'Does it bother you that she hasn't?' I ask.

'I want to say it bothers me less. When I think about it, I feel it's not personal, it's perhaps the way she is. The whole family, in fact, lacks basic etiquette in communication. But it makes me sad. Sometimes angry,' she says.

We made several appointments to meet again. Confessedly, I cancelled quite a few of them. In April, she texted me to ask if 'our project' was still on. Yes, of course, I reassured her, let's meet in a few weeks. By the time I got down to fixing a time and place for that meeting, it was May. I called her a few times, but found her phone was switched off. My text messages were not delivered and eventually, in mild panic, I emailed her. She replied the following day saying she was back in Austria. We set up a Skype call.

Carla was seated in a study. The room had high ceilings supported by rich wooden beams. She seemed a lot more relaxed. When we met in Delhi, she often took a while, weighing the words, before she spoke them. Now she speaks far more openly and answers questions immediately. It is only when I see her smile on Skype that I realize I've never seen her smile before.

'Things have been up and down these last few months,' Carla began. 'We had some good times but only when I behaved. When I didn't behave well, things were bad.'

She air-quotes the word behaviour for extra emphasis, 'Good behaviour is when my mother-in-law tells me what she expects me to do and I obey her. Bad behaviour is when I tell them what I expect them to do.'

What did Carla expect? Equality. She assumed that, like in Austria, her husband would help with the chores. That if her mother-in-law expected her to help in the kitchen, she should expect her sons to do that too. Asking a man to help with the cooking and cleaning wreaked horror in the corner of west Delhi. Ankit's mother found the notion laughable. To be fair, Ankit did try. But every time he went to the kitchen, his mother kicked him out and told him to stay out. 'That is no place for a man,' she told him firmly.

Indian men have a long but uncomplicated history with domestic chores. It's just not their business. In a recent survey conducted by the International Center for Research on Women and Instituto

Promundo, 86 per cent of Indian men thought household chores were a woman's responsibility. Even in developing countries, this is an abnormally high number. Ten per cent men in Brazil thought the same way. And even in Rwanda only 61 per cent men agreed.

In Indian families, girls are always asked to help in the kitchen and around the house. Boys can relax because mummy will take care of them. So when Carla came in with her notions of 'equal chores for both genders' her mother-in-law initially found it amusing and later annoying that her little boy was being ordered by his wife to dip his hands in the dirty kitchen sink. It is to Ankit's credit that he was willing to see his wife's point of view and take a cultural step forward. But really, if he was being teased about it, there was nothing he could do, right?

A sample chore-related conversation would go like this:

Carla to Ankit: If your mother thinks I should help around the house, you should too.

Ankit to Carla: I want to, but my mother won't let me.

Carla to Ankit: If you tell her you must, she will.

Ankit to Mother: I want to do the dishes.

Mother to Ankit: Why, are you a woman?

Ankit to Mother: No, but my wife says I must.

Mother to Ankit: I was going to do the dishes, but now that I think about it, it's your wife's turn.

Ankit to Carla: Yeah, you have to do the dishes.

Carla to herself: What the fuck?!

'For me it's normal that my husband helps out in the house and for her its normal that the woman pampers her husband and he sits and enjoys while the wife does everything,' she says. When she put her foot down, all hell broke loose.

Forget equality between her sons and daughters-in-law, Ankit's mother is struggling even to treat her two daughters-in-law equally. When she feels that she is totally losing control with the new daughter-in-law, she takes it out on the older one by either snapping at her or freezing her out. Carla has been allowed to wear jeans. But if the older daughter-in-law wears them, she will not talk to her for weeks. The desi daughter-in-law is allowed to run the chocolate business from home. Working outside is out of question. 'I find that very uncomfortable,' says Carla, even though she is better off in comparison herself.

Things have come to such a pass that in less than eight months Carla is questioning the wisdom of her marriage. 'I get doubts. Why did I marry this guy? Why did I go there? This is not the life I want to live. I am happy to be back here for five weeks. It gave me a much-required break. The situation was so difficult I couldn't live with it,' she says.

The day before she left, Carla wore a pair of capri pants. She was inside the house all day and both her pairs of jeans were in the laundry. Because of this clothing transgression, her mother-in-law did not even say bye or wish her a safe trip when she left.

'You all talk about family values all the time. I am not sure what the family value is when a pair of pants is more important than wishing your family members well,' she asks, safely tucked away in Austria.

I ask Carla for some photographs of the family. While she sends them, her mother appears on the screen. She sneaks in behind Carla and makes funny faces. Carla turns around and playfully shoves her out of the frame. Carla's mother and I exchange pleasantries and with a breezy 'ta' she disappears from the screen.

In the photographs that Carla sends, Ankit—boyish, spiky-haired and trim—is in Austria. In one, he and Carla's mum are roaring with laughter. In another, he has his arm around Carla's grandmother. The atmosphere in all the pictures is warm and happy. Carla sends me two photographs of her with her mother-in-law. In one, dressed in a red salwar kameez, Carla is accepting a gift of saris and jewellery. Her mother-in-law is dressed in a simple sari draped neatly. Her hair is tied in a low ponytail at the nape of her neck. She looks like any other middle-class lady in urban India. She could be your friend's mother.

What's comical about the photograph is how rigidly both of them are standing. They are smiling, but you can tell by the gritted teeth that they are both wishing the photographer would hurry up and click already. In another, she is in the kitchen while Carla is sautéing something in a steel kadai. The photographer seems to have popped up midway through a cooking lesson. Carla is leaning in towards the kadai, and her mother-in-law stands in front of her. The contrast between the families in Delhi and Austria is obvious even through the filter of a camera lens.

Carla updated me that the loan had come through and the construction of the first floor was nearly complete. The structure was up, the plumbing was done. Once the marble floor is laid, it will be a matter of weeks before they do up the interiors, and then Carla will move in. The young woman is not looking forward to that at all. It will mean that she is completely robbed of all privacy.

Ankit and she have drawn up a list a dos and don'ts to be settled with his mother. Carla hopes that while she will abide by her mother-in-law's rules downstairs, upstairs she will be allowed to live the way she wants. But she isn't holding her breath. Even if they follow the rules, there are likely to be issues. The matter of having friends over, for example, is a tricky one. Carla does not know if she will be allowed that, and if she isn't, how she will likely deal with the situation. 'I feel perfectly sure there will be many reasons for not being happy there,' she says. 'But I want to go in with an open mind and see how it goes.' These few weeks away have helped, she says, everyone has had a chance to step back and see the big picture. But what kind of a marriage needs a time out in less than a year?

Has her mother-in-law spoken to her while she was away, I ask.

Carla laughs till tears appear at the corner of her eyes. 'Of course not!'

I ask Carla if she thinks her mother-in-law has had to 'adjust' on her behalf. 'Of course, the fact that she attended our wedding is the biggest adjustment she made. I think she has adjusted reasonably well to this bad luck that fell on her—her son going ahead and marrying a foreigner.'

Through all of this, Carla has been certain about Ankit. Even when she questions the wisdom of having married into an Indian family, she has never questioned the man. Ankit, she realizes, has also had a difficult time. He does not want to hurt his mother, and he does not want to lose Carla. He has been mediating endlessly. 'He is the perfect guy for me,' Carla gushes, 'and I can't wait to go back to him.'

When I prod her further she opens up a little more. In many ways, Carla is caught in a bad place. If she leaves Ankit—no matter how valid her reasons—she will end up proving her mother-in-law right. She had always told her son that the Austrian girl would walk out when the fun and games were over. She doesn't want to give her mother-in-law the joy of being right.

'Maybe I hope we can move out one day and live in another part of the city. Or another city,' she says and then brightens up, 'or another country!' She is not certain how long she will continue to 'adjust', but she reckons at some point she would want to live the life she has dreamed of. 'Like in a home, you know, not a prison.'

In the meantime, there is a new house and new battles to prepare for once Carla gets back. She and Ankit have some family weddings to attend as soon as she returns from Austria.

'That might be fun, you must be looking forward to that,' I tell her.

'No, not sure of that,' she says. It's a small matter but Carla knows the wedding will involve her touching 'thousands of feet'. She is not a believer, she thinks it's a sham. She even complained to Ankit about it.

'What did he say?' I ask.

'He said I should adjust!' she yells.

3

The Family That Eats Together

Name	Age (in 2013)	Husband	Married
Payal	36	Parag	2005

Often, we incorrectly assume that the rich and the real-estate endowed are too sophisticated to indulge in multigenerational family conflicts. It is difficult to imagine people who live in fancy homes in expensive parts of the city getting down and dirty and slugging it out with their daughters-in-law. What would they fight over, you might wonder, they have everything. It only stands to reason then that everything is what they have to fight for.

Truth is, the more expensive the real estate, the harder it is to break free of it. The streets of Delhi's Golf Links, Mumbai's Cuffe Parade and Chennai's Boat Club Road are strewn with stories of women braving bitchy mothers-in-law because walking away would mean leaving behind multi–million dollar inheritances.

Nowhere is the lure of real estate greater than in Mumbai. When I worked in the city, I had a young colleague—the proud possessor of a sailor's mouth on a model's body—who often rather casually unveiled the truth about Mumbai and revealed my small-town stupidities. J, as I'll call her, lived in Borivali, the suburb at the wrong end of the western line. Often she turned up at work looking like she had jumped out of bed. We'd leave office around eleven and usually board a train to go to south Mumbai—'town'—for our meetings. The minute the train crossed Mahalaxmi station, J would bring out a hefty pouch and start working on her face. Concealer first, followed by powder, then mascara, eyeliner and, with a flourish and much smacking of lips, a bright red lipstick.

'Why do you always wear make-up when you cross Mahalaxmi?' I asked her once.

'Because it only matters from here,' she said. 'Who cares about looking good for the other side?'

I was a recent postgraduate, with views that favoured both feminism as well socialism and couldn't dismiss this with an eye roll.

'But how can you peddle yourself like this? And how can you be so discriminatory?' I asked her, outraged.

'I want to turn heads from Mahalaxmi, get a boyfriend from Peddar Road, get engaged to someone on Marine Drive and marry a man from Cuffe Parade,' she told me coolly. 'This is Mumbai, the only thing that matters here is real estate.'

'But even in a marriage?' I asked incredulous.

'Especially in a marriage,' she told me before turning back to give her face the once-over in her hand mirror.

So I sought a south Mumbai daughter-in-law. Sensing that asking around for women who had married into expensive homes would not be the best strategy, I spread the word that I was looking for someone who lived in a joint family in south Mumbai.

Payal was the friend of an acquaintance. We met on a Monday morning at a mall in Parel. She was waiting for me outside Marks & Spencer. On the phone, she had called it Marks, with the Mumbaiite's typical economy of words. I walked past her twice. Of average height and build, Payal's nose was buried in her phone. When we discovered we were standing right next to each other and waiting, she burst into a smile which made her look like a five-year-old. Her straight hair fell below her shoulders and she didn't wear make-up or any loud accessories. She was dressed simply, in a printed shirt and a pair of capri pants.

Initially Payal seemed rather formal and withdrawn. When we sat down, she got straight to the point. 'Let me tell you at the outset,' she said, 'there will never be peace between a mother-in-law and a daughter-in-law. That relationship will never find a balance. You can write it down.' I nodded my head. 'No, really, you must write it down,' she said and so I did, in big loopy letters to reassure her that her prediction was properly documented. I was worried that having proclaimed this, she would draw the meeting to a close. Fortunately, she did not.

Payal met her mother-in-law for the first time in a typically formal Indian setting. At their home. With her parents. Dressed in traditional wear. The whole shebang. She had met Parag a few months earlier. He had opened a luxury car showroom on the ground floor of the apartment complex in which she lived. Payal had finished her master's degree in the UK and come back to India. She began working in her father's business, a complicated set-up which manufactured and traded in chemical products. It was what people in her father's generation and their Marwari community may have described as a son's job; but neither Payal nor her father worried about things like that. When Parag's showroom opened, Payal's father, an ardent car lover, began spending quite a lot of time hanging around with the new boys downstairs.

One day, when Payal went down to drag him home for dinner he introduced her to Parag. They just said hi-hello, she thought he was cute and that was that. After that, she bumped into him often and they would chat a little. Soon, she found herself spending more time in a car dealership than she ever thought she would. Parag seemed 'chilled out and like a really cool guy'. Payal thought he was fun to be around and the more she got to know him, the better she saw his warm and caring side. He was a bear of a man and she felt safe with him.

Often, the women I met would give me very detailed reports of how they had met their husbands. They would have a timeline and a series of anecdotes. And because they had told the story so many times—to friends, cousins and random co-passengers—the narrative always progressed in a linear fashion. Several times, they would go back to fill in a minor detail that they had perhaps skipped in this particular retelling. But Payal did none of that. 'So we hung around a lot and eventually started going around,' was the sum and substance of her romance.

The hanging around which led to the going around progressed well, and in a few months, 'when it became official,' Parag and Payal decided they wanted to get married. Since Parag was already familiar to her family, the first step was for the parents to meet formally.

If it is true that there are only seven degrees of separation between any two people on this planet, in south Mumbai that is reduced to 1.5 degrees. Not only was Payal's father aware of who Parag's parents were, he had in fact even gone to school with his mother. And this prompted him to ask Payal to reconsider her decision. He hadn't heard good things about the family, he told her. Even by the standards of Gujarati Jain families in south Mumbai, Parag's family was considered especially conservative. He had raised Payal and her sister to be achievers, to stand shoulder to shoulder with men and pursue their careers and interests. He wasn't sure Parag's parents would offer her similar liberties. He wasn't even sure of their business acumen.

Most of all though, Payal's father was unhappy that, socially and financially, Parag's family was weaker than theirs. In Mumbai real estate terms, if Payal was Cuffe Parade, Parag was Peddar Road. Both are worth painting your face for after Mahalaxmi, but while Peddar Road was south Mumbai, it wasn't the southest of the south like Cuffe Parade. Payal didn't think that was a problem, the going around was good enough for her to make that slightly northward journey.

Her parents grudgingly agreed, after announcing the statutory warning that they had made her aware of their objections and that she couldn't come running back to them if things went wrong. She agreed and an official meeting was arranged. Parag's mother told Payal's father that she should be dressed conservatively since Parag's father was an orthodox man. Only a salwar kameez would be considered appropriate attire, she said. 'Hmmm, well . . . OK' went Payal's thoughts and she went and bought herself one. On the appointed day, she went home from work, changed into the salwar kameez and went to see her future in-laws for the first time. Left to herself, she would have gone straight from office, wearing whatever she was wearing.

'I am always nervous when I meet new people and I felt like I was being judged,' Payal said of the first meeting. 'They were scanning me.' She does not recall much of what transpired at that meeting but she came away feeling certain that the visit had not gone well. Parag said, 'Whatever. It doesn't matter.' And that was that.

Payal admits the difference in their financial status was enough of a non-issue to be an issue. That even though no one was actually talking about it, it was on everyone's mind—the Swarovski crystal laden elephant in the room. 'In our society,' she says pointing in the general direction of Malabar Hill, 'a financial match is very important, perhaps the most important aspect while finding a match.' But Payal herself didn't think the fact that she was wealthier than Parag was reason enough not to marry him. It wasn't an issue with her. And Parag's parents were happy that the daughter-in-law came from a wealthy family.

Payal, however, knew what she was getting into. It was told to her in no uncertain terms that she would be living with Parag's family. This included his grandmother, parents, brother, the brother's wife and their two children. Parag and his brother, jointly, managed the family business. Everything was tied together and pulling one thread would imply that the whole big ball would unspool, leaving everyone with nothing. It was imperative, not just as a lifestyle choice but as a livelihood choice, that they all live together. There hasn't been any other way in their family for generations. 'At the time, I didn't really understand what living in a joint family really was about. I thought OK, his folks would be around, but since I would now be married and treated like an adult, I would be able to do what I pleased,' she says.

When she saw his house, Payal thought it was a good layout for a joint family. They owned two flats, one on the ground floor and another right above it on the first. They had then connected these with a staircase, so it was a two-storeyed home in an apartment complex. Parag's grandmother and his parents lived downstairs, his brother and family and the two of them would live upstairs. It was, on paper, a good idea. Payal could live her life upstairs, and intermittently mark her presence downstairs.

She thought she would be able to live a semi-independent life within the confines of the larger family. But there was a kink in the plan, one that Payal did not foresee. That of the kitchen. You cannot live a semi-independent life in a residential unit if the kitchen is a shared one. 'We had all kinds of problems,' she tells me, 'but eventually I figured out that the crux of the problem was the kitchen.'

The kitchen is significant not just because it is the source of sustenance. In fact the shared kitchen poses no problem on the food front at all. In Parag's home, for example, the food is cooked by a maharaj so there is no issue about who is doing the cooking. And members of the family can ask for anything they feel like eating. Variants can always be rustled up—diabetics get food with no sugar, those who like their food well seasoned are served portions with an extra dash of salt, all kinds of snacks are fried, people can pick and choose.

The significance of the kitchen is in that it is a meeting point. The kitchen forces you to interact and in large families, interaction comes with an easily bundled 'combo' of interference. If you are forced to say hello, you are leaving yourself vulnerable to being asked why you are so late. Payal's was a meta real estate story. The disputed territory of the kitchen was the most valuable space inside a most valuable home.

'It wasn't like I was given a set of house rules when I first got married. No one really told me what was acceptable behaviour and what was not. So of course, you behave like you would in your own home, right? Because that is the assumption—now this is your own home. But it never is,' Payal says. The rules came gradually. The first one was about wake-up time. Payal and Parag liked to party. Even if they weren't heading to the hot and happening club of the moment, they liked to go out in the evenings, hang out with friends and come back home at 1 or 2 a.m. So naturally, they woke up late. That was the cause of the early complaints.

'My mother-in-law started passing these comments saying this is no time to wake up. You have to see and supervise things around the house. Then she would work herself into a temper and ask what it was about me that I had to go out all the time. Things like that,' Payal says. At times, she would say these things directly to Payal, but most of the time, she would complain about her to Parag. Not wanting to hurt his new wife, Parag would not pass these on to her, but she could sense that things were unpleasant. 'I would know as soon as I saw his face that she had gone to him with an issue about me. I would be like what the fuck, man,' she says.

Part of the problem was that Payal's mother-in-law was expecting a different kind of bahu. Parag's brother had got married in 1998 ('it was a whole other era') and his wife projected the ideal qualities that a traditional family looked for in a daughter-in-law. This largely involved unquestioning compliance. Daughter-in-law #1 was only twenty-two when she got married. She was too frightened to take on the family or lay down her wishes. She was too frightened, in fact, to even harbour any desires. All she did was listen and obey. After being blessed with this ideal for almost eight years, Parag's parents had assumed that this was how the younger daughter-in-law would be too.

As she spoke, I felt Payal warm up towards me. When she said 'what the fuck man' for the first time, I knew we had turned some kind of a corner. We could relate then as individuals, as people tied together by her story. Now that the ice was broken, Payal spoke easily and more descriptively.

In comparison to her sister-in-law, Payal was twenty-seven when she got married. It was 2005; life had changed significantly in the preceding eight years. Payal was not going to take 'any shit'. She saw compromise as a two-way street. She wasn't the sort to put her head down, bite her tongue and live a life that was defined for her by others. 'Initially, everything I said or did was an issue. I was always told but your sister-in-law never behaved like this. She would wake up in the morning, serve them their food, then sit down to eat, etc. She would never go out anywhere. Things like that. I wasn't going to spend the rest of my life living like that,' she says.

So, silently at first, but vocally soon after, Payal started asserting her right to live the way she wanted to. Her rebellion began with her clothing. 'I prefer to wear Western clothes. The first time I bought salwar kurtas was, in fact, for that meeting with the in-laws and subsequently as part of my wedding trousseau. So, I started wearing jeans—not around the house—but when I went out. But even then, in deference to their preferences, I would wear it with a long top or something. Since I had to go through the in-laws' quarters in order to get out of the door, my mother-in-law would see me and she would say "*Chee, accha nahin lagta*" and things like that. I learned to ignore her,' says Payal. Soon, her sister-in-law also got on the style bandwagon and, using Payal as an excuse, she too began to sport a pair of jeans.

If you dump a frog in boiling water, it will jump out. But if you place the frog in tepid water and slowly increase the temperature a few degrees at a time, the frog will just sit there until it's boiled. Payal successfully applied this to resolve the dress code issue and her sister-in-law quickly followed. They began with the long tunics and jeans. Then the tops got shorter. For about eighteen months or so, they stuck to kurtis, so that 'offensive' areas like the butt and upper thighs were well covered. Eventually, they raised the hem higher and settled on T-shirts. Over time, the sleeves too got shorter and shorter till finally one day, she wore a sleeveless top and no one really noticed. 'Even if they did, they didn't say anything. Or even if they did say something, by then I didn't give a shit,' Payal says.

The second battle was about religion. Parag's parents are devout Jains. While Payal's family did believe in God, they weren't ritualistic. They have a Diwali puja once a year, but not much else. Once she was married, Payal was asked to pray every day. 'And it's not even prayer. It's an apology. You have to apologize to God every day. Now if you do it without really believing it, it's just a farce,' she says. But it became a big issue that Payal wasn't in the home temple every day. Also, truth is, when she first met Parag, she noticed that he had no dietary restrictions based on his religion. He ate what he liked, drank what he wanted—onions, potatoes, garlic, the whole unJainly lot. So Payal did not expect him to come from a home that was so religious.

Even as the arguments about the absence of Payal in the puja room were raging, the pilgrimages began. In the first couple of years, they had to accompany the in-laws to nearly half a dozen temple trips. Jain temples are usually atop mountains and, after climbing up, devotees have to bathe in dipping pools and change into fresh new clothes before doing the puja. These are coarse fabrics that have to be kept pure. Payal couldn't eat while dressed in these nor could she visit a washroom. It was a tough regimen to follow.

She found it totally irksome to climb a mountain, dip in a common pool, wear horrid clothes and do a puja she didn't believe in. To make things worse, Parag never did the puja and that didn't seem to be a big deal. 'I thought if I don't put my foot down now, I'll be doing this puja for the rest of my life.'

After the long trek up on her eighth or ninth pilgrimage, Payal politely told her mother-in-law that she wasn't planning on doing the puja. There was much shouting and crying. 'It scared me to take her on like that,' Payal says, 'but I thought if my husband gets to choose not to do it, it's only fair that I get that choice too.' It was a year-and-a-half since she had got married. By then she had a feel for what her mother-in-law was like. Payal thought she could either stay unhappy or put her foot down, deal with some immediate unpleasantness but eventually live a life that she wanted. She preferred the latter.

And then came the third battle. This one was about their evenings out. She stuck with it, no matter what Parag's Ba said. Once Ba realized that haranguing Payal about what time she woke up wasn't working, she started harassing the couple about the amount of money they were spending on going out. Soon though, the brother and sister-in-law began joining them.

'It was annoying at first because then Parag would tell me you have to be "proper" in front of them. My deal was, listen, I am putting up with this shit all day, you can't tell me I don't even have a chance to unwind in the evening,' she says. Still, initially, she dressed a little more conservatively when out with her brother- and sister-in-law. She did not drink or smoke in front of them either. Eventually, she decided if they were coming out with them then they had to deal with how she behaved. Also, times had changed. South Mumbai was crawling with hipsters who wore what they wanted, drank what they pleased and blew smoke at whoever passed by them. They saw girls from the neighbourhood, friends they had gone to school and college with, all living this new modern version of life. It was easy then to imitate and eventually assimilate.

Ba muttered about this every day. When she realized that Payal's bad influence had corrupted her older son and daughter-in-law too, she was livid. She constantly nagged her sons and yelled at Payal. Increasingly, Payal spent most of her time upstairs. But she couldn't avoid mealtimes. And across the dining table accusations and curses flew. No one was happy. And no one could be trusted.

Despite the fact that Payal initiated the way for her sister-in-law to get out and live it up a little, the relationship between them was not friendly. When she feels a bit 'insecure' about things, she goes to Ba and complains about Payal. 'Think of us,' says Payal, 'we are three women—intelligent and educated—who are sitting at home all day with nothing to do. We were obviously tearing each other apart.'

Resentments and suspicion built up furiously. Her mother-in-law's position was an unenviable one. Not only could she never take control of this new daughter-in-law who knew her mind and stood up to her constantly, she was quickly losing her grip on the older daughter-in-law as well. They had several unpleasant exchanges, some in front of the men of the family, most while they were away at work. But none of those were as bad as what was to come.

Payal was pregnant with her first child. She cannot recall the genesis of that argument, but remembers that it was about her parents. Parag's parents expected to be treated in full accordance with their status as the 'boy's parents' by Payal's folks. They had to be called and greeted for each festival. If there was a delay, Ba would start off about how Payal's parents were disrespectful of them. Her parents threw a dinner party once a year. For that, Parag's father and mother had to be called and invited, first individually, then jointly. 'After all this, my mother-in-law would come and sit there with a long face and ruin everybody's evening,' she says.

Parag's parents were in the middle of an important week-long fast. The seventh day was the most important one, a swing was brought home and a lot of ceremonies were involved before the fast was ultimately broken. Parag's parents did it every year and each time Payal's parents had to call daily and inquire about it. This particular year, Payal's parents were leaving to spend the weekend in Khandala and, in their hurry, they forgot to call and wish them on the seventh day. That was the breaking point.

It started with Ba scolding Payal about her parents and all the frustrations and complaints about the previous months came tumbling out. Ba shouted and screamed for half an hour. Then her father-in-law joined the tirade and all kinds of ugly words were exchanged. Finally, he told her that she had to decide—she could either stay with them or choose her parents and walk out of the marriage.

'I was like fuck off, I am getting out of here,' she tells me. She called her parents who 'freaked out' and sped from Khandala all the way back to Worli. Her in-laws weren't letting her leave the house, but they weren't letting up on their complaints against her either. 'I was fighting with my husband telling him I wanted to leave. My mother-in-law wouldn't let me out of the house. She stood at the door. I was like this is not happening, no one asks me to choose between my parents and anyone else,' she says. Her father waited at the gate of the building, too anxious to leave and too worried to come in lest things take a turn for the worse.

'This went on for a long time. My mother-in-law would not let me walk out of the house and she would not stop yelling at me. She just stood there and harangued me telling me this was not the way to behave. That everything was my fault. That I was a bad person. Things like that,' she says. Parag tried desperately to mediate between the two sides and he refused to let her leave. 'I knew that he had faith in me, but I thought he had to know that if he didn't put a full stop to this, it was never going to end,' she says. After enduring this for over two hours, Payal finally relented and decided to stay. She was six months pregnant and she had no fight left in her for the day. 'But I came very, very close to leaving that house for good, that day,' she says.

Eventually, she just stomped off upstairs. She was livid, she wanted to neither see nor talk to her in-laws for a while. But in a couple of hours, she felt famished. There was nothing else to do but repress her anger and go downstairs for a bite. This is where the kitchen got tricky. If she lived by herself, or at least had some provision to take care of her immediate needs, Payal could have stewed in her anger until things cooled off. The time away would help put things in perspective, she could even face up to where she was wrong in the fight. But the fact that the kitchen was common made all of it impossible.

'You are forced to see, interact and sometimes re-confront your adversaries before you have had the time to process the trauma of the argument,' she says. Her mother-in-law had steadfastly refused to allow the daughters-in-law to affix a water filter upstairs. So they couldn't even drink a glass of water without coming to the kitchen. 'My sister-in-law has also had fights with my mother-in-law. After which she would refuse to come downstairs and eat. But how long can you do that? My mother-in-law knew that in a couple of days she would be back—tail tucked in, ego and issues swallowed. The joint kitchen was the bane of our existence,' Payal says.

So things bumped along. The fight was not forgotten, but it wasn't brought up either. The secret to the longevity of joint families lies in pretending things don't happen. It might be eating you up inside, yet the outside world shouldn't hear even a whimper. But, Payal did not even have the comfort of that. She would walk into the house to overhear her mother-in-law complaining about her on the phone to her friends. She'd seize up mid-sentence on seeing her, and would hold on to the phone silently, until she walked out of the room.

Payal complained to Parag and threatened she would do the same too. Caught between his conservative mother and his modern wife, Parag was not of much help. He assured them both of his love and support and did not carry complaints from one to the other. What more could he do? When things got particularly bad with his mother, Payal would take it out on him—withholding sex and then communication. It was nerve-racking. 'We were all boiling, the house was like a fucking pressure cooker,' she says.

Right then her phone rings. She excuses herself to answer it. 'I am meeting that person I told you about, who wants to hear about my mother-in-law,' she says and looks up at me and smiles. The conversation ends quickly. 'Sorry, that was my husband,' she says.

'Is he OK with you talking about his mother?' I ask.

'That's the deal you know. My husband is a wonderful guy. I hide nothing from him. He is the most loving, most amazing man, ever. Which is what makes all of this even harder. I know how much he hurts in the middle of this, but what can I do?'

I had seen pictures of Parag's on Payal's Facebook page. Most of them were shot at parties or during a vacation. Tall and on the heavier side, he was often dressed in funky printed shirts and sported a pair of glasses with a red frame. He seemed colourful; quite likely the centre of the party. In most of the photos Payal had a wide grin while Parag held her tight. And every other status update of Payal's is an affirmation of love for her two little daughters and their father. Not surprisingly, her in-laws appear in none of the photographs. It is clear that despite whom she lives with, her definition of family is just the four of them.

After that first near walk-out, Payal started talking to Parag about getting their own kitchen. She thought about moving out, to a place of their own. Since Parag worked in the family business, that decision would not just be a personal one, it would also be a professional one. Economically, it would be a stupid move. South Mumbai is one of the most expensive places to buy a home, in not just India but the world. And moving out would mean they would also have to cobble together enough capital for Parag to start a new business.

It would be impossible for him to find the money and the manpower that had been built over so many years if he decided to strike out on his own. If they moved out they would have to more or less write off a substantial chunk of the inheritance. So Payal focused on the kitchen. If she had a kitchen of her own, she could live in the house without having to see her mother-in-law three times a day. Parag was fine with the idea of a separate kitchen, but his mother would have none of it. Each time he broached the topic, she would come up with an old proverb comparing mashed potatoes to broken families or some such. And things continued despite this impasse.

A couple of months after that big fight, the family sat down to discuss the living situation. Upstairs wasn't big enough for two full-fledged families—Parag's brother's and now Parag's own growing brood. Ultimately, they managed to buy the adjacent apartment on the ground floor. Mother-in-law said while the two of them could move in immediately, eventually they should look at breaking the wall and 'combining' the apartments. Payal said nothing. This was not a game she was going to lose. But she had to play her cards right. Even though Payal and Parag now had a house of their own, there was no question about using their kitchen there. They would all continue to eat from the main kitchen, mother-in-law mandated. That was final.

Payal was determined to win the kitchen war. But she knew that, as with the clothes war, she would have to move slowly and stealthily. First she would fight for a fridge. She complained constantly about not having her own fridge to store her baby's milk. Mother-in-law was not happy about that at all. 'How far is the fridge here that she cannot store the child's milk here?' she asked. Parag pointed out the inconvenience of coming from one apartment to the other three times a night. Yet, she grumbled. By the time Payal's daughter was eighteen months old, she had been allowed to buy a fridge to store the baby's night-time feed.

So it went on until the second tipping point. Payal doesn't remember exactly what happened or she isn't keen on laying out the dirty to me. But there was something, she says, something her mother-in-law said or instigated her father-in-law to do. They called her in and yelled at her. Payal didn't argue, she stood there, head hung low, eyes firmly fixed on the floor. When it was over, she went across to her apartment and told Parag she was going to her parents' place for a few days. Even though they had been married for many years by then and her parents lived a few kilometres down the road, it wasn't a simple affair. Often, her mother-in-law insisted that her mother call and 'seek permission' to have Payal over.

Parag didn't suspect a thing. Payal packed her stuff, took her child and left. It was only when she was in the car that she called him and said this was no ordinary trip home. 'I told him I'd had enough, that I wasn't going to take this shit any more,' she says. A frenzy of phone calls followed. Her father-in-law called the driver and ordered that the car be turned around immediately. Payal insisted he stay the course. Her mother-in-law called, told her this was no way to behave. Parag called and asked her to not make such a big deal out of things. But she was certain. She was going to stay with her parents until things were fully resolved.

The phone calls, of course, had reached her home before she had. Her mother told her that she hadn't known Payal to be a screamer and a fighter and if her marriage had reduced her to that, it meant her problems were serious. Her father told her now that she had taken the big step, she should go back only if changes were made and things were resolved. 'There is no point going back to the same issues. Solve them now and only then go back was his advice. That gave me confidence,' she says.

When Parag came to talk to her about going back, she told him she wouldn't move unless the kitchens were separate. That was her ask and she was not prepared to budge from it. She would accept no halfway solutions, no vague promises of doing it after a few months, nothing. If she were to go back, it would only be to her own kitchen. Nothing less. Nothing else.

Eventually, Parag yielded. She gathered her things and her baby and moved back the following day. She arrived with one additional piece of luggage though, a cooking stove. She set it up, hired a maharaj and got her kitchen going in less than two days. 'Even those two days that I had to eat from the main kitchen were horrible. Things were so bad, all our anger and animosity towards each other had gotten so toxic, that I found it impossible to swallow the food.'

None of this went down well with the mother-in-law. She gritted her teeth and bore it initially. But she was determined that this wouldn't be a permanent arrangement. She nagged Parag constantly about it. She tried various tricks to shut Payal's kitchen down. She fired the maids Payal hired. She paid the maharaj money to not go and cook for her. But Payal was determined that no matter how difficult it was to run her kitchen, she wouldn't go back to the previous regime.

Still, never having lived in a joint family, I could not fathom why the kitchen was so important. Other than the Hindi movie vibe of a happy family sitting around a dining table, what is the emotional significance of having a common kitchen? 'It isn't about the food,' Payal says, 'it's about what it symbolizes to the outside world. That we are a happy family which is still together.'

'Look at our case,' she says, 'We are three women from three different homes. It's impossible that we gel. We can try and be cordial but after some time even that becomes difficult and forced. We aren't cooking in the kitchen ourselves, but we are expected to manage things. My mother-in-law then interferes in every decision. So if she thought I should be in charge of ordering the groceries, she should just leave me to it, right? No, not only do I have to order the groceries, I should also do it her way. So if she bought stuff on the fifth, tenth and fifteenth of the month, I should too. My argument is that if you want me to do things, you should let me do them my way. And for God's sake, I'm a postgraduate and I helped my dad run his company, surely I know how to buy atta and chawal!'

The most important change that splitting the kitchen has brought is in Payal herself. With the common kitchen and the issues that it threw up, she had become a person she didn't know and like. She wasn't one to squabble, but that was what she found herself doing. She wasn't a screamer and fighter, but that's who she had become. The only expressions her daughter saw on her face were anger and misery. With her own kitchen, she could finally go back to who she was. 'I feel like a weight has lifted off my shoulders,' she says.

In the three years since she won the battle of the kitchen, Payal had another child. The girls run freely from one home to the other and treat both as their own. Parag visits his parents once a day, usually in the morning before he goes to work. Payal goes over every once in a while, for a quick chat or to plan something if there is a festival or some such.

She is certain that splitting the kitchen saved her marriage. Since she now fights less with her mother-in-law, there are fewer fights between Parag and her too. She isn't steaming in the house all day waiting for him to come in the evening so she can rip into him. He too is happy to be liberated from being constantly caught in the crossfire. Ever so often, there is talk about merging the houses. But Payal points out to Parag that he is thirty-five, an age where he wouldn't want to be told what to do and what not to do by his parents.

There are still some issues. At some point, Payal wants to make a reasonable routine of when the kids will visit the grandparents.

They are spoilt silly there. 'Some completely illogical things go on there,' she says, 'they feed them chocolates before mealtimes. They give them ice cream if they ask for it, even when they have a cold or a sore throat. They feed them supari if they ask for it. Can you see the shit I am dealing with?' she leans forward and asks me. But she does not want it to become another mighty row.

So she tells Parag about them and, concerned father that he is, he jumps into action. Payal does not want to stop the grandparents from having access to the kids. Her issues are her own, she does not want to influence the kids with them. Earlier, her mother-in-law would tell her that she had raised kids herself and did not need to be instructed how to do so. Now that the older daughter is five, her grandmother merely tells her I want to give you this chocolate, but your mother will yell at me if I do. 'I don't know how to explain it to them any more. Earlier I used to pick my kids up and bring them back. Now I think, let their father deal with it,' she says.

Payal has learned to pick her fights. And focus on the good things in her life. Her loving husband, her two adorable girls, that rock on her finger and the fact that she owns the most priceless real estate in south Mumbai: her own kitchen!

4

You Are (Almost) like a
Daughter to Me

Name	Age (in 2013)	Husband	Married
Anshika	26	Rohit	2009

It is safe to say that from the day her son is born, every Indian mother dreams of his wedding day. As she slings a water bottle around his neck and sends him off to kindergarten, and years later lovingly sorts through his semester's worth of dirty laundry, she is thinking about the day he'll dress up like a maharaja and stride into a shamiana bedecked with marigolds and fairy lights. It would be a 'grand' reception and the bride's father will have paid for all of it.

Over the next two decades, Mummyji works on her dream, filling in the details. She will choose the bride from among a thousand applicants. The girl will be fair, tall and thin. She will be educated and smart, and eager to forsake her career for her husband. For the wedding, the bride will wear a sari with a six-figure price tag, and her son will buck tradition and land at the venue in a helicopter. No expenses will be spared, she'll make sure she'll tell the bride's father that the flowers have to be orchids from Thailand

and the DJ has to have played a whole season in Ibiza.

It is inevitable that, when her son comes home and gently breaks the news that he knows whom he wants to marry, Mummyji's heart will break. She will clap her palm to her mouth, shake her head in disbelief and run to her room to cry. She has seen this happen on TV, but had never thought it would happen to her. Slowly, over the next few days, Mummyji passes through all the stages of grief. From disbelief, she leapfrogs to anger at the vixen who has waylaid her son so, and eventually to a vow of retribution.

No matter whom the son has picked, Mummyji is not going to be swayed. Even if she ticks all the boxes and would have been the kind of daughter-in-law Mummyji herself would have chosen, the fact that she wasn't the one to choose is reason enough to never accept her.

Anshika Dewani would have definitely been in Rohit's mom's shortlist of potential daughters-in-law. She belonged to not just the same Sindhi community as Rahul's family, but even the same sub-community. And they had both grown up in the same Mumbai suburb. In fact, there already were marriages between the two families. Anshika's aunt had married Rahul's uncle. On paper, Rahul and Anshika's was a match made in arranged-marriage heaven.

I met Anshika outside the Siddhi Vinayak temple at Dadar on a Tuesday evening. 'I'm wearing a yellow salwar kameez with a hot pink print on it,' she had told me over the phone earlier, 'you can't miss me.' She was right. Even in colourful Mumbai, she stood out like a tropical macaw. The twenty-seven-year-old teaches in a posh Mumbai school. It was the beginning of the year and she had promised herself she would go to the Siddhi Vinayak temple eight Tuesdays in a row, directly after school.

She couldn't meet me after work on other days. It would require permission from her Mummyji and, in all probability, it was likely to be refused. So we decided to chat on the slow commute home from the temple. This way she could continue with her campaign of trying to be the good daughter-in-law. She'd been trying for three years and things weren't going well on Project Good Daughter-in-Law. But Anshika was determined to make it work.

'But why,' I asked her when she told me how hard she was trying to please her mother-in-law.

'Arre, because,' was her reply.

Anshika is one of the liveliest people I have ever met. She sprinted to the taxi I was waiting in, and before she had set her bag down or caught her breath, she started talking. Her straight hair was pulled away from her face and some of it was tied on top of her head, in what I later discovered is called a half-pony. What stood out about Anshika's looks were her eyes; they were expressive and mischievous. Her mother-in-law hadn't yet managed to wipe out their sparkle.

Throughout our car ride, Anshika spoke non-stop. I could barely get a question in. She has a really zingy sense of humour and is the first to laugh at what she says, often even before she has said it. Her voice has a strange pitch, as though she is just recovering from a cough and that made her laugh a cackly boom. I found myself laughing a lot with her. If I had to guess, I would have thought she was the kind of woman who would walk up to her future mother-in-law and charm the diamonds off her.

'So Rohit and I were childhood sweethearts,' she began. She remembers meeting Rohit for the first time at a common friend's birthday party. They were both in the fourth standard. But because they were both Sindhis living in the same locality in Mumbai and they even belonged to the same sub-sect, it was possible that they knew each other 'practically since birth.' When they were in class nine, they went to the same place for their tuitions. They began to see a lot more of each other and, eventually, before the year was over, they were 'going around'. They were one of those inevitable couples, two people that everyone around them knows will end up together. Anshika was certain even then that this was the guy she would marry.

Despite the close circles they moved in, Anshika managed to avoid meeting her future mother-in-law. She knew from Rohit that she was strict and conservative. In fact, among their gang of friends, they called Rohit Cinderella, since he had to rush home at midnight, or else his mother would get mad. 'Can you imagine a big group of people and this one guy says my mummy will scold me if I go home late? We used to tease him all the time. Like, I mean, ALL THE TIME,' she says.

Though Anshika and Rohit were dating for years, they were careful to hide it from their families. Anshika avoided the family and community events where she was certain Rohit's mother would be present. They both graduated. Rohit started working in the family business, trading in textiles and fashion accessories. Anshika's parents decided to move to Guwahati to pursue their business interests there. But she wanted to stay on in the city.

Her parents had raised her to be independent and ambitious and they had no qualms at all about leaving their daughter of 'marriageable age' alone in the city. Anshika found a job teaching the junior programme in an international school and her parents let her continue living in their Mumbai house. The cook and two maids were instructed to look after her. But then suddenly, in the midst of this, everyone came to discover her relationship with Rohit.

Anshika's parents were shocked and her mother was appalled. Her aunt who was already married into Rohit's family had told her enough horror stories about Rohit's mother. She knew her daughter would not have an easy life there. She sat Anshika down and told her graphic stories about her future mother-in-law and tried to convince her that she was making a mistake. Eventually, when she realized that Anshika wasn't going to listen to reason, she gave up with the ultimatum that she was not to come back crying to her in the future. 'But you know how it is when you are in love, no?'

Anshika asks me. 'You don't want to think of anything negative and you just agree to everything. To be honest, at that time, I was sure I could handle anything. Or anyone.'

Pandemonium reigned in Rohit's home too. How could he be audacious enough to choose his own wife? That was Mummyji's dream! And if he did have to go and choose his own wife, couldn't he have chosen someone who was fair and thin? Why didn't he consider his poor mother before making this decision, Mummyji asked him. Did he not think of the humiliation she would now have to endure? Taking this dark, fat girl and introducing her as her daughter-in-law? Why, everyone would be laughing behind her back.

As Anshika tells me this, I nod my head absently. It is only after she has progressed further into her story that I sit up with a start. Because, Anshika *is* fair and of average build. 'But you are fair,' I blurt. 'Well, no. I am only wheatish,' she says. After a long pause, she adds, 'I don't think I can ever be fair enough for my mother-in-law. I mean, even if I was the colour of milk, she still wouldn't think of me as being fair enough.'

At first, Anshika couldn't believe Rohit's mummy would not accept her. Even Rohit was surprised. Not one to give up, Anshika began working on becoming the ideal daughter-in-law. First, she gathered as much information as she could about the family. This was easy as they knew many people in common. Soon Anshika discovered where the chink in the armour was. The daughter! Rohit's sister, Reshma, was married and lived a few buildings away in Lokhandwala. It was she and her husband, Anand, who made all decisions for the family. If Reshma or Anand said a spoon was a fork, then it was a fork. No questions asked.

The way to her mother-in-law's heart, Anshika decided, was through her daughter. So she set out to woo Reshma. She called and spoke to her every day. She bought her presents. She would visit her on all special occasions—early in the day, before her mother-in-law appeared—for her birthday, her daughter's birthday, her husband's birthday, for a puja, for an anniversary, sometimes simply because it was a day that ended in 'y'. The effort paid off. Reshma put in a few good words about Anshika to her mother.

Soon, a family wedding came up. It was the son of Anshika's aunt, the one who had pioneered liaison with Rohit's family. It was inevitable that Anshika would meet her mother-in-law there. She spent the day in the beauty salon, trying to get as 'fair' as she possibly could. She also dressed in clothes that would make her seem thinner and taller. At the wedding, Reshma took her over and introduced her to her mother. 'I don't remember what she asked me. It was very formal and quite stiff. I don't think it would have lasted more than a minute, but it felt much, much longer,' she says. She focused on smiling and trying to look coy and proper.

After that first meeting, Reshma started talking in slightly more concrete terms. The conditions under which she could possibly be considered as a daughter-in-law of the family were laid down one by one. She would never get permission to work, she told her. Anshika agreed. She would never be allowed to wear revealing clothes. Anshika agreed. Not even sleeveless. Anshika gulped but nodded her head.

A few days later, Anshika received a call from Reshma asking her if she was free to meet. The venue—in typical Mumbai fashion—was 'below the building'. Below Rohit's building, that is. Sensing that this might be significant, Anshika went appropriately dressed—in a long top that nearly fell to her knees and full sleeves. Reshma met her downstairs and told her that her mother wanted 'to talk'.

By talk, she meant, Rohit's mother would ask questions. 'It was like a rapid-fire round in a quiz show,' Anshika recalls. She was asked what she did all day, what time she went to work, what time she came back home. Whether she went out at night. If yes, how often. But the questions always returned to the central one—did she know how to cook?

Most of Anshika's answers were truthful, she says. 'I told her that I didn't know the C of cooking, to which she said, don't worry, I'll teach you; which I thought was very sweet, you know.' Then Mummyji stated her first non-negotiable rule. She would not be allowed to continue working. Anshika nodded her head in earnest agreement.

'She was quite open and direct,' Anshika says. 'She told me I expect you to cook, I expect you to clean, I expect you to stay home and do whatever I ask you to.' Anshika nearly headed to the kitchen right then to start doing the dishes. She had nothing to ask her future mother-in-law. Rohit's mother did not speak English and Anshika just kept saying 'OK aunty, OK aunty' to everything. 'Then I ran off from there,' she says.

The promise to teach her cooking was the sign that she had been approved. Preparations for the wedding could now begin. This was going to be a three-round affair, spread over twelve months. Stage one, was a roka. Stage two: an engagement. And stage three: the grand finale—a destination wedding in Goa was what Anshika and Rohit had in mind.

The Indian wedding industry is worth 35 billion dollars and Anshika was determined to help it grow. She had dreamed of this day all her life and she wanted it to be as perfect as possible. No costs would be spared. She was going to beg, plead, cry and cajole to get things done just right.

Anshika's parents came from Guwahati to formally meet Rohit's parents and seek their approval for the roka. It went well. Though they were a bit jittery with the family, they absolutely loved Rohit and couldn't be happier for their daughter. Things progressed at a fast clip to the roka. There was no talk about dowry, but her mother-in-law told her parents that all the wedding functions must be grand. Several times.

Of course, as the bride's parents not only do they have to pay for all the functions, but they also have to take prior approval from Rohit's mother and brace themselves for all kinds of criticism later. Anshika's parents shortlisted a venue for the roka and took Rohit's parents for a walk-through. They looked happy enough about the place and said it was OK. 'Of course, after the wedding they told me they hated the place!' says Anshika.

Unaware of this at the time, Anshika's parents went into full-blown 'Sindhi parents of the bride' mode. Rohit's mother sent a long list of things that were needed for the puja. This was the Holy Grail and it was followed to a T. Then Anshika's parents sent twenty-one goody baskets—one contained the best whiskies, another the best chocolates, the third had an assortment of the best mithai and so on. This was so Rohit's family could distribute it to their relatives and friends. The baskets of goodies are a sign that the announcement of an engagement will soon follow. For the roka, Reshma called Anshika early on and told her not to wear a sleeveless dress. 'No one in our family wears it,' she said. Of course, come roka day, Anshika was in full sleeves and Reshma herself had her shoulders on full display!

But Anshika was too thrilled to finally be Rohit's fiancée to care about her undisplayed arms. Soon after the ceremony, she decided to quit her job and go to Guwahati. There was less than a year to go for the wedding and she had to learn to cook. But before she left, her parents came to Mumbai to discuss the details of the wedding. Both Rohit and Anshika were keen on getting married in Goa. Rohit's mother said if the wedding was in Goa, Anshika's parents would have to book hotel rooms for all their guests as well.

Her parents agreed, but Anshika thought this was highly unreasonable. If the wedding was in Mumbai, Rohit's parents would foot the hotel bills of their relatives; it was only logical that they did so in Goa too. She tried to get Rohit to reason with his parents first—since a Goa wedding was a shared dream—but he was unsuccessful. Much back and forth ensued. Anshika had already planned quite a few of the finer details of the Goa wedding. But eventually, she decided it wasn't worth being bullied so much for.

So they gave up the idea and decided to marry in Mumbai where Rohit's family would at least take care of lodging their guests. Having settled on a date and a city, Anshika left with her parents for Guwahati. There she started her cooking lessons. Since she had been living in an apartment in Mumbai by herself with three people to cook and clean for her, her first lesson was on how to boil water.

In a few months, of course, wedding preparations moved up one gear and things were beginning to get to that frenzied state of anxiety and excitement. With a couple of months to go for the wedding, Anshika went to Delhi to shop for her trousseau. According to the custom in their community, the boy's family is expected to gift the bride one outfit—usually the one that is worn for the reception. In Delhi, she found her dream reception outfit. It was a lehenga in a rich shade of maroon, embellished with embroidery in an antique gold polish. It was classy and elegant. It was everything she wanted it to be.

So, in a fit of shopping-induced euphoria and confidence, she called her future mother-in-law up. With her fingers firmly crossed, tentatively and shyly, she asked if she could go ahead and buy the outfit. Her mother-in-law could pay for it later so that it would be a gift from her. Mother-in-law said no. 'I was wondering if I heard her wrong for a moment. Then she came down on me. She said what kind of a girl are you? What kind of a person is your mother that she allows you to call me—your future mother-in-law—and ask for money for an outfit? You can't choose it by yourself. It's our outfit. She went on and on like that,' Anshika says.

But Anshika was so sold on that dress that she told her mother she would buy it nevertheless and that when she returned to Mumbai before the wedding, she would somehow manage to convince her mother-in-law. It cost 35,000 rupees and Anshika felt certain her mother-in-law would love it when she saw it.

A few weeks later, she came to Mumbai and met Mummy. She showed her the stuff she had bought. 'When would you wear this?' her mother-in-law asked picking up the disputed dress. 'That's the dress I really, really loved and thought I could wear for the reception,' Anshika said, shaking the dress out and displaying it properly.

'Reception outfit?' her mother-in-law asked, her face turning wedding sari–red.

'Yes, I really, really loved this one,' Anshika mumbled.

'No,' her mother-in-law said, 'we will go and buy your reception outfit. It has to be EVERYBODY'S choice.'

Anshika pleaded with her. But her mother-in-law remained firm. 'I don't care what you do with the outfit you bought. Return it, burn it, whatever. What you will wear is what we will all go and choose. Together,' Rohit's mother said.

In retrospect, Anshika feels she should have put her foot down then. But at the time, she didn't have the courage to take her mother-in-law on like that. So with a broken heart, she resigned herself to the fact that she would not be able to wear what she loved. 'I knew that she didn't approve of me. I knew that I don't have the physical attributes she wanted in a daughter-in-law. And I was so low in confidence because of that, that I was a pushover,' she says.

The following week, six of them—Rohit's parents, Reshma and Anand, Rohit and Anshika—went shopping for the reception dress. While Anshika had shopped for her entire trousseau in two days in Delhi, it took two weeks for them to eventually find that one outfit. Everyone's choice mattered, except of course her own. Eventually, they decided on a blingy, crystal-studded 'as Sindhi as you could possibly get' outfit. Anshika hated it, but her brother-in-law said that was the one he liked the best. So that was the dress she wore.

Even though Anshika was telling me the story three years on, it was evident that she was still affected by it. The flowers she held in her hand—the prasad from the temple—were crushed to pulp in her hands and her sunshine smile dimmed. She stared out of the car window and shook her head slowly as we crossed Bandra and then Juhu. In many ways, Anshika thinks of this as the battle that changed everything. It showed her up as weak and as a person who could easily be bullied. 'Well, at least I made sure they bought a more expensive dress than the one I had,' she shrugs.

Anshika was a nervous wreck by the time the wedding came around. There were so many 'instructions'. She had to alter pretty much most of her outfits in keeping with the mother-in-law's wishes. 'I was running around like crazy, keeping up with her orders. I was constantly going shit, shit, shit, she should be happy. I told my make-up artist to paint me as fair as possible. She would keep telling me and other people in front of me, "*Mera beta kitna gora hai.*" My mother, of course, just washed her hands off me. She told me she had warned me about this and I had to suffer for my choices.'

Anyway, despite all the heartache, the wedding went off well and Anshika was thrilled to be Rohit's wife. Then, there was the matter of where to go for the honeymoon. But wiser from her experiences, Anshika merely waited for her brother-in-law to decide and went to Australia on an itinerary that he had planned. I was a bit surprised when she didn't add that Anand and Reshma joined them on their honeymoon. I was pretty certain that was where this story was headed.

Back in Mumbai, Anshika tried to settle into the rhythm of her new home. Her mother-in-law welcomed her into the house and told her that she was almost like a daughter to her now. *Almost.* Mummy began every sentence with 'in our house', which implied this was a rule to be obeyed without any questions. Not only were there rules, there were also admonishments.

Within the week of starting her married life, Mummy began scolding her. She nagged her for waking up late, for leaving her shoes askew, for switching on the bathroom light two seconds earlier than was necessary. Anshika did her 'yes Mummy, sorry Mummy' bit and tried to get into her good books. That same week, the cook was relieved of his responsibilities. Anshika was told that she would have to take care of breakfast and lunch. This meant waking up early in the morning and cooking two meals before nine so that Rohit could take his lunch box with him.

Dinner was supposed to be her mother-in-law's responsibility. But soon, the dinner parties began. They had guests over at least a couple of times a week and, as the new daughter-in-law, Anshika was expected to demonstrate her superb cooking skills. Like the operations head of a company, her mother-in-law had a system for her dinner parties. As soon as the guests arrive, they should be given water. Exactly, two minutes later a tray of dry fruits should be presented. Six minutes after would come the snack. Then the first starter, the second, and so on, until dessert. 'I would just kill myself getting all of this done. Then she would criticize everything. This doesn't have any chillies, that is undercooked, this is overcooked, things like that,' she says.

Initially, Mummy was kind. She wouldn't say that a dish was awful, outright. She would say she taught her daughter to cook it so beautifully that once you ate that version, you would know how bad this one was. The implication of this was that Anshika's mother had done a bad job raising her. After a few weeks, she stopped bothering with the insinuation. As soon as the guests left, she would come into the kitchen and yell at Anshika, telling her how badly brought up she was, how her mother was evidently useless, and things like that.

'One dinner, they criticized everything I did. And she came into the kitchen and started banging the vessels. "What was this rubbish you gave us! The food was so bad it wasn't even worthy of feeding the servants!" She was clanging plates and cutlery barely inches from my face. I was so scared; I didn't know what to do. I just ran into my room and burst into tears,' she says.

She hoped Rohit would tell her what she should do. Rohit is a boyish twenty-seven-year-old. In photographs he looks like he is in his teens. He has always been scared of his mother and had never felt the need or had the gumption to question his parents' authority. When they married, he had just started in the family business and was still learning its ropes. He wasn't at a place where he could make a bold move or even suggest his new wife take one. He was entirely sympathetic about what Anshika was going through but he did not know how he could set that right. He asked her not to take his mother seriously. He loved her and that was all he could do.

Anshika was caught between trying to make her post-wedding romantic fantasies come true and dealing with the daily dirt that was reality. What she wanted to do was spend time with her new husband—go for movies and candlelit dinners and long drives late in the night. What she was stuck with was spending most of her waking hours cooking and cleaning under her mother-in-law's watchful eyes. Real married life, she was beginning to see, was not as fun as she'd imagined it would be. But she was a chirpy sort, so she hung on to hope and got on with her life.

Rohit, thankfully, made it all worthwhile. He was kind, gentle and loving; everything Anshika had wanted in a husband. He was her biggest fan and supported her in everything she wanted to do. But despite his best intentions, he simply could not take his parents on. He had always lived under their authority and he had always been a little scared of them. In many ways, he was in competition with that perfect specimen of manhood—his brother-in-law, Anand.

Some four months after the wedding, Anshika met a friend who was wearing a lovely pair of earrings. Rohit's family had given her some jewellery, but since they had shopped for them without her, none of it was of her choice. They were all lying in the locker, never to be worn. When Anshika saw these earrings, she loved them so much that she asked her mother-in-law if she could redesign one of the pieces they had given her.

Mummy did not say anything at the time. That evening, Rohit and Anshika were leaving home to go watch a movie. Like a scene straight out of a Bollywood film from the 1980s, mother-in-law's voice boomed 'Stop!' as they were opening the door to leave. Rohit and Anshika froze.

'Do you know that your wife wants to sell the jewellery we gave her?' she asked. Then she really began to scream. 'What kind of a family are you from?' she yelled at Anshika. 'In our family we don't believe in redesigning our jewellery. We don't believe in being disrespectful.' That was the warm-up exercise. Then she quickly moved to: 'You don't do any work around the house. You should clean the refrigerator. You should clean the cupboards.' Anshika couldn't quite fathom how she had moved from earrings to the cleaning. Rohit was frozen. She sat down and began to cry.

Then, not one to waste a good fight, her father-in-law joined in too. He began by abusing Anshika as well as her father. 'What does he think of himself? He did not give us enough respect during the wedding. He does not give us enough respect now.' Then, since he had come so far, he let loose a string of abuses against her dad, in the kind of language Anshika had never heard used in her family—motherfucker, sisterfucker, all in pure Hindi.

When the father-in-law's abuses ended, mother-in-law resumed. It took Anshika a few seconds to understand what she was saying, but she was complaining about the venue for the roka ceremony. 'That place was so bad, how could your father be so cheap and pick a place like that?' mother-in-law screamed. 'And the DJ played such loud music,' father-in-law backed her up. And when they were done with that, mother-in-law brought up the 'covers'. These were envelopes of cash, which were gifted to Anshika during festivals before the wedding. She had accepted the gifts and spent the money.

That evening, she learned that she was actually expected to bring that money back. 'You should have brought it back. You have no culture. And now you dare tell us you don't like the design of our jewellery?' At last it came full circle. Anshika was too distraught to even try defending herself or her family. Rohit was aghast. 'What are you saying?' he kept asking his parents and tried to talk some sense into them. They asked him to shut up and carried on. Finally, her mother-in-law asked the two of them to get out of the house for the evening. She didn't want to see their faces.

Anshika and Rohit sat in the car and cried. This was a trap neither of them could see a way out of. Rohit couldn't possibly abandon the family business. His parents would never allow him to move out and live with his wife. It was all too complicated and all too messy. There was nothing to do but cry.

The next morning, Anshika began to try even harder to please her mother-in-law.

'Why?' I ask.

'Arre because na!'

She stopped going out. She didn't spend time chatting on the phone with her friends. She called Reshma and paid her 'respects' every day. She cleaned the refrigerator. Thoroughly and often. She buzzed around her mother-in-law, like a little puppy. 'What shall I cook Mummy?' 'What shall I clean Mummy?' 'What shall I get you Mummy?' Rohit was shocked. He asked her not to bother. He warned her nothing would come out of this. He told her she should just do what she wanted and ignore his unreasonable parents.

'But the minute Rohit left for work, I'd go Mummy, Mummy, Mummy. I think life is too short to live in an unpleasant manner. I don't have much of an ego. And most importantly, I wanted her to be happy with me. That was the only way I could be happy living with her,' she says.

But how long can you be fake? Five or six months later, Anshika began to forget who she should be and slowly reverted to who she was. She and Rohit began going out again in the evenings. The refrigerator wasn't at the receiving end of multiple daily clean-ups. The cupboards saw the duster more rarely. Three months later, there was another 'meeting'. The same issues were aired out. Earrings, refrigerator, respect, roka, culture, get out.

Maybe because it lacked the element of surprise this time, Anshika felt it sting less. She cried but 'not full on' like the first time. Rohit asked his parents to stop, but not with all his might. When they were asked to leave, they didn't sit in the car and cry for hours like the first time. Anshika sobbed for a bit, then fixed her make-up and they went on with their evening.

The following morning, mother-in-law started some stealth operations. It was entirely based on unpredictability and injecting an element of surprise in everyday tasks. Anshika would ask her what she should cook to which she would pointedly turn her head away and ignore her. She would then come to the kitchen and taunt Anshika, calling her names, insulting her mother. Then just as suddenly, she would stop talking to her.

Even though a new cook had been hired by then, Anshika's mother-in-law insisted she do the cooking. Mummy told her that her relationship with her husband and in-laws would be strengthened only if she slaved for them over the stove every day.

Anshika was becoming a nervous wreck. She had to take deep breaths to steel herself before she walked out of her room in the morning. It wasn't the kind of life that a young, educated woman living by herself in Mumbai would want to live. It wasn't the kind of life anyone would aspire for, in fact.

Due to this stress and anxiety, Anshika often fell ill during the first eighteen months.

'You know how when you are sick your mother would make you khichdi and you get to relax? Here, she would tell me that if I was too lazy to do the housework, I could just sleep. You don't have to tell lies over and above all this, she would tell me,' Anshika says.

In the meantime the taunts over Anshika's appearance hadn't ended. Mummy would yell at her to go to the gym and work out every day. '"Look how fat you are," she would point out. All the time. ALL.THE.TIME. I'd be like, you just told me I was fat ten minutes ago. Surely, I haven't grown fatter in ten minutes that you have to say it again!' she tells me.

Anshika decided that there was only one solution to her problems. The obvious solution—moving out and living alone with Rohit—was not an option. No, the only way she would be able to stay sane in this marriage was if she managed to go back to work. Project back-to-school took shape in her mind and she immediately started work on it.

Like a North Korean dictator, one of Mummyji's orders was that Anshika was to sit with her from 2–5 p.m. for a 'chat session'. That is, Mummyji would chat and Anshika had to constantly and continuously maintain eye contact and nod her head in agreement. Usually, these conversations were about Anshika's shortcomings and how 'perfect' their family was. Her mother-in-law would tell her how the five of them—that is the two parents-in-law, Reshma, Anand and Rohit—were the five fingers of a hand. So obviously there was no room for Anshika. Anshika would listen and agree with her mother-in-law about everything.

Once the back-to-school idea germinated, Anshika began using this time to push the idea with Mummy. She began telling her how posh the school was and regaled her with stories and gossip about Bollywood stars and business leaders who were the parents of her students. She thought if she made it aspirational, her mother-in-law would like the reflected glory of being part of this institution.

Once the school bit was over, Anshika would move on to praising Reshma and Anand. She told her mother-in-law how much she idolized Reshma, how Anand was such a perfect gentleman. 'I brainwashed her every day. I tried to keep the conversation positive and cheerful. I took all the insulting things she said about me and my family without a whimper. I knew this was my only chance,' she says. Finally, when she thought she had softened her mother-in-law enough, she came right out and asked her. 'Mummy, can I go back to working in the school, please? I would really love it, if I could.' Mummy didn't bat an eyelid. 'No,' she said.

So she took it up with Rohit. She told him she was going crazy sitting at home. Their marriage was crumbling under the pressure of his mother. Every evening, Mummy would have a list of at least five complaints about her, which she would relate to Rohit as soon as he came home. Then, when he entered their room, Anshika, in her frustration, would start a fight with him.

Some days Rohit would calm her down. Other days, he would snap at her and the two of them would end up fighting. Anshika wouldn't allow him to hold her. She withheld sex. Rohit was patient and understanding, but months of crossfire wore even him down. They went to bed fighting. And woke up sour at each other. 'My mother-in-law was beginning to be the cancerous tumour in our marriage,' Anshika tells me. And since Mummy often behaved super sweetly with her when Rohit was around, Anshika began to wonder if Rohit thought she was making up all these stories about his mother. There were more shadows than people and they were all slowly going crazy.

Rohit thought Anshika's going back to work was a good idea. If nothing, it would get her out of the house for a large part of the day. So he talked to his father first and asked him for permission to allow his wife to take up a job. Father refused. Then he spoke to his mother. She also refused. It was against the family's custom, he was told; their honour would be dragged through mud.

Then Anshika hit up on her fail-safe plan. Getting Reshma and Anand to agree. Apart from Rohit, Reshma was the only one who even bothered to listen to her. And although she wasn't supportive of everything Anshika said, she was at least open to some amount of reason. Anshika went to Reshma's house and did the sell. She told her about the star kids in school and shared some inside gossip. And she eventually pleaded with the 'modern woman' in Reshma to see the benefits of her going back to work. She kept at it, day after day, week after week. Finally, Reshma said OK. And that evening, Anand came over and told his in-laws casually that maybe Anshika could go back to work. And just like that, she was granted permission! Customs, honour, none of it mattered, now that the plan had the son-in-law's approval.

The rules now had to be rejigged. The dress code was further tightened. There was to be no work-related excuse for coming home late in the evenings. Since she had to leave for school by 6.30 a.m., Anshika was exempted from cooking on weekdays. Weekends continued to be her responsibility. There would be no weekends out, no matter what came up at school, and she couldn't bring home and entertain any of her colleagues or friends. Despite these conditions, Anshika was thrilled. She got to do what she loved, she got to stay out of the house and away from Mummy's disapproval all day. She also got a chance to talk to people. 'I feel that, after three years, I am finally living,' she says.

Anshika's horror stories about her mother-in-law caused shock and consternation in the staffroom. Earlier, she would tell herself that this was how most people lived. Now she is certain her situation is abnormal. This has given her more courage. She does a lot more of what she wants to do now. She has a mini-wardrobe in her car, for example. So if she is going out with Rohit to a nightclub, she leaves the house in Mummyji-approved gear and strips off the tights and scarves and changes to what she wants in the car.

The first time she officially stood up to her mother-in-law was three months before we met. It was another dinner party. There were about eight guests and the sequence of events had unfolded in the usual militarized fashion. When it was time for dinner, the sequence broke down a bit. The chapattis weren't coming fast enough. Once the first round was over, there was a wait as Anshika went on a rolling-and-flipping frenzy in the kitchen. Still, she wasn't quick enough and her mother-in-law popped in several times and hissed at her to serve the chapattis quicker. Finally when she came for the sixth time, Anshika lost her cool and snapped, 'Shall I just sit on the tawa myself?'

'Is that the way to talk to me?' Mummy asked her, set her lips tightly and walked away.

'I don't know what came over me,' Anshika tells me, 'but she was stressing me out and I just blurted it.'

After the guests left, of course, there was a detailed dissection of this. All the old issues—starting with the earrings and ending with the roka venue—were once again given an airing. But it hurts her less and less. It's just noise; in fact, she doesn't even really hear the words any more.

Anshika has made several other subtle changes too. For instance, each time a gift came for her, it would be sent directly to Reshma's. During festivals, especially, her mother and aunts would send her loads of stuff: clothes, jewellery, accessories, bed linen, crystal vases. Anshika would not even get to see any of this because they were just dispatched straight to Reshma's house.

Finally, Anshika told her family to stop sending her stuff. If they wanted to give her gifts, they could give her cash. When the next festival came around, the lack of gifts from her family was observed and commented on. Her mother-in-law came right out and asked her why her mother wasn't sending anything. Anshika quietly told her they had changed the system. 'My mother sent me money so I could buy something of my choice,' she said quietly, 'maybe a new pair of gold earrings.'

Other battles are still on. As part of the whole 'respect' exercise, each time anyone in her family visits Mumbai, they are expected to call her mother-in-law. This is not just her parents and siblings, but also includes a wide range of assorted uncles and aunts. Once they call to pay their respects, they may or may not be offered a dinner invitation. If offered one, they are expected to turn up gift-laden and spend an evening listening about Anshika's many shortcomings.

'Look how fat she has become. And going back to work has tanned her so she is even darker now than she was,' they are told. After enduring this evening, they are obligated to call and speak to Mummy at least once more before they leave town. 'My uncles and aunts are tired of them. They are like we can't suffer them any more,' she says.

But since the families are related, it is inevitable that her mother-in-law will discover if someone was in town. 'Half the time I am stressing out, making sure they call and visit and all that. And someone or the other is always coming over. My brother was here fifteen days ago. He called, came over with a bottle of whisky etc. and he left yesterday. He is coming back in a week's time, when he is expected to do all of this all over again,' she says.

It isn't like Anshika gets away with her newfound cattiness. She is also sufficiently punished for it. Her mother-in-law's favourite strategy is to terminate the services of the domestic help and make her do all the work. She doesn't even bother making an excuse about it. The help is told that she needn't bother coming for work the following day because the lazy daughter-in-law is growing fat and needs the exercise.

The Sunday before we met was her birthday. Anshika hoped she would be able to celebrate it just with Rohit, but that was of course out of the question. It had to be the whole family. She suggested then that they go for a continental brunch, since it was a Sunday and they always ended up going for dinner. Eventually, of course, Anand decided that it would be Chinese food and it would be dinner. And so it was. Even though the birthday was hers. 'I sometimes think about what my mother-in-law said—that I would be like a daughter to her. And I can't stop laughing,' she says.

The pressure to have a child has begun, now that it's three years since the wedding. Her mother-in-law is beginning to insist that she go to a doctor. 'I am sure there is a problem with you,' she tells her constantly. 'I tell her that Rohit doesn't want to have kids yet because, really, even I know how foolish it sounds if I tell her that I have a choice too.' So then she takes off on her about how much she has 'damaged' Rohit. 'My son was never like this,' she tells Anshika. 'You have ruined him.'

We had reached Lokhandwala and were parked in front of her apartment for more than half an hour by then. 'I am glad I started giving it back to her a little bit,' she tells me. Her colleagues are supportive of her and they have continuously encouraged her to stand up to her mother-in-law. 'I am brave now, I am not scared of her any more,' she says. Just then her phone rings. She fishes it out of her bag and flips it open. 'Mummyji,' she gasps and in less than a second she is out of the car and running home.

5

The Unforgiven

Name	Age (in 2013)	Husband	Married
Seema	34	Srini	2006

The most puzzling aspect of Mummyji behaviour is her desire for absolute control. There is no room, usually, for negotiation. Like a certain American president, the Mummyji philosophy is that you are either with her or against her. Even if you agree to all her conditions bar one, that one exception will be held against you. None of the things the daughter-in-law has complied with ever find mention, but the one thing she hasn't is talked about till the end of time.

The ways in which daughters-in-law respond to this authority often differs according to their seniority. The older daughters-in-law are usually the ones to bear the brunt of the tyranny. Friendless and without an ally in their new homes, these daughters-in-law also capitulate easily. The younger daughters-in-law I spoke with said they were expected to be the ones to bring in the revolution. The wives of the older brothers hoped the new bride would liberate them. Some were successful, most succumbed. But irrespective, in all cases, Mummyji began to re-evaluate the 'goodness' of the older daughters-in-law once she had a modern, more radical, younger one. No matter how bad she thought the older daughter-in-law was, the younger was often much worse.

When Seema married Srini, the eldest of three boys in a Tam Brahm Chennai family, she knew that she would encounter some traditional Brahmin conservatism. She was prepared for it. But she did not think that her one transgression—that of not wearing a nine-yard sari for the wedding—would be a burning issue for years after her 2006 wedding. She should have known better. Although originally Seema and her family are from neighbouring Kerala, they had lived long enough in Tamil Nadu to know that just as Horlicks boosted the ability to do mental mathematics, the three extra yards in the sari made the difference between upper-class Tamil Brahmin and the rest of the world.

Like most people who grew up in Chennai in the eighties and nineties, when Seema finished college, she too joined an IT company. She met Srini there. Actually, she spent the first few months hearing about him. Everyone knew him, everyone loved him. Even people who didn't know him, loved him. When Srini came to office, it was like a movie star was visiting. You couldn't see him from the crowd thronged around him; he was a corporate Rajnikant.

In a company that employed thousands of project managers and tens of thousands of employees, Srini's team was the most coveted. People strategized and schemed to get into it. And women were apparently ready to kill just to be on a project that he managed. For the longest time, Seema stood back and watched this circus. Then suddenly, she found herself on a project he was managing.

It was after she became a part of his team that she realized why everyone wanted in. Turns out, Srini had what was hardest to find in Chennai: a liberal mindset and a sense of humour. He was also very women-friendly and was one of those rare managers who didn't treat his female staff like ticking time bombs who might leave the project in a lurch by getting married or pregnant.

The project, as these things tend to, moved to the US. So not only was Seema working in Srini's team, they were working together in a city far from home. What were the chances of them not spending all their time together? 'I know I am plain-looking. My sister is the beauty in the family. And Srini always had such a huge fan following that I never thought I would catch his eye. But in the US, it was a bit easier,' she says, with a self-deprecating smile.

Tossed together in a strange country, they began spending a lot of time together. When Seema heard that Srini played the violin, she immediately proclaimed it to be her favourite instrument (favourite instrument, *ever*!!) and requested that he teach her the basics. D minor led to Love major. 'It was worth it,' Seema says of her brief digression into music.

I met Seema on a Sunday morning at eight. The venue was a fruit juice shop! When I reached there, under-caffeinated and overly grumpy, I was told by a rude watchman that I was too early and the shop was yet to open. 'How can I be too early? This is Chennai, everything opens at 5 a.m.'

'Madam, please leave. You are looking dangerous to me,' he said.

After twenty minutes of aimlessly driving around the area, I found a coffee shop. The sign said 'closed', but the staff was inside. I begged to be let in and texted Seema about the change of venue.

'This is the first time even I've heard of being too early anywhere in Chennai,' Seema says as she walks into the coffee shop. She is dressed in a non-descript salwar kurta, with a muted print. Her wispy, curly hair is cut short, just above her shoulder. And when she smiles, a deep dimple emerges in one cheek.

As we talk, Seema's dupatta slides off in various directions, lying eventually in a heap by her feet. She appears very comfortable in her skin and possesses a wry sense of irony. If Srini was known for his sense of humour, it isn't hard to understand why he would have liked Seema.

Seema comes from a typical Malayali family. Her father, liberal and easy, treated her mother like his secretary. She had grown up observing this lopsided balance of power in the family. Around the time that Seema was pretending to be deeply moved by the violin, her sister was going through a very painful divorce. So even though she was really keen on Srini, she wasn't all that sure about getting married. She didn't want to end up either like her mother or her sister.

'Srini and I spoke a lot about marriage. Our views were nearly the same. It wasn't the most important thing,' she says. But Srini was nearly thirty and he was certain his family would soon start pushing him to get married. He would be able to resist it for a couple of years, but eventually it would get too complicated and he would be forced to go and see some girls. After much discussion, they decided since they wanted to be in each other's lives, the best way forward was to get married. Seema told herself that Srini was a man different from her father, and she wasn't the sort to get bullied easily anyway.

At this point, Srini warned Seema that his mother was 'a difficult lady'. She didn't think too much about it at the time. 'Srini is not the sort to say a bad word about anybody. Perhaps I should have read more into what he said then. It is significant that he chose to warn me about her. I should have been worried,' Seema says. She was flushed with love and was feeling generous. What the hell, she thought, we are all difficult ladies.

When her part of the project wrapped up, Seema came back to Chennai and told her parents about Srini. That he wasn't from Kerala or that he was a Brahmin weren't things her parents had quibbles with. 'Like good Malayalis, they said, "Oh good, good, very well," and did nothing about it,' she says.

But when Srini told his parents, his mother couldn't wait to get off the phone to speak to her prospective daughter-in-law's parents and 'firm the whole thing up'. She rattled out details of the wedding—oh we need to have three kinds of sweet dishes, I wonder if this wedding hall will be available, we will have to go to Kancheepuram and buy the saris—even before Srini could finish his sentence. When he ended the call, he wondered about the monster he had set forth.

In less than a minute, his mother had called Seema's house. She picked the earliest available 'good day' to come and see the bride-to-be and discuss the details of the wedding. At the café we were in, the staff was just beginning to clean up before throwing the doors open. All around us were buckets of water with diligent staff mopping the floor while we kept our feet up on some chairs that were turned upside down.

'My house looked like this,' Seema said, pointing to the water and the mops, about the days leading up to her mother-in-law's maiden visit. 'My mother was a furious cleaning machine. She may even have cleaned the neighbours' homes, in case the prospective in-laws looked sideways and happened to spot some dirt there,' Seema says. 'I was telling her to please relax, but she was hyper.'

Everything was sparkling when Srini's parents turned up. Seema, who was a bit anxious herself, was at first amused and then annoyed by her parents' behaviour. 'We were very hospitable,' she says. 'Water is coming, then vadas are coming, then laddoos are coming. My mother worked on the assumption that Srini's parents had never eaten and this was her God-given opportunity to feed them.'

The two fathers talked about their work. Since Seema's mother was mostly in the kitchen, she was left to entertain her new mother-in-law. Srini's mother had a lot of questions for her. Wise as I now was to guess how these things proceed, I asked her if she asked if Seema knew how to cook.

'Of course she asked me that. It was one of her top three questions. I told her I knew survival cooking,' she says.

Srini's mother's main concern, though, was that the wedding

be conducted according to Tamil Brahmin customs. 'Pretty much every second sentence she spoke was—the wedding should be proper Tamil Brahmin, proper Tamil Brahmin, proper Tamil Brahmin,' Seema tells me, pronouncing it 'prahper'. Like two Chettiar dolls, her parents sat there with their heads bobbing incessantly. Srini's mother then painstakingly detailed every single custom and tradition.

'I don't think she spent a moment wondering whether I was right for Srini, all her energy was focused on explaining and insisting on every aspect of the wedding,' Seema says. After a while, when it began to feel like it wasn't her wedding that was being discussed, she tried to catch her parents' eyes to signal to them not to agree to all the demands. But they were too hypnotized to even notice her.

When they finally left, Seema's mother expressed a sliver of doubt. 'Your mother-in-law seems really conservative; how will you adjust?' she asked her.

Seema screamed at her in reply. 'Why did you agree to everything she said?'

'We have to, Seema, that's our duty,' her mother calmly assured her.

Seema was so livid, she immediately called Srini and asked him if the wedding could be a more 'mutual affair'—one that borrowed from both their customs instead of being a prahper Tamil Brahmin one. In fact, she suggested, why don't they just get married at the registrar's office and then throw a party for friends and family? But in the ten minutes that had passed since his parents left her home, his mother had already called and told Srini that Seema's parents were not only insisting on a big wedding but they were also keen on doing it the Tamil Brahmin way. Srini, who was thousands of miles away, couldn't really figure out what was going on. His mother was saying one thing and Seema quite another.

Seema feels she should have called out her mother-in-law's

duplicity then. But with Srini in the US, her parents playing the ready-to-please bride's family and his Amma bulldozing them with her demands, it was impossible to unknot the twisted threads that each of them spun.

Amma's phone calls began from the day after the visit. Every morning, at 10.30, the phone would ring and it would be Srini's mother at the other end with instructions and advice about the wedding preparations. Every single day. The first point on her agenda was that there should be an engagement ceremony. Both Srini and Seema were against the idea of throwing one party to announce another. But Amma was insistent and said with absolute finality that she wasn't going to back down from this.

Srini came back from the US and a suitable date was picked. A fortnight before the engagement, Seema's cousin met with an accident and passed away. The family was plunged in mourning and wanted to call off the event but Amma stood firm. The engagement would progress as scheduled, she said. People were invited and the pandit was booked. She wasn't willing to back down, and eventually the ceremony took place as planned. No one from Seema's family attended. Seema herself was fraught.

'My mother kept telling me it's OK, it's OK. At the end of the day, I was wondering if I could divorce my mum. She was being so servile and it made me even more angry,' she says. Seema asked herself how she felt the day of the engagement and she realized that she was 70 per cent unhappy and 30 per cent relieved that it was over. Suddenly, it seemed like the wedding was not hers but Srini's mother's in which she was only a benign participant.

Seema's parents thought that by putting their grief aside and toeing Srini's mother's line, her tacit bullying would end. They were mistaken. The frequency of her phone calls only increased. Over the phone, Amma was incredibly polite. Maybe, she actually did think she was helping. She wasn't ordering them around, but constantly informing them about the Tamil Brahmin way of doing things. 'This is our tradition,' she would remind them.

One of the reasons she was so stuck on everything being her way, Seema reckons, is because none of her three sons follow her diktats on anything. They don't wear the sacred thread, they all eat non-vegetarian food—although they don't do so at home—and none of them are into any rituals. Seema was her mother-in-law's way out. She might have thought that if she could make her a proper Brahmin wife, that success would sufficiently wipe out her failure with her boys.

Seema thought this was getting out of hand. But it was a delicate time—the one between the engagement and the wedding. She considered all options, but felt like things had progressed too far for her to take any drastic action. Yet, at the same time, she knew that she was laying down the pattern for the future. She started dropping hints to Srini. 'I would call him ten times in a day and tell him that the lists were growing. In retrospect I feel I should have just been very direct with him,' she says. 'I suppose that's how weddings are, but it wasn't the kind of wedding I wanted.'

Srini, though, picked up on what she was hinting at and decided to take some amount of control over the situation. This was a project that needed management, and he was the best project manager he knew. He scheduled conference calls. He recorded the minutes of these meetings. He created excel worksheets in which every little detail was recorded and responsibilities assigned. His family offered to pay half the expenses of the wedding, but Seema's parents quickly declined it and announced that it was their honour to pay for everything Srini's mother wanted. 'Take the money,' Seema hissed at her father. 'I still have my dignity,' he informed her.

Since Srini's mother had hijacked the engagement and all the preparations for the wedding, the one thing Seema did not want to concede was what she would wear for the wedding. From day one, Srini's mother had started talking about the nine-yard sari. She told Seema and her parents about her preferred colours, designs, and stores from which to buy the sari. Seema categorically told her parents that she would not be wearing a nine-yard sari for the wedding.

The more Srini's mother insisted, the more determined she was about not wearing it. 'I decided this would be my rebellion. Not wearing a nine-yard sari,' she says. She explained it nicely to Amma. Her grandmothers would be at the wedding, she said, and they would want to see her dressed in an off-white Kerala sari. Srini's mother flipped. This was not the 'prahper Tam Brahm' wedding she'd envisaged. The sari would ruin everything.

She persisted. When she saw that she was not making much headway with Seema, Amma called Seema's mother and asked her to reason with her daughter. Her mother begged, pleaded, cajoled and threatened her. 'My mum had succumbed to the pressure big time,' Seema says. But Seema was steadfast. The more Srini's mother talked to hers, the more Seema's mother fought with her. Eventually, fed up with her daughter's stubbornness, she declared that she wished she had never had this child. 'So much emotion, can you imagine, over one sari?' Seema asks me.

When her mother failed to convince her, the task fell on her sister. She called Seema one day to ask her why she was making such a big deal about wearing a nine-yard sari. 'She was like just wear the sari and get it over with. I told her I was doing everything else—sitting on my poor father's lap for the ceremony; ready to be jerked on a swing at the wedding; putting up with the charade that my husband had developed cold feet and was going to remain a bachelor. All these are Tamil Brahmin wedding rites. So much silliness I was putting myself through. I told her I am allowed to have one choice, and that is the sari,' she says.

Now that mother and sister had failed, Seema's aunts were called to action. One of her aunts spoke to her and promised that if she wore the nine-yard sari, they would all wear one to show their solidarity with her. Seema said they could all wear bikinis to her wedding if that's what they fancied, but she herself was not going to wear a nine-yard sari. As the wedding day approached, Srini's mother was so anxious about the sari she was calling every hour. And each call was followed by a fight between Seema and someone in her family.

The day before the wedding, Amma called and nearly broke down. Then she told Srini that she would refuse to attend the wedding the following day if he didn't convince Seema about the sari. Nonchalant as ever, Srini said she was free to stay away from the ceremony. On the day of the wedding, Srini's mother carried a nine-yard with her to the marriage hall. She hoped that Seema would have a last-minute change of heart. Sadly, Seema did not change her mind. She came to the hall in a Kerala sari and wore it through the day. Amma clutched the spare nine-yard sari in her hand tightly.

Even though no expense was spared and all the Tamil Brahmin customs were followed, neither Seema nor her mother-in-law was happy about how the day turned out.

Seema moved into her in-laws' home after the wedding. She and Srini had bought an apartment but, until it was ready, they were going to live with his parents. Seema continued to work; there was no question of her quitting the job. Her mother-in-law had also worked through her life until she retired and she was of the view that daughters-in-law—even those who didn't dress appropriately for the wedding—were entitled to their careers. But this did not mean that Seema was allowed to use her work commitments to shirk any of her duties as a Tamil Brahmin wife.

Every few weeks there was a festival or mini festival of some kind. 'All of them involve fasting and then feasting after it,' Seema explains. She tried to do what she could. She carried her mangalsutra and sindoor in her bag and had an alarm on her phone to remind her to put these on before going home for a puja. After a few months, her relationship with her mother-in-law settled down largely, but it never recovered from the saga of the sari. Ever so often, her mother-in-law would raise the subject of the unworn nine-yard sari. She would start off on a note of wistfulness and regret, then take it up a notch to anger and hysteria and end with tears.

The two of them are still suspicious of each other. Seema believes that her mother-in-law is rather immature. She has lived her life surrounded by men—her husband and three sons—who indulge her whims but ignore her desires. Living with her, Seema noticed strange things about her mother-in-law. She loves gifts. And her favourite things are teddy bears! 'Can you imagine? A sixty-something-year-old lady who squeaks with delight on ripping open the wrapping paper and seeing a teddy bear?' She has to be constantly complimented. If Seema accompanied her for a wedding or a family event, Amma always walked ahead of her. She had to be the first one in.

At home, her mother-in-law talked incessantly and bitched about other family members. She even told Seema about her struggle to gain control over her kitchen from her own mother-in-law. Since Amma was employed full-time, her mother-in-law lived with them and helped raise the boys. When Amma retired, she wanted to take charge of her kitchen. She noticed that her mother-in-law was waking up at 6 a.m. to start cooking. So she began waking up at 5. Mother-in-law noticed this stealthy takeover, and woke up at 4.30. So Amma set her alarm at 4. And this went on, until her mother-in-law gave up and Amma was queen of the kitchen. 'Don't try these stunts with me,' she warned Seema. 'Little does she know that I have absolutely no intention of doing any of that. I am happy that I don't have to cook myself. I am already loathing the day I will have to start taking over the kitchen,' she tells me.

Seema would nod along to these stories, and if the conversation turned to vile family politics, she tried to bring her back to some neutral, harmless ground. 'She wanted me to be her friend. Take her for movies, go on car rides with her, things like that,' she says. Despite the fact that Seema paid her mother-in-law the attention she sought from her sons, she still couldn't live down the sari story. She brought it up all the time. No matter what the discussion was about or how happy she was, the conversation eventually turned to the fact that Seema had refused to wear a nine-yard sari for the wedding. Seema didn't bother arguing with her.

Amma also continued to try and brahminize her. She was asked to give up eating non-vegetarian food, even though Srini and his brothers ate meat. She was told that she could eat only after the menfolk were served their food. These things grated at Seema and she discussed them with her mother whose advice was that she should ignore them and not get into a fight with Amma.

Her parents, in the meanwhile, were rapidly brahminizing themselves. They sent gifts for every festival and fast. A silver plate here, a rice cooker there. Seema found out that some of these were demands that Amma was surreptitiously making to her parents. She was livid and forbade her parents from sending gifts to her in-laws. But it was a bit of a lost cause.

Srini is one of the most supportive husbands I encountered in these interviews. He paid no attention at all to his mother's whines and complaints and exhorted Seema to do the same. This allowed Seema to draw her own boundaries with her mother-in-law. She did not want to ignore her altogether, but she knew she had Srini's support on issues that she wanted to back out of. It allowed her the liberty to engage with Amma on her own terms. Unlike many other daughters-in-law, Seema didn't have to really worry about what his mother was filling Srini's head with. Srini's head was his own. Their marriage was a happy one. And a few months after the wedding, when their apartment was ready, Seema and Srini moved out.

A couple of years after the wedding, Seema was pregnant.

Amma was thrilled and quickly brought out the Tam Brahm book of rules for expecting mothers. Seema followed some of them and pretended to follow the rest. Amma insisted that there be a Seemandham—the Tam Brahm equivalent of a baby shower. Once again, the process of painfully informing her parents about every aspect of the ceremony began.

Pregnant and on full-time employment, Seema was too exhausted to put up a fight. Still, she did not wear a nine-yard sari. She had a baby boy and took nine months off work. Amma began to worry that Seema was an overtly possessive mother who wouldn't allow her access to her grandchild. Seema had no such intention though. When her leave got exhausted, she resumed work. While her mother helped with the baby during the week, they spent weekends at Srini's. The baby brought a sense of perspective and contentment and, despite some occasional Tamil Brahmin–related hitches, things were going reasonably well for both Seema and her mother-in-law.

Alas, peace was not to last. Another wedding came up and the nine-yard sari reared its ugly head again. Ganesh, Srini's brother who lived in the US, seemed interested in a girl in Bangalore. Even though they dated for nearly three years, Ganesh wasn't forthcoming about this relationship to the family. But there is no fooling an Indian mother. She found out about the girl, discovered she was not a Brahmin and pleaded with Ganesh to give her a chance to find him a proper girl. Eventually, he just popped up at home one fine morning with her and introduced her as the girl he was going to marry.

The first question Amma asked her was, 'Will you wear a nine-yard sari for the wedding?'

Seema collapsed in laughter when she told me this. 'First question! Can you imagine? The girl was still standing at the door. She hadn't even been asked to come in. Will you wear a nine-yard sari for the wedding?'

Srini's mother put aside her disappointment about a second non-Brahmin daughter-in-law and dusted off her 'Brahmin mother of groom' cape. The 10.30 a.m. phone calls started. The new daughter-in-law came from a small family—it was just her and her mother. So, unlike Seema's parents, they didn't get into a tizzy over the wedding arrangements. More often than not, they did not even answer the phone. Amma insisted on a big engagement ceremony. Daughter-in-law #2 flatly refused. Then, when she bore down on them, she agreed to a small ceremony.

'This was in Bangalore. And when we reached the venue, they hadn't even put up the lights. We had to help in setting things out—laying the table, getting the room cleaned, things like that. 'I knew that my mother-in-law was quite unhappy, but she didn't say anything to me,' Seema says. Later on, she took it up with Ganesh and they had huge fights about the poorly arranged engagement ceremony. But, in front of Seema, she put up the pretence of being entirely charmed by the new daughter-in-law.

The date of the wedding was fixed for a few months thence. Just before the preparations were to start, Ganesh called his mother to say that they wanted to postpone it to the following year. Some work commitments had come up, he said. The next year, his fiancée decided to move to the US to study. The wedding date was once again fixed and postponed. This went on for three years. The third year, Ganesh was graduating with his second master's degree and he invited his mother to attend his convocation. She was thrilled to go. Ganesh's fiancée was there too and they spent a few weeks together.

Amma took the visit as an opportunity to instil Brahminical values in this younger daughter-in-law. She told her that she should serve Ganesh first and only then should she sit down to eat. She said no way. 'She was, in fact, quite rude to my mother-in-law. She would tell her off to her face, in fact. They began to fight all the time,' Seema tells me. Srini and she were constantly called in to mediate.

On one computer, Ganesh would be complaining to Srini about

their mother, and on the other, the new daughter-in-law would complain to Seema. And mother-in-law would end up calling home and crying. The new daughter-in-law was blunt and belligerent. Seema actually began to feel sorry for her mother-in-law. 'When she came back from the US, she was a changed woman,' she says. 'It was visible to everyone. With me, she kept up this pretence of being fascinated by Ganesh's fiancée, but I knew the truth.'

Like most mothers-in-law, Srini's mum too began to look at Seema favourably when confronted with the more radical second daughter-in-law. Earlier, she had focused only on the things that Seema didn't obey, but now she began to count her blessings with Seema. Compared to Ganesh's fiancée, Seema seemed god-sent, even though she hadn't worn the nine-yard sari.

Eventually, Ganesh's wedding took place. On a budget of 65,000 rupees! None of the Tamil Brahmin customs were followed. The girl's family did not bend over backwards to please the future mother-in-law. Not one of her diktats was obeyed. There was no swing, the bride didn't sit on her father's lap, Ganesh didn't pretend to renounce his worldly life and stay a bachelor. But having been privy to the story of Seema's wedding, in a move as strategic as the Boston Tea Party, the bride wore a nine-yard sari. Mother-in-law was thrilled. Nothing else mattered. She pointed out her new bride in a nine-yard sari to everyone. She couldn't stop gushing over her.

Other slights abounded. After Srini and Seema's wedding, her parents had sat down with her mother-in-law, shown her each of the photographs, written down the ones she liked, and presented her with two albums. Ganesh's bride handed over a USB stick with the photos and asked her mother-in-law to print them herself. Even now, for festivals like Pongal, Amma discreetly reminds Seema's parents about a gift and they send her what she likes. The new daughter-in-law's mother does not even remember to call and wish her.

These differences are stark and are as visible to her mother-in-law as they are to others in the family. Because of this Amma has stopped challenging Seema. In fact, Seema is certain she actually appreciates her a lot now. But even so, every once in a while she makes it a point to mention that the other bride wore a nine-yard sari. 'She was a perfect Brahmin bride,' she says. All because she wore a nine-yard sari. When she hears her mother-in-law talk about it, Seema just bursts out laughing.

6

The Centre of the Universe

Name	Age (in 2013)	Husband	Married
Deepa	44	Sandeep	1994

The two big reasons for strife in a marriage are stepchildren and infidelity. A close third is in-laws. This isn't the view of a sociologist with a Mummyji hang-up, but a theory propounded by the well-known evolutionary biologist Richard Alexander. He argues that a successful marriage is all about protecting your genetic interest. Stepchildren cause dissonance because one of the spouses does not have a genetic interest in them. Infidelity signifies that the adulterer's genetic interests are outside the marriage.

Similarly, Mummyji has a very strong genetic interest in her son, but none at all in her daughter-in-law. She is free to wreak havoc on her. And each time she tells the story of how she is acting against her daughter-in-law in order to protect her son, there is perhaps a biological compulsion to it. Her concerns might be misguided, but she does have a genetic reason to meddle in her son's marriage.

I met Deepa a couple of years ago when I was waking up at 2 a.m. to harvest my squash and plant my pumpkins. We had some friends in common and, through that extremely stressful half-year, we had each other's backs—sometimes I fertilized her strawberries and often she gave me a milking can or a grain silo. We were Farmville friends—that increasingly common social group brought together by too much time and an eagerness to obey the ludicrous just because it flashed on a screen.

Over the next few months, I got glimpses into Deepa's life through Facebook—some corny jokes, lots of forwarded internet humour and some amazing vacation photographs. I knew her husband was in the army and that she was the mother of a teenage boy. We'd exchange a couple of 'Likes' and write a comment or two—always positive, often an adjective, like 'Brilliant', 'Lovely' or 'Awesome'.

In many photos, I noticed Deepa and her son exchanging extensive comments. They seemed really cool with each other. Deepa, especially, came across as someone really easy, the kind of mother you could talk to about anything. My curiosity piqued, I pored over earlier photographs. Deepa always had a wide grin in the photos. She was often surrounded by friends; they all had their arms round each other's shoulders. She seemed like a fun person.

I noticed a lot of the comments were from her son's friends. They were all gushing over her, calling her the coolest mother ever. In the latest set of photographs, Deepa, her husband and son were evidently in Goa. Their dog, a lovely black Dobermann, was there too. Deepa had a big wide grin in all the photos. The son was goofing around like a typical teenager. Her husband—tall, well built and with the upright stance of a typical army man—was often standing at the back in the photographs, a slight smile on his lips.

To me he looked like a patient man who was happy to indulge his family members and their craziness. There was one of Deepa in shorts and a vest, riding pillion on a bike. Her tattoo stood out and her long hair flowed down her back. She looked a veritable happy hippie. Her arms were stretched upwards and her index and middle fingers formed a V. It was the kind of picture that one aspired to—a happy family, a sunbeam of a mother. Every day must be joy and laughter in this family, of that I was certain.

When we chatted once on Facebook, I told her that I was travelling the country listening to stories about mothers-in-law. 'Here's a story,' she told me. 'This daughter-in-law is diagnosed with a terminal illness. They are at the doctor's office. And the mother-in-law's first and only question to the doctor is, "How long does she have? I have to make plans accordingly."'

'Do you know this person?' I asked.

'Babe, I am that person,' she said.

I had, by this time, heard all kinds of stories about mothers-in-law. But this was a new low. I had to go to Bangalore and hear more. We fixed a date and Deepa flooded me with questions about what I would like to eat. A tremendous back and forth ensued and she finally fixed a menu of yakhni pulao and mutton curry. She sounded so excited and enthusiastic on the phone, I felt like I couldn't wait to get there.

'It'd be so good to finally meet you in person,' we said in unison.

The evening that I reach Bangalore though, she calls me with a change of plans. Captain, her Dobermann, has taken ill and she has to spend the day at the veterinary clinic, where Captain will be hooked on to an IV and undergo some tests.

The next morning, I head for the animal hospital to meet Deepa. It takes a flurry of phone calls to find the place, and after almost thirty minutes of delay, I spot a tiny lady with a big dog stretched at her feet. Deepa is much smaller than she seemed on Facebook. She has a wide, toothy smile and her hair, exaggeratedly brown, tumbles all the way down to her butt. Thin and short, she could pass off for a college-going kid. But I was right about her joie de vivre. Even in the dim and dingy hospital, she is bright and chatty.

She smiles easily, and instantly seems like the kind of person you would want to have a fun girls' night out with.

We walk inside the hospital and find a corner where we can wait until it is Captain's turn for the IV and an X-ray. Young vets whizz past us bearing cats, rabbits, hamsters and even a pet parrot as Deepa talks about her mother-in-law. At first, it seems like an odd choice of a place to talk. But if you think about it, there is no better place to vent spleen about the vicious and bitchy than an animal hospital.

Deepa's marriage was one of those made-in-India specials—an arranged love story. Sandeep and she were both non-Bengali Kolkata kids. Their parents moved in the same social circle, although they weren't really friends. The two families were liberal and cosmopolitan. Deepa's and Sandeep's mothers were both working women, which was rare for their generation. Deepa's mother was a doctor and Sandeep's mother was an air hostess in an international airline.

The kids were around the same age and the thought occurred to both their mothers that maybe they should look at setting something up. Sandeep once came to drop his mother at Deepa's for high tea and Deepa's mother thought this strapping, handsome and quiet boy was rather suitable. Soon after, Deepa and her parents went for lunch at a friend's home and Sandeep's mother turned up, ostensibly, to check her out.

But, being a modern woman, she was not comfortable with the whole business and didn't look beyond a glance. Later, she asked Sandeep's younger brother Deepak if he took a good look at Deepa. He had seen her and had also spent time with her. He found her easy banter, sharp sense of humour and quick laugh very endearing. 'If Sandeep isn't marrying her, I will,' he said. That was endorsement enough.

Since Sandeep was in the army, it was arranged that the two of them would meet the next time he came to Kolkata. His mother insisted that it should be without parental supervision. While this was not unheard of, it was quite progressive for the 1990s. Usually, the prospective groom and bride were allowed a little walkabout in the garden while the adults kept a discreet watch on them. 'I was thrilled at how cool she was,' Deepa says.

The meeting with Sandeep went well and she was warming up to the idea of getting married to him. But then she realized that, with his life in the army, she wouldn't be able to pursue her own career. Deepa was a graduate in hotel management and, at the time, she was working at the Oberoi in Kolkata. She told him she wasn't keen on abandoning her career. He conceded that it was a problem, but since he was home on leave and did not have many friends left in the city, he asked if she was OK spending time with him.

Polite to a fault, Deepa said yes, of course. They had a fabulous time that fortnight and Deepa felt a deep pang when it was time for him to rejoin his platoon. Then she got a letter from him, talking about his post-vacation life. She wrote back, and this carried on for months. By the time his next vacation rolled around, they had become a couple.

Just before his vacation, Sandeep got his transfer orders. He was to be posted in Lucknow. Since it was a city and not a mofussil border town where he had been stationed earlier, Deepa had an option to find work. Sandeep suggested that she continue to stay in Lucknow and work even if the following posting was somewhere far-flung. There were solutions to her career conundrum, he said, and he was willing to make the sacrifices that entailed. Having resolved this, Sandeep went down on his knees and proposed marriage to her. Deepa happily said yes.

Now that the two of them had come round to their mothers' plans, Deepa had her first conversation with her future mother-in-law. She doesn't remember a lot of details; it was largely about the specifics of the wedding. Deepa was nervous meeting her, but she had heard good things about her from all of Sandeep's friends. They all loved her. "'Neeta Aunty is the coolest. You are *so* lucky to be her daughter-in-law." That's what everyone told me. I was like wow,' Deepa says.

Neeta Aunty had been a flight attendant with an international airline for most of her life. When she quit, she had taken up a desk job and was still working full-time. She still had the air hostess's bearing, confidence and sharp sense of style. When Deepa visited their home the first time, she was shown all the family albums. Neeta Aunty was everywhere, flaunting her ace body in two-piece bikinis at poolsides around the world. When she spoke, she said things like 'screw this shit' or 'get that bugger on the phone' or 'he was such a bastard but I do love him.' Who wouldn't want a mother-in-law so modern? Deepa thought that her biggest stroke of luck in this marriage was winning the mother-in-law jackpot.

That's not to say that Neeta Aunty did not have her own set of quirks. Deepa found it a bit weird that, just before the wedding, Neeta Aunty opened her wardrobe and asked her to pick the saris she wanted. Then she opened her locker and laid out her jewellery. 'It was the done thing, I suppose, and she wanted me to pick the stuff I liked. But then it got weird when she offered me her bikinis and said I could use them as underwear!' she says. Shocked, Deepa was unsure if Neeta Aunty meant to humiliate her or was just obtuse. She mumbled that there was enough time to discuss this after the wedding and managed to get out of there. Once home, she rationalized that her mother-in-law meant well. It was all good, really.

Soon after the marriage, Sandeep had to go back to Lucknow and apply for family accommodation. It would take a few months to get a house allotted and it was decided that Deepa would join him only after that. Neeta Aunty suggested the new bride move in with her and Sandeep's father. It would give them a chance to know their daughter-in-law better, she said.

Deepa moved in with her in-laws and was looking forward to a roaring good time with her cool, new mother-in-law. It began well. In the mornings, she would go to the kitchen to help her cook and Neeta Aunty would wave her away. 'You have the rest of your life to do this, she would tell me, you go and take it easy now,' Deepa says. After cooking breakfast and lunch, Neeta Aunty headed out to work. Deepa stayed home with her father-in-law. It was boring, obviously, but it was a sacrifice she didn't really mind making.

After a couple of weeks, small changes began to creep in. If Deepa helped with the salad, Neeta Aunty would remark at the table that the carrots were to be chopped and not shredded. Deepa would immediately apologize but wonder why Aunty hadn't pointed it out in the kitchen when she had begun to shred the carrots. Since she didn't have much to do all day, Deepa spent most of her time chatting with her friends on the phone. Neeta Aunty complained about this too. Not quietly to her, but loudly when there were others in the room. Deepa was quite horrified at her own faux pas, and she immediately corrected them. She didn't think they were big enough to be damaging in the long term.

One day her friends called to ask if she would be keen on joining them for an evening out in town. They planned to have dinner some place and then maybe go to a club. Neeta Aunty insisted that Deepa go. 'No, no, you must go. You are young. Why should you be locked up in this house? Meet your friends, have fun,' mother-in-law was insistent. But when she got ready and emerged from her room, Neeta Aunty was not pleased. 'Are you wearing jeans?' she gasped. 'What if someone sees you?'

Deepa was shocked. 'But how can I go to a nightclub in a salwar kameez or a sari?' she asked.

In the meantime, her friends had arrived. Aunty said hello to them nicely and warmly. Then she pulled Deepa into another room. 'You are married now. You can't dress the same way you did before you came into my family. I can't afford to have someone see you like this,' she hissed.

'But-but,' Deepa stammered.

'No buts,' Aunty said, 'you have to change out of this right now!'

Deepa went to her friends, who were waiting for her in the living room, and told them Aunty wanted her to change her clothes and wear a salwar kameez. She was nearly in tears. Her friends—who were all fans of Neeta Aunty—rallied around her. They said they would bring the car around the building so she could hop into it from the lobby and minimize the prospect of being spotted by someone in the building. But no, Neeta Aunty was having none of it. She stood firm. 'If you are a married woman, you should dress like one,' she said. Ironically, Neeta Aunty herself was dressed in a pair of jeans at the time. Deepa pointed it out gently. 'How is it that you can wear jeans and I can't?' she asked.

'Well my dear, that is how it is,' Aunty proclaimed and walked into her room.

Deepa changed into a salwar kameez and followed her shocked friends to the car. They were all puzzled by Neeta Aunty's obvious double standards. But they put it down to social pressures and tried not to dwell too much on it. Over the next few weeks, Deepa was consistently shocked as Neeta Aunty's true self revealed itself. She realized Aunty was not as cool as she seemed to be. She would say things in order to win popularity points. But the minute she realized that someone else was stealing her thunder, she would come down hard and heavily on them.

Still, being easy-going and inherently cheerful, Deepa shrugged things off. She didn't want to react rudely or make a scene. She obeyed what Aunty said and nodded along with her inconsistencies. A couple of months later, Sandeep wrote with some good news. He had managed to get family accommodation. He came to Kolkata to take Deepa back with him. That week, her friends said they should spend a day together so that they could get to know Sandeep as well. It was decided they would all go to an amusement park just outside the city. Neeta Aunty's permission was sought and given.

The morning of the excursion, Neeta Aunty announced that Sandeep's dad would go with them and that two of Deepa's friends were to come back to the city to pick her up from office so she could join them at the amusement park. Sandeep nodded his head. As soon as breakfast was over, Deepa pulled Sandeep into the room.

Why were his parents coming along? 'He was of the general view that his parents are usually right and they have a reason for the things they do or say. I was too, but despite that, I could see how unbelievably ludicrous this particular idea was,' she says. How could her friends ever hope to get to know her husband if his parents were hovering around them all the time? She tried to get Sandeep to convince his mother, but he refused.

There was no point arguing, and when her friends arrived, they all piled into the car and went. A bunch of twenty-somethings and a fifty-seven-year-old man constituted the group. Sandeep's father was, at the time, recovering from a triple bypass surgery. He could barely walk a few steps at a time. There was no question of his going on any of the rides. Angry and awkward, Deepa said she would stay back with her father-in-law and urged her friends to go on some of the rides. Sandeep said if Deepa wasn't going, he wasn't either. And their friends said well, if the two of them weren't going, they weren't going too. And so they all just sat around the amusement park all morning, making polite conversation with her father-in-law. At noon, two of her friends went back to the city and brought Neeta Aunty to the park. She joined them and regaled her friends with zany stories of her experiences in amusement parks around the world. Deepa tried to enjoy herself but she couldn't hide her disappointment. She spent the day in a sulk.

The next morning, Deepa's mother got a phone call. Neeta Aunty had decided that enough was enough and she wasn't going to take any shit from a youngster who couldn't even extend her the courtesy of enjoying her stories. She told Deepa's mother that her daughter was extremely ill-mannered, that she didn't help around the house, that she was very aggressive and was trying to take her son away from her.

Deepa was sitting right there by the phone. Neeta Aunty hadn't mentioned any of these concerns to her. So when she picked up the phone, Deepa had no idea it was to call her mother and complain about her behaviour. She was shocked and fled to her room and began to cry.

The following day, Deepa's worried mother sent a friend to inquire what had happened. It was while relating events of the past weeks that Deepa realized how wrong it had all turned out. 'Nothing is what it seems from the outside. Here everyone was going Neeta Aunty wow and Neeta Aunty yay and I allowed myself to believe that she was cool. I realized she wasn't. She has a pattern. She is cool about herself, but she doesn't want me to do what I want. That realization was shocking to me. That someone could project one thing about themselves and be the exact opposite to their daughter-in-law,' she says.

Sandeep was unable to assess things objectively. He hadn't lived at home with his parents since he finished school. Because his parents got so little time with him, he was treated 'like a god' when he was home. Then he decided to join the army and became an even bigger god in his mother's eyes. Armed with ten years of fussy love from his mother, he couldn't understand why his wife was making such a big deal about his mother. He couldn't find any fault with her, and his friends have always told him how much they loved his mother. All of them couldn't be wrong, he thought. It was just easier for him to assume that the problem must be Deepa.

'At the time, Sandeep's brother was dating this girl and she would come over on their way to the disco. And Neeta Aunty would tell her, come on, why are you all buttoned up, this is no way to dress to the disco. Now imagine my telling her that Aunty wouldn't even let me wear jeans. How would she ever believe me?' Deepa says. A couple of times, before Sandeep came to take her to Lucknow, his brother and girlfriend would insist that Deepa go along with them.

You should go, Neeta Aunty would insist. And when she went to her room to change, she would follow her in and tell Deepa softly, 'Poor Sandeep must be at the border, I wonder if he's eaten, I wonder if he's safe. But don't worry, you should go to the disco, Deepa.' So she wouldn't. Obviously.

Deepa had thought she would cry buckets when it was time to leave her hometown to go to Lucknow. But because of this 'mindfuck' with Neeta Aunty, she was quite relieved to get out of Kolkata. In Lucknow, she set up home for the first time and settled down to live the life of an army wife. In a couple of weeks there was a letter from Neeta Aunty. In it, she told Sandeep that his wife was evil, spoilt and a selfish brat. She said that she was badly brought up and, although it was sad that things had come to this, Sandeep had to choose between his wife and his mother. Sandeep showed Deepa the letter and told her that he didn't want to choose. 'You have to work at getting my mother to like you,' he said.

So she did. In her next letter, Neeta Aunty wrote to Sandeep that Deepa shouldn't go to work for a few years so that the two of them could get to know each other better. That was essential to making a marriage work, she wrote. But in reality, a break like that at the beginning of the career never works out professionally. More often than not, in a couple of years there is a baby on the way and then there is never a good time to go back to work. It was a trap. And Deepa fell right into it. 'It was all a bit bizarre because Neeta Aunty herself worked right through her marriage. I wonder how she got to know her husband. But by then I didn't want to fight any more. So I just said yes, you know better, and stopped looking for a job in Lucknow,' she says.

While we are chatting, Deepa's phone rings a few dozen times.

Each time she looks at the screen and disconnects the call. 'God, she is going to live for a million years: here we are talking about her and that was my mother-in-law calling,' she says. I tell her she could take the call, I am happy to wait. 'Oh well, I know. I just don't feel like talking to her,' she says.

By now it is Captain's turn and we abandon the story of Neeta Aunty to pin the Dobermann down on an X-ray table. Deepa talks soothingly to him, promises him many treats and tries to get him to hold still. It's a battle loaded against her, much like the story she was telling me. The technician manages to take one shot, but then comes back saying he would have to do it again. Poor Captain is hauled on the table again; he isn't pleased about that at all. Eventually, the third X-ray is deemed acceptable. We pile into her car, then, Captain taking up all the room in the back seat, and go to Deepa's home.

Deepa's son, Sanjay—a sixteen-year-old—opens the door. In the surly tone that teenagers universally deploy, he informs his mother that dadi has been calling like crazy. 'I don't want to talk to her, Sanjay,' she tells him. Our yakhni pulao has been reduced to pizza and we settle down in her modest but tasteful living room. The phone rings again, this time it's the landline. Deepa asks Sanjay to answer it. Sanjay picks it up. 'Mom is not back yet,' he informs her drolly. Then a long silence. 'I am studying,' he says and sticks to single-sentence responses over the next couple of minutes. 'I ate Maggi,' he says after a minute or so, in a tone which suggests that he couldn't wait to get to the end of this phone call. Finally he hangs up. 'Mom!' he rolls his eyes before walking out of the room.

'It's OK darling, come here and give me a kiss,' Deepa pulls him in before stepping out for a cigarette. In the balcony, she whispers to me, 'I am happy he discovered her unpleasantness on his own,' she says.

Back in Lucknow, things weren't going too well for the newly-weds. Each time Sandeep's parents came to visit, there would be an issue. On one of their visits, Deepa recalls having made upma for breakfast. Neeta Aunty belched at the sight of it and said, 'We don't eat such rubbish.' Deepa offered to make her an omelette. 'No thanks,' she said, 'I'd rather make it myself.' That evening Sandeep got to hear about the substandard food his wife was serving his mother. Expectedly, there was a row.

On another visit, Deepa fell ill on a weekend when an army picnic was scheduled. Sandeep suggested they skip the picnic but Neeta Aunty would have none of that. 'The commanding officer is expecting me to be there and I can't go if she can't go. Pop a Crocin and come along,' she commanded. And so Deepa went— burning up with fever, in a bus with forty other people bouncing through potholed roads for four hours on a hot, sunny, Lucknow day. I ask her if Sandeep didn't see the cruelty in this. 'She would present it to him as something she was doing for the sake of his career. Everything would get twisted. At the end of that day, she said, she saved her son's job which apparently I was determined to screw up,' she says.

Sandeep was truly torn between his mother and wife. But the fact is, he has always known his mother was on his side. And with all the stuff his mother was filling his head up with, he wasn't sure if Deepa, a woman he had known relatively recently, was on his side as well. The marriage had begun on a note of suspicion and doubt and, no matter how hard they tried, they couldn't get past it.

On one particular visit, Neeta Aunty made a long list of complaints about Deepa to Sandeep, who of course repeated them to his wife the minute his mother had left. It was the last straw. 'The next day when he went to work, I just walked out of the house. I didn't know where I was going or whom I should call,' she says. She found a shared rickshaw and spent the little money she had on that. It took her to the railway station. She didn't know what she should do, so she just sat there on the platform bench, contemplating her life's chaos. 'I had been an independent working woman and I felt my life was reduced to being a wife and, from the feedback I was getting, not a very good one at that,' she says. Sandeep found her there at eight in the evening and took her home. He said she was free to leave when she wanted, but she should let him book her a ticket and make sure she was safe. So she left.

She went back to Kolkata and stayed with her parents for some time. But she began missing her husband and he was missing her too and, over hundreds of phone calls, they decided that they should work at things. And she went back. Over the next couple of years, this was the pattern of their marriage. Her mother-in-law would visit or write, create chaos between the two of them and Deepa would go back to her parents.

At one point, Sandeep told her he was determined to cut off all communication with his mum. But these were promises made in the throes of desperation and Deepa knew honouring them was not his intention.

'It is difficult, especially in an arranged marriage, to build trust and be each other's biggest champion. The only way that will happen is if you both start out with a clean slate. I never got that clean slate from Sandeep. His mother had already told him I was bad and put him in a position where he had to choose between her and me,' Deepa says. When she went to Kolkata after her fights, she stayed home with her parents. Her mother would advise her to see things from Sandeep's point of view. She would tell her that marriages are difficult, they need work. She should learn to ignore Neeta Aunty and just live the way she wanted.

But each time Deepa talked herself into warming up to Neeta Aunty, she did something entirely unforgivable. When Sanjay was small, he suffered terribly from asthma. By then Neeta Aunty was widowed and had moved to Bangalore. Deepa and Sanjay were visiting her. When the baby started wheezing helplessly, Deepa was panic-stricken. Neeta Aunty told her she was overreacting. New mothers are anxious and there was nothing wrong with the child, she assured Deepa. But as the child started to struggle for breath, Deepa asked that Neeta Aunty allow her to speak to her mother in Kolkata. She was a doctor and she would know whether this was serious or not, she told her. These were the days before mobile phones, so Deepa couldn't make the call herself. Neeta Aunty had a landline, but the STD facility was locked.

She refused to unlock it and kept telling Deepa that there was nothing wrong with the child. Finally, Deepa sneaked in a local call to Sandeep's brother and begged him to get her mother to speak to her. When her mother called, she described little Sanjay's symptoms. Her mother prescribed a medicine and told her if the baby didn't improve within thirty minutes, he had to be taken to the emergency room. It was a very serious attack and, for a baby that young, a delay in medication could prove very serious.

Sandeep, who always believed his mother was right, refused to budge. Deepa called her brother-in-law again and pleaded for the tablet. He brought it home and, soon after taking it, Sanjay's breathing normalized. 'How can you get past events like this?' she asks me. Neeta Aunty's response was to complain to Sandeep that his wife was disobeying her and sneaking phone calls behind her back.

A few years later, Sandeep's faith in his mother was also shaken by another asthma attack. This time, he was visiting his mother with Sanjay. Deepa had refused to go. In the middle of the night, Sanjay had an attack and Neeta Aunty advised her son to give the child a steam inhalation. Four hours and several inhalations later, Sandeep realized there was no improvement at all. Finally, at around 2 a.m., he called Deepa to ask her what he should do.

She gave him the names of the medicines and through the call she could hear Neeta Aunty yelling in the background asking Sandeep to decide if he wanted listen to her or Deepa. He took a chance and listened to his wife and immediately saw his son's condition improve. For the first time, it occurred to him that his mother might not always be right. 'It was just the two of them in this situation. When there are people around, things get diluted. If this had happened while I was there, he would simply have thought of it as something between her and me. This time, he could think about his mother's words and deeds in isolation from those of others. That made a big difference. Also, Sandeep is the rare man who accepts and acknowledges his mistakes. That's what has helped me stay with him, despite these troubles,' Deepa says.

But all said, Sandeep is unable to shake off his mother's grip on him. 'He knows the truth about her now, but he still can't accept it,' Deepa says. Without a foundation of trust, their marriage has been wobbly. The couple rowed frequently. It didn't help that they were posted in small towns with no distractions other than the cantonment. Deepa focused on raising Sanjay and helping out in the Army Wives' Clubs. Sandeep and she enjoyed spells of happiness but they always ended with a letter or a visit from Neeta Aunty.

The phone rings again. 'What is wrong with her?' Deepa grumbles but does not answer it. Nor does she ask Sanjay to get it. 'Now she is old and she needs me,' Deepa says, 'and I suppose I am also a little tough with her. Too bad. She asked for it.'

A few years after the asthma incident, Sandeep was diagnosed with a medical condition after he came down from the Siachen glacier. It was clear this would prevent him from proceeding beyond a certain rank in the army. When he told his mother that he was thinking of quitting the forces and finding a corporate job, she opposed it vehemently. She told him he lacked the ability to cope with life outside the armed forces. To Deepa, it was evident that part of her resistance came from the loss of bragging rights about having a soldier son. But Sandeep listened to his mother and decided to stay put.

The next five years were a struggle. Sandeep's career was going nowhere. He was stuck at his rank in the army with no prospects of being promoted. Once again, he decided to quit. Neeta Aunty called Deepa to urge her to talk Sandeep into staying. Deepa said that she agreed and that becoming a civilian's wife would be the worst thing that could happen to her. She would be lost without the big army accommodation and her batmen. That was that! Neeta Aunty withdrew all her objections. If Sandeep quitting the army was a bad deal for Deepa, then she was all for him going ahead and doing it. Sandeep found a job with an international consulting major and moved to Bangalore. He is on a fast track in the company and, even though it has dispelled his mother's notions about his inability to 'cope with life outside the forces', he has never pointed it out to her.

In the middle of all this, Deepa fell seriously ill. After a week of tremendous pain, it was diagnosed that she was suffering from a serious condition called polycystic kidneys. The doctors were unsure about how quickly the cysts would multiply. But they knew it wouldn't take too long, less than a decade perhaps, before her kidneys were entirely dysfunctional. The condition was terminal.

Sandeep was on his way out of the army, but was on a remote posting. Neeta Aunty came to Delhi where Deepa and Sanjay were stationed, 'supposedly' to help. After ten days, she was discharged from the hospital and sent home to convalesce. She was advised to eat small meals, freshly cooked, every couple of hours. Neeta Aunty couldn't be bothered with the details. She cooked a very spicy khichdi and froze it, so that it could be reheated and given to her. Deepa found it impossible to eat.

Finally, Sanjay decided to take charge and, even though he was barely in his teens then, he got the batman to help and cooked some nutritious and bland food for her. 'Neeta Aunty would be constantly talking on the phone in my bedroom. He would come in and tell her please dadi, let mama rest,' she says. She was of no help at all. The IV drip routinely formed air bubbles, her medicine schedule went awry, her mealtimes would come and go while Neeta Aunty was busy calling all and sundry and talking about this 'calamity that has befallen her'. 'I was ill and dying,' says Deepa, 'but she wanted first dibs on the calamity and the resultant sympathy.' The only reason she insisted on coming to Delhi was so she could call everyone and tell them about being the mother-in-law of a person with terminal illness.

It was then that Sanjay realized the truth about his grandmother. The beloved grandson started withdrawing himself from his dadi. He started reading between the lines of her conversations. He was often too polite to take his grandmother on and call her bluff, but he would come and talk to Deepa about it. Deepa was glad that he himself saw Neeta Aunty for who she was and made up his own mind about her. Sandeep offered no explanations for his mother's behaviour.

'One of those days I had to go to the doctor for a check-up and Neeta Aunty insisted on coming with me. When we reach the doctor's office, the first question she asks is, "Doctor, could you tell me how long she will live exactly? Because we have to make arrangements. I now live in a rented place in Bangalore; if we don't have too long then I won't buy a house but move in with Sandeep instead." The doctor nearly fell off his chair. He was so angry, he couldn't speak. Finally, he stood up, towered over her and said, "Ma'am, I am not God."' Deepa herself was too ill to react. 'What can you do when all your mother-in-law cares about is whether she should rent or buy a house while she waits for you to die? You can only laugh.'

The diagnosis transformed Deepa's outlook on life. She sat down and thought about what she wanted to do with whatever time she had. She wanted to make sure that Sanjay was independent, as well as ground him in the principles that were important to her. And she wanted to make sure that she lived her life the way she wanted to. Like really *live* it. She told Sandeep that she was going to do her own stuff now and not worry about everyone's approval.

'I told him, if you are with me, fine; if you aren't, to hell with you, go live with your mum. I am now going to do everything I denied myself in order to make you and your mum happy.'

First up, she decided she wanted to go on a holiday to Goa. Usually, all the family holidays involved going to visit Neeta Aunty. She announced that she was going to Goa and Sandeep and Sanjay were free to join her if they liked. They did and the three of them had a fantastic time. Then, when they moved to Bangalore, she put her foot down and refused to live with Neeta Aunty. And little by little, Deepa wrestled control of her life away from Neeta Aunty. Her health has stabilized now, but there is no predicting when the cysts in her kidneys will grow out of control.

I ask her how much of the problem in her marriage was caused by her mother-in-law. Hundred per cent she answers without blinking, proving Richard Alexander the evolutionary biologist's theory right. Even today, she and Sandeep are constantly circling each other's shadow. They can't fully trust one another—she, because she is wary of what his mother would have filled his head with and he, because his mother has told him so many bad things about his wife he can't be certain what his wife's intentions are. 'And I also notice, even today, how negative he gets when he talks to his mother. He will get off the phone with her and the first thing he says will be something negative. It could be about the house, about me, about the weather, about the city, about anything. She has that effect on him,' she says.

It's now nearly twenty years that she has been married to Sandeep. Deepa has, in her orderly and clinical manner, tried to analyse what the triggers were for Neeta Aunty's transition from Aunty cool to monster mother-in-law. They are both a lot alike, actually. They are both the 'coolest mums' their kids' friends know. They are both extroverted, the life of the party. That was the role Neeta Aunty played all her life.

Then, when Deepa entered the family, she reckons, her mother-in-law felt the attention shift away from her. If nothing, here was someone who was new and seemed interesting. It couldn't have sat well with a narcissist. She had to get rid of this competition. People would tell Neeta Aunty how wonderful her daughter-in-law was and she would immediately call Sandeep and tell him what a monster his wife was. If there is a lesson in this story, it certainly is that a mother-in-law who offers to hand down her bikinis does not really have your best interests at heart. Deepa should have trusted her instincts and run at the first sight of elastic and padding.

A few months later, I notice that Deepa has been missing on Facebook. I send her a few messages. I get a reply a fortnight later and we set up a chat on Facebook. She has been ill, she tells me, and has come to her mother's for some rest. She cracks a few jokes, we have a good laugh. And then she slips in that Sandeep and she have decided to separate. Sanjay will finish his schooling in a few months and leave home for college. There is no point staying together after that. 'We live like two room-mates,' she writes, 'there is no marriage left. He still slavishly follows his mother's diktats and I am done living on her terms.'

I write and delete several sentences. I don't know what I should tell her. Eventually, she writes, 'Babe, you are taking too long. I'll tell you the same thing I told myself when I decided I should get out of this marriage. I don't have forever, you know!' This she followed with several sunshine-yellow smileys.

7

The Peacekeeping Mission

Name	Age (in 2013)	Husband	Married
Supriya	39	Robert	2001

All relationships are the result of strategy. That first meeting might be pure serendipity, though in some cases even that is the result of years of planning. If you don't believe me, you haven't been reading enough trashy newspaper stories about how Kate Middleton picked the college that Prince William was going to just so she could plan to accidentally bump into him. But even for us non-aspirants to royalty, the evolution of a relationship is the result of how we decide to play the game.

In the strategy-laden universe of all relationships, it can safely be said that there is none more tactical than the one with the mother-in-law. Every daughter-in-law has a strategy for Mummyji even before the first meeting. Some think they should be coy and conservative. Others are belligerent and spoiling for a fight—'I am not going to take her bullshit, I'll have her know.' Some others pretend to be pushovers—they agree to everything they are told and then go ahead and do what they wanted to anyway.

Then there is a small minority of reformists. Like a UN

peacekeeping mission, they decide that they will be the glue that holds together the mother and the son. These are women who have known their husbands long before they marry them. They are privy to detailed accounts of family feuds. And as the objective third party, they can see the situation for what it is—a miasma that can be fixed with some magic dust.

Supriya was one such reformist. She met Robert through her brother. The boys were best buddies and spent an inordinate amount of time in each other's homes. Supriya's brother and Robert qualified as architects and, while her brother left the city to pursue his career elsewhere, Robert found a job in Delhi and stayed on. Supriya and he continued to meet. They were friends. And confidants. The redeeming part of a bad day, for both of them, was the telling of it to the other, over a glass of beer in the evening. Even though they felt a strong physical attraction to each other from the day they met ('We wanted to do each other from the word go' as Supriya put it to me), they didn't get together until much later. This was a relationship that was firmly rooted in friendship and, through good times and bad, the friendship stayed.

Robert often talked to Supriya about his family. It was a difficult relationship. Robert felt that they hadn't supported him and regarded them as a source of a great deal of anxiety. Inevitably, Robert's most complicated relationship was with his mother. He did not get along with her at all. They have always fought, often over trivial reasons. But when he told Supriya about these fights, it was as a joke. The worse the incident, the funnier would be his story. Supriya did not catch on about how intensely damaged the relationship was until much later.

I've known Supriya for a few years. Vigorous and outspoken, she is an activist, one who bravely takes on issues of gender and sexuality. Yet she is emotional and high-strung. You have to walk carefully around her, although if you do end up triggering a fight, she is likely to be the one making a peace-offering telephone call the following day. Born to Bengali parents and raised in Delhi, Supriya is a perfect blend of intellectual high-mindedness and big-city smarts.

Although she barely reaches the shoulder of most people in a circle, hers is often the loudest voice. My enduring image of Supriya is of her dressed in a clumsily draped handloom sari, hair twisted in a careless knot, a cigarette in one hand and a beer in the other, loudly denouncing right-wing politicians while quoting Camus and Kafka. I haven't heard her having a single conversation that didn't slide into a debate. Robert is the perfect calm to Supriya's constant agitation. I often find him standing by her, calmly smoking a cigarette. He seems perfectly comfortable in his own skin. Supriya and Robert are the kind of couple who prove that opposites do attract.

Supriya met Robert's Mum for the first time when Robert and she were still friends; before they began dating, that is. The plan was to go to Robert's home and then go for a party from there. 'It was really cold and for some reason I hadn't dressed appropriately. I remember he went in and talked to his mother and she came and opened this cupboard and handed me a lovely coat. She was very concerned and kept asking me if I was fine and did the coat fit well and all of that,' she says.

Supriya and Robert had a few drinks at the party but then decided to go back to his house for dinner. His mother is a fabulous cook and it was Supriya's first introduction to Goan food. She was bowled over by the meal. By the time they were done with dinner, the Delhi fog had descended. Robert said it was too risky for her to go back home and his mother insisted she stay. They all sat and chatted for a while and, later, she showed Supriya to the guest room.

Robert's mother went to church every morning at 5.30. At 5, Supriya woke up to see her quietly moving about the room—getting her things ready, and making an incredible effort to do it quietly so as not to wake her up. She rasped good morning and the older woman sprung around and apologized for waking her up. 'Go back to sleep,' she urged. Supriya was delighted by how considerate she was.

She was bowled over by her future mother-in-law. She couldn't fathom how this caring, warm woman could be the nightmare mother of Robert's stories. She met her a few times after that and she was consistently charmed.

Then her friendship with Robert evolved to romance. Obviously, all that chemistry couldn't be suppressed for too long. Sometime before Robert popped the question, his mother had asked him if she should start looking out for a good Goan girl for him. For no real reason, Robert said yes. Grateful for the opportunity to find someone within the community, Mum immediately set the wheels in motion. Friends and family in Goa lined up prospective girls. So chaos reigned when Robert finally informed his mother that he was marrying Supriya. Mum felt betrayed, cheated and pissed off. Supriya wasn't Goan. She wasn't a Christian. She wasn't a Catholic. And she felt compromised in front of her friends and the community because she had begun the bride hunt.

Supriya stayed out of it. For the next couple of months, she didn't go to Robert's place. She would call, of course, and if Robert's Mum answered (these were the days before mobile phones) she'd hang up. No one was fooled, his mother would tell Robert it was a blank call and quite likely to be from 'his girl'. Two months later, she went to Goa and wept to her sisters about this calamity. And from there, she went to Portugal to visit her daughter.

In Lisbon, Robert's sister and her in-laws, whom his mother really respected, knocked some sense into her. They told her she was foolish to be stuck on a Goan daughter-in-law. She should accept whoever makes Robert happy. This worked. When she came back, she was not only willing to accept Supriya, but had also carried some presents for her new daughter-in-law.

Thus began the honeymoon. Not one involving Robert and

Supriya, but an altogether special one: that of Supriya and her mother-in-law. The first time they met after her mother-in-law returned from Portugal, they both knew it was to an altered relationship. She handed Supriya the gift and sat her down and showed her all the family photographs.

The honeymoon progressed splendidly. The two of them went shopping, they dined out by themselves, they chatted on the phone. Mum loved to ramble on and Supriya indulged her. 'She had an endless way of talking, jumping from one thing to the other, and in many ways what parents of kids who have grown up crave is just someone who would nod along. I nodded along very well,' she says.

It was in the flush of this honeymoon that Supriya decided it was her job to bring Robert and his mother together. 'I sensed a lot of pain in both of them about not getting along with each other,' she says. Among the three children, Robert was the one who was most vocal about his mother's injustices. He had been a good cricket player in school, but that was neither encouraged nor praised at home. He was a very good artist. That too was ignored. Eventually, he began hiding his accomplishments from his mother.

Supriya thought she had to ensure that Robert's family saw him for the amazing guy he was. 'I was shocked that they didn't think he was fabulous. His mother didn't think anything about him. She would tell her friends—in front of Robert—that she doesn't remember Robert much as a child and things like that, she says. There is no force greater than a woman on a mission, and Supriya was on hers.

Supriya told Robert about his mother's good qualities. She constantly made excuses for the way his mother behaved towards him. When Robert refused to alter his views about his mother, Supriya and he fought. She couldn't fathom why Robert thought badly of his mother. On her outings with her mother-in-law, she made sure to recount good stories about Robert. She complimented him constantly and even thanked her for raising him to be the wonderful person he was. Mum didn't actively oppose her views, but she always had a rather quizzical expression as she listened to Supriya, as though she wasn't certain they were talking about the same person.

By then Supriya had begun planning the wedding. She shared all the details with Mum, who was quite involved in the event. There was never any discussion about Supriya's converting to Christianity, but Mum did mention a couple of times that their children would have to be baptized. 'It was said casually and I took it casually. No one really paid much attention to religion,' she tells me. They first had an engagement—a small family affair—where a secular priest came and spoke beautifully about love, marriage and family. It was a very touching ceremony. At the end of it, Robert and Supriya turned to both their parents and told them they would be calling them Mum and Dad from then on. Everyone was thrilled.

About this time, there was some talk of their living together after the wedding. Robert's Mum sat him down and told him that both Supriya and she were independent and strong-willed women and it was absolutely unlikely that they would be able to share a house without friction. It was best, she said, that they live separately. That way they would see each other often enough—on weekends and holidays—and yet not grate on each other's nerves. Supriya adored Mum even more for that. 'It was a very rational and realistic thing to say and I was amazed at her foresight and tact,' she says.

The wedding went well. Supriya and Robert moved into a *barsaati* close to his parents. Life was perfect. When they visited, Mum would cook her favourite dishes. They shopped, dined, joked, laughed. If they weren't on a jaunt somewhere—Mum and she—they were planning one. They were perfectly suited. If Robert got into an argument with his mother, Supriya would always take her side.

The honeymoon bobbed along for a couple more years. There were some issues—mostly minor and immensely forgettable—and

Supriya and Mum stayed friends. Robert was talking less and less about his mother. Supriya patted herself on the back. The peacekeeping mission had gone well, she told herself. She had managed to bring love to a little corner of Delhi where earlier there was only angst and anger.

Three years after the wedding, Supriya was pregnant. Both sets of parents were thrilled when they announced the news. One evening, towards the end of her first trimester, Supriya decided to stay over at her in-laws' as Robert was out of town. After dinner that night, Mum sat her down and, in a tone of voice Supriya had never heard before, laid down her rules. This baby will be raised a Catholic, she said, and it is your responsibility to do so.

Supriya was taken aback, she had not seen this coming at all. In the three years that she had been married to Robert, she had participated in important religious activities at his home. Since the issue of religion had never really come up—barring those early suggestions that the kids should be raised Catholic—Supriya was quite blindsided by the force with which Mum laid down these rules and the zeal with which she repeated them. 'That evening Mum demonstrated a different kind of ownership altogether. It wasn't a warm and fuzzy one, but a horrible dictatorial one,' she says. Supriya was horrified, she knew this was only going to get crazier once the child was born. She couldn't sleep that night. And she went back home the following morning with a severe migraine.

When Robert returned from his trip she told him about the conversation. He didn't think it was a big deal but reassured her that his mother wouldn't do anything against her wishes. But this became the beginning of an endless discussion about their unborn child's baptism. 'Robert and I fought a lot about this, right through my pregnancy. And Mum started making it clearer and clearer that this baby would be baptized and there was no other option she was even willing to consider,' she says. In many ways, the arrival of Jesus marked the culmination of the honeymoon.

It was the end of an era. In a matter of a couple of weeks, Mum became a source of endless stress for Supriya. Since she didn't want to take her on or be rude in any way, she would listen to whatever she was saying and then come home and yell at Robert about it. Supriya and Mum no longer had anything to chat about. All Mum could talk about was the baptism—and her tone would go from reasoning, to pleading, to rage—and all Supriya did was listen to her and suppress all her instincts to get into an argument.

Then came blow number two. The baby was born and she was a little premature. In movies and advertisements, the baby arrives and brings some zen-like magic with her. In reality, everyone around the baby is sleep-deprived and rattled. When the baby is premature or has some health issue, the atmosphere in the house is even worse.

Supriya, like most new mothers, had assumed she would be breastfeeding the baby for at least four months. But since she was premature, the baby was unable to suckle. Like a manic machine, Supriya was expressing her breast milk and trying to feed the baby from a bottle. Expressing too often triggers severe post-partum depression and Supriya fell into a chasm. She felt inadequate and unhappy. As if that wasn't bad enough, she also developed an abscess in her breast. Her gynaecologist told her she had to switch to formula. 'She told me she could talk to my mother-in-law, if I wanted her to. I wondered why she was saying that. So I told her no, thank you, I'll tell her myself. I didn't realize it was going to be a big issue,' she says.

When she went home, she told Mum that she was switching the baby to formula. Mum wasn't nice about it at all. 'So you aren't giving her any breast milk at all? Not even a little bit?' she would ask her several times a day. 'And she would ask that in a very whiny tone, which made me feel sad and angry at the same time,' she says. Mum would then list out all the problems related to not breastfeeding the child. 'She would tell me that my child would not have a bond with me. Or this is your first failure in motherhood.

Things like that,' Supriya says.

Around this time, Robert's brother had a baby too. Mum harped on about how her other daughter-in-law was breastfeeding the baby exclusively till he was six months old. A couple of years later, Supriya found out that this was untrue. Her sister-in-law had also stopped in a couple of months. But she was sensible enough to not tell her mother-in-law this. All things considered, if the choice is between being honest and appearing correct, the golden rule is to choose the latter. 'What hurt the most about all of this,' says Supriya, 'is that Mum knew how low I was feeling. And she knew I was a new mother and I was fraught with doubts and that her words had a powerful effect on me. Still, she persisted with her taunts.'

Every evening, when Robert got home, she would burst into tears and tell him about the taunt of the day. He tried to comfort her. The only way to deal with Mum, he told her, was to distance oneself from her. It was then that Supriya saw why Robert was not close to his mother. Suddenly she felt foolish about the entire honeymoon.

In the larger context of the relationship between Mummyji and the daughter-in-law, Supriya's might seem like a mild story. But it tells us one of the big truths about the mother-in-law story. Even among the cultured, sophisticated and the well-intentioned, the Mummyji relationship eventually crumbles. All it takes is for one small issue to pop up.

Within three months of becoming a mother herself, Supriya was quite done with Robert's Mum. But she was still a part of Supriya's life and an active participant in most big decisions. And the baptism question was a large, unresolved issue on the table. After the postnatal depression and the challenges of looking after an infant, Supriya didn't have enough fight in her to take the issue on. So she let it be and Mum went ahead with her plans to baptize the baby. She picked the date, the venue, and even decided who the godparents would be. Supriya and Robert remained largely divorced from the proceedings and decided to just turn up for the event and stay out of everyone's way.

Going through the motions of the baptism helped no one. Supriya found it really difficult to let go of how badly Mum had bullied them. So she kept chipping away about it with Robert. And although Robert was patient and understanding initially, he began to lose his temper with Supriya. The two of them fought constantly. The fight would start with something Mum had told Supriya and quickly escalate to name-calling and hurling really hurtful things at each other. They were going weeks without talking to each other. Their relationship had been built on the bedrock of communication. They were losing that.

Finally Robert and she decided to see a marriage counsellor. They could neither ignore Robert's damaged relationship with his mother nor live in denial of what it was doing to their marriage. Through the course of the therapy, they managed to separate the strands of their relationship and issues. What they discovered was that a large majority of their disagreements with each other stemmed from something that his Mum said or did. That was immensely helpful, says Supriya, this ability to see that if they took away Mum from the equation, there was ample warmth, cohesiveness and intimacy in their relationship with each other. It also forced Supriya to deal with the fact that, through the honeymoon, her efforts at bringing Robert and his Mum together had actually been counterproductive.

Therapy gave Supriya new modes of engaging with Mum. She would no longer sit down and listen to her complaints and demands and come back and yell at Robert. She would call her on her bullshit right away. 'Not in a nasty manner, but I would say Mum I am not happy with that remark, or Mum that wasn't nice of you. Things like that,' she says. This tilted the balance of power. She and Robert also began absenting themselves from the Goan community dos and kept them to the bare minimum.

Mum noticed the changes; she even talked to people about

it. A lot of it would come back to Supriya, including complaints about how much she had changed. They were still meeting every weekend but the meetings were rather unpleasant and, more than that, uncomfortable. There was always an undercurrent of anger and suspicion.

This state of affairs continued for the next three years. Mum and Dad both retired and decided to move to Goa. Supriya felt pangs of guilt. She wished things had worked out differently. But there was nothing she could do. In Goa, Mum too felt disconnected and out of touch with her son's life. Yet, she continued to meddle in their affairs unnecessarily. She would call the home number when she was certain Supriya was out and ask the maid whether the granddaughter was going to church on Sundays. By then, Robert had entirely given up on his religion. Supriya would take her daughter to church whenever she expressed a desire to do so. 'So every once in a while she would come up with these issues, but the distance helped me brush them off,' Supriya says.

A year after Mum moved to Goa, Supriya's daughter had a terrible accident. She was admitted in the hospital and endured weeks of painful battle. Mum and Dad came down immediately. Mum visited the hospital every other day and she would just sit there in a devoted vigil, next to Supriya. Trauma, by its very nature, strips one of pretence and posturing. And so, for both Supriya and Mum, this was a time of great honesty. Often, Mum told her about how she had failed with her children, especially Robert.

Supriya found herself advising Mum, telling her that Robert loved her food, and that was a connection she could build on. At the same time, Supriya also learned to understand and appreciate the power of Mum's faith. She prayed for her grandchild every day.

Six years after the first child, Supriya discovered she was pregnant again. This time the baptism arguments were reversed. Supriya was in favour of it and told Robert that they should pick the godparents and let Mum do the rest. Robert went on a rant threatening to disown his family. But she convinced him. Religion is still an issue that pops up but, with their renewed respect for each other, Supriya and Mum deal with it better.

A few months ago, when Mum and Dad were visiting, Supriya's daughter ran into her room yelling, 'Mama, we are Catholics.' Supriya called Mum into her room—her territory—and told her politely but clearly that religious differences weren't a topic of discussion with the children. That her daughter did not even know the difference between Hindu, Christian, Sikh and Muslim, and it was too early to bring Catholicism into her life.

'I told her that I love that she tells her stories, even biblical ones. But she can't tell her you are this, or you are that. The thing is, Mum is an intelligent person; it is not that she doesn't understand this. But religion is something that she is so close to that she can't think properly when it comes to that. She can't understand the concept of choosing your religion as an adult,' she says. Mum, on her part, said 'of course, of course' and let the point drop. It didn't become the next hundred-year war.

The problem with honeymoons is that they end, no matter how hard you try to stretch them. And when they do end, you land with a painful thud. In Supriya's case, the trauma of the accident helped Mum and her put their differences aside. Now when Mum says something annoying, Supriya can ignore it, because she knows in the larger context of what really matters—the health and happiness of the family—that remark carries no weight. Or else, she can just laugh and says, 'Please Mum, you know that's bullshit.'

In many ways, Supriya is closer to Mum now. She can see Mum making overtures to Robert, although Robert is yet to start accepting these. In time, he probably will. But having learned her lesson, Supriya is not restarting her peace mission. Nor is she keen on a second honeymoon with her mother-in-law. That is for the delusional, she says.

8

The Ugliness of the Indian Family

Name	Age (in 2013)	Husband	Married
Keisha	40	Ashwin	1995

When I started this project, I set off thinking it would be fun to listen to stories about other people's mothers-in-law. Usually, family stories, no matter how horrid, tend to be coloured with love and glossed over with tenderness. People tend to say things like, 'My father whacked us hard if we didn't wash our hands before mealtime, but it was only because he loved us so much.' Which is not quite the same thing as 'That man beat me.' This allowance for cruelty within families is universal, but it is especially pronounced in India where the family reigns supreme. I was conditioned for it and, really, I was looking for some laughs. The mother-in-law as a comical relief was my original motif.

It was only when I began talking to daughters-in-law that I realized how much more serious the mother-in-law issue was. More often than not, I was speaking to strangers—people I had met on the internet or were referred to by a chain of people. Without the threat of being judged by someone familiar, the women were more honest. They didn't bother to dress it up as a joke or a forgivable flaw. What I was left with, usually, were stories of raw callousness and abject cruelty. Often I found myself blinking back tears. Days later I would try to match my first impressions of the people I had met with the reality of their stories and would shudder at how little we know about what goes on in other households.

Keisha's was the final nail in my coffin of Mummyji humour. As I heard her story, I was reminded of an essay by the writer Mukul Kesavan called 'The Ugliness of the Indian Male'. In it he observes that Indian men are measurably uglier than Indian women. 'Why are Indian men like this?' Kesavan asks. 'How do they achieve the bullet-proof unselfconsciousness that allows them to be so abandonedly ugly? I think it comes from a sense of entitlement that's hard-wired into every male child that grows up in an Indian household. That, and the not unimportant fact that, despite the way they look, they're always paired off with good-looking women.'

Of all the ugly Indian men Kesavan wrote about, Keisha's husband Ashwin is the ugliest. And his sense of entitlement came from his Mummyji's constant feeding of it. Throughout her telling of it, I constantly wondered why she married him.

I met Keisha in Kolkata. She was waiting for me outside a Haldiram's outlet. Her Mummyji was so legendary that I heard about her awfulness from a friend's friend's friend. Keisha and I hadn't communicated on email or phone before we met each other (the meeting was arranged through the friend's friend's friend), and we were quite awkward initially. Added to it, was my disappointment that I was in Kolkata and eating at Haldiram's (Keisha's pick of venue) and not wolfing down rolls at Nizam's or biriyani at Shiraz. In the event, I put my professional self ahead of my gluttonous self and settled for pav bhaji. We grabbed a table and placed our order.

Keisha is beautiful with a model's cheekbones and wide-set eyes. Dusky and straight-haired, she held her chin up in a stance that sometimes seemed like a challenge, but was quite often a disguise. She had outlined her lips in a dark shade of brown and filled it in with a shimmery light lipstick. This gave her mouth an odd exaggeration, as if she had painted on a reluctant smile.

Through lunch and the rickshaw ride to my hotel, I struggled to break the ice. Keisha's responses to my inquiries were monosyllabic. I was doubtful about what she would tell me and in how much detail. Once in the room, she sat ramrod straight on the chair—stiff and formal—while I scurried around offering water and soft drinks.

'Can I start?' she asked.

'Yes,' I said.

And she began. I didn't have to ask her a question or prod her to go deeper as I had with so many of the women I had met. She launched into the story of how she had met and married Ashwin like it had been bursting inside her for twenty years.

Keisha came to Kolkata from a small town in Karnataka called Bellary. She was conceived before her parents married. Being a staunch Catholic, her paternal grandfather told her expectant mother that if the baby was his son's he wouldn't allow her to abort it. Her mother, who was barely out of her teens then, agreed to keep the baby as long as the old man was willing to look after it. A shotgun wedding was organized. Seven months later, she delivered a baby girl. Fifteen days after Keisha was born, her mother had her baptized and, to everyone's shock, handed her over to her grandfather, reminding him of his promise.

He kept his word and took the baby in. In Kolkata, Keisha grew up in her paternal grandparents' home. One of her aunts, her father's sister, donned the mantle of being her foster-mother. When it was time for the aunt to get married, she was so fraught with the prospect of being separated from Keisha that she declined matrimony entirely.

When Keisha was a little older, her parents asked that she live with them. Keisha went to Bellary and stayed in a 'normal' family for the first time. When she was twelve, her parents had another child, a boy this time. So once again, Keisha was sent back to Kolkata where she resumed her life with her grandparents and aunt.

She rejoined her previous school in the city. By this time, she and her fellow students were nearly in their teens and the context of their conversations had significantly altered. They were pairing up, the boys were writing love letters, they were jostling to make eye contact and exchange greeting cards with the girls.

When Keisha was in class ten, she met Ashwin who was in class twelve. His friends told her that he thought of her as his girlfriend. They exchanged sly glances and, later, spoke an occasional word or two to each other in the school corridor. Then he gave her a love letter. And she accepted it. That was it. Like the white smoke that signals the choice of a pope, in the eighties in India accepting a love letter was the universal sign of 'an affair'.

'I was very naïve when I came to Kolkata. Then suddenly I was getting letters and cards and this boy was paying me so much attention. What can I say, love was in the air,' she says. From the beginning, Ashwin was quite possessive about her. He hated seeing her talk to other boys; he hated it if she even walked past boys.

In the way when one is young, stupid and insecure, Keisha was totally flattered by how much he loved her. Her one guiding principle in life was that her first boyfriend would become her husband. 'In Kolkata, especially, people think of Anglo-Indian girls as loose. I didn't want to live the stereotype by having multiple boyfriends. I was determined that I would marry my first boyfriend,' she says.

When he finished school, Ashwin decided that he wanted to join the merchant navy and work as a naval radio operator. That was his father's profession and he wanted to follow in his footsteps. He graduated from college and signed up for a course in radio technology. But in a short while he gave that up. His father bought him a store and he began trading in bits and bobs of ladies' fabrics—blouse pieces, sari falls, embroidery threads, buttons and

such. Keisha wanted to become a teacher, but that did not work
out, so she took a secretarial course and started working soon after
she turned twenty.

After seven years of courtship, Ashwin and Keisha decided
they should get secretly engaged. They even picked a date. Perhaps
Ashwin's father overheard some conversation between Ashwin
and his friends, or he was just prescient, but he decided that
Ashwin should be sent away from Kolkata. He was worried about
the influence of this 'Anglo-Indian' girl and concerned that she
would convert him to Christianity. In Kolkata, especially among
the community from UP, dating an Anglo-Indian is a big deal.
Ashwin followed his father's orders and without a whimper just
upped and left. He went to Delhi and stayed with some relatives.
His older sister, who was married, also lived there. He didn't even
tell Keisha he was going. One fine morning, she woke up to hear
from a common friend that her boyfriend of seven years had just
left the city for good without telling her.

She cried. She sent him letters. She got no reply. She cried some
more. (Here occurred my first 'Why did you marry him?' query.)
Then a friend told her that she should just forget about him. She
had heard that his wedding was fixed; his parents had chosen a
girl for him from within their community. Keisha cried till she
could cry no more. And then decided she had cried enough. She
was ready to move on.

She showed me her photographs from around this time. Thin,
tall and glowing, she looked like a model. Since Ashwin had left
and there was no one holding her back, Keisha did in fact become
a model. She got a few assignments and her pictures appeared
in local magazines. During this time, she also found work in an
international airline as ground support staff. In all respects, she
had become quite a catch. She had a lot of suitors and she started
meeting some of them so she could get to know them better. News
of this reached Delhi rather quickly. Sure enough, there was a call

from Ashwin. Her aunt answered it. Keisha was away all weekend, attending a friend's wedding.

A dozen questions tumbled out of Ashwin's mouth. Where was she? Whom had she gone with? When would she come back? Why was she spending the night away from home? Her aunt simply answered that since he had decided to move on, none of this was his concern. She said Keisha was happy and he should just let her be. He hung up then, but called back a little later and told her aunt that he would move on only if Keisha told him so herself.

Her aunt briefed Keisha when she returned on Sunday evening. The following day he called and spoke to her. Even though she was really hurting inside, Keisha managed to project an inner calmness that she didn't feel and told him that she wished him a good life and hung up. 'He couldn't believe that this small-town girl from Bellary would stand up to him. Of course, as soon as he hung up I burst into tears. I was a mess for a few months,' she says. Coincidentally, this conversation took place on the day they were to get engaged.

Three months later, Keisha heard that Ashwin was in town. He was working then for a company that sold costume jewellery and they were hosting an exhibition. Keisha and her friend decided they would 'accidentally bump into him'. She walked into the exhibition hall and, even though her legs were jelly, she knew he was 'zapped' when he saw her. He came over and said hello. She told him she worked in an airline now. He was 'zapped' again with her fancy new job. She thought if she spoke any more, she would break down, so she just left.

'But I knew from the look in his eyes that he would pursue me. And he did,' she says. He called the following day and, even though Keisha figured he had had a couple of drinks, she was thrilled by the fact that he cried on the phone. He pleaded with her to come back to him. He told her that, each time he went to see a girl his parents had shortlisted, he would come back and look at her photograph and tell himself that she was nothing compared to his Keisha. She told him it wasn't so easy to bounce back and she needed time. But in her heart she knew she would get back with him.

'Why?' I ask.

'Because of my first boyfriend theory yaar,' she explains.

I am no psychologist, but I am certain Keisha's unusual upbringing had a lot to do with her reluctance to give up the relationship. Having heard the story of being abandoned by her mother quite early on in her life, Keisha is afraid of losing relationships. She was also raised with the story of commitment, especially her aunt's, in taking charge of someone else's problem and pledging a lifetime to it. Keisha too wanted to be the steady, stable person in someone's life; one who wouldn't run at the first sight of trouble.

Over the next few months, Ashwin turned the charm on. 'Full force.' And eventually, she said yes. This time when Keisha told her aunt, though, she wasn't all that thrilled about it. She told Keisha clearly that she had to take a final decision whether she wanted to be with Ashwin or not. She couldn't keep at this on-again, off-again relationship. Keisha promised her that it wouldn't ever be off-again.

When his grandmother passed away, Ashwin landed in Kolkata. He came over to her house and met her aunt and grandmother, her grandfather having passed away a few years earlier. They had a long conversation. He promised her aunt that he was going to marry Keisha. He told her she would be able to continue with her career and her faith. Her aunt asked him if he was absolutely sure. He said yes. She told him that they knew his parents did not approve of this relationship. He said it was his life and it would be his decision. He was firm and seemed determined. He left a letter for Keisha with her. Within a fortnight, he returned to Kolkata and took charge of the shop. Keisha and he became a couple again.

One not so fine day, Ashwin told her he was taking her home. By then, they had known each other for nearly ten years but she had never been there. He asked her to wear a salwar kameez and she raised an eyebrow. He said, come on, you are meeting my parents for the first time, and so she agreed. It was a really wet day; it had been raining since the previous night and by noon all the streets were flooded. But Ashwin wasn't going to let a small matter like the weather change his plans.

Late in the evening, after work, Keisha waded through knee-deep water in her salwar kameez and reached Ashwin's home. And what a welcome she got! The first thing Ashwin's father said was, 'You are not a good girl.' Then he asked her why she had come so late—it was 8 p.m.—and didn't her family know better than to let their daughter gallivant around town after dark? Softly, Keisha said Ashwin had asked her over so that he could introduce her to them. At this, her father-in-law lost all interest in her and started yelling at his son.

'I was like oh my God, what is going on here? I was nearly in tears and I told Ashwin, please, let's just go,' she says. All the while, her mother-in-law just stared at her unblinkingly. She looked at Keisha from head to toe, like how you'd examine a dead fish in the market, part spurious delight and part revulsion. Keisha was spooked. 'From that first day to today that's what she does—stare at me. It makes you very very uncomfortable to be stared at like that,' she says.

Finally, after a long silence, her mother-in-law asked her what her name was. Keisha said her name. And mother-in-law barked '*Kya? Kya?*' like she couldn't understand it. It was a gesture of dismissal—this chit of an Anglo-Indian girl who didn't even have a pronounceable name thinks she can traipse into their home and marry her son? Eventually, Ashwin said you could call her Kate—which was what her family called her. 'Whatever your name is, don't you have a brain?' her mother-in-law asked. 'Do you wander into everyone's home uninvited like this?' Keisha feels she should have put her foot down then. But she felt sorry for Ashwin.

On their way back that evening, Ashwin promised her that once they married the two of them would be living on their own. In which case, she thought, it wasn't really important how his parents treated her. When she went home, her family asked her how the meeting had been. Too scared to tell them the truth, Keisha said it had gone well. She told them that Ashwin's family had welcomed her warmly.

So they carried on. 'Then suddenly one day, his father decides to die,' she tells me. He was suffering from cirrhosis of the liver and was admitted to the hospital. It was clear that he wouldn't return home. Ashwin called Keisha and told her that he would follow his father's last wish. 'I said OK, fine, whatever. If his father's last wish for him was to marry an illiterate fourteen-year-old from a village, let him do it. I told him whatever it is, just let me know. Please don't run away like the last time,' she says. Ten days later, Ashwin's father died.

Ashwin's sister told him that their father had told her that Ashwin could do whatever made him happy, even though he himself was not thrilled about the prospect of an Anglo-Indian daughter-in-law. When she heard about the death, Keisha got home from work, changed into a black salwar kameez and went to his home. At the gate, Ashwin's sister stopped her and told her if her mother saw her, she would die of heartbreak. She pleaded with her to go back and so Keisha returned to her aunt's. Once again, she lied. She told her that everyone was sad, but she had been treated as a part of the family.

A few days later, once the initial grief and shock had passed, Ashwin's uncles started teasing him. Where was this great girlfriend of his, they asked, who couldn't even come to pay the family a visit in this difficult time? Since he'd heard from his sister about Keisha's visit, he narrated the incident to them.

The uncles were naturally horrified. There was to be a puja marking the final day of mourning for Ashwin's father and they asked him to invite Keisha for the puja and make sure that she came. In fact, they wanted her to bring her family as well. Keisha didn't dare take her aunt with her. Instead, she went with a Hindu friend, hoping it would somehow present her in a favourable light. There she was introduced to everyone by the uncles as Ashwin's wife and blessed by the entire family. The mother-in-law, though, wouldn't even look at her or acknowledge her presence. Sister-in-law also did not speak a word to her.

Once the relatives left, Keisha started on her plan to get her mother-in-law to come around. She began visiting her every evening after work. She would carry something for her—fruits or sweets or a snack—and spend some time in her home. Mother-in-law accepted the gifts but did not warm up to her. Often she ignored her queries or answered her in monosyllables.

Eventually, Ashwin and she picked a date for the wedding. (My second why.) First there was to be a registered marriage. Her mother-in-law told her she had to wear a sari to the registry. It wasn't a suggestion, but an instruction. On the appointed day, the two families and some friends went to the registrar's office where Ashwin and Keisha signed the files and were officially declared wed. Keisha's aunt had thrown a small get-together at their club that evening. Everyone had fun; a lot of photographs were clicked. Ashwin's mother did not attend the party as she was still in mourning for her dead husband.

When Ashwin had spoken to her aunt, he had assured her that they would also have a church wedding. But his mother refused him permission. She told them that they would have a registered marriage and, upon completion of one year from his father's death, there would be a Hindu wedding.

When Keisha went to Ashwin's home the day after the registered wedding, her mother-in-law asked her to fold her hands in front of a photograph of his father and seek his forgiveness.

'For what?' Keisha asked.

'For marrying his son and causing his soul so much unhappiness,' Mataji said.

So, even though she wasn't feeling apologetic at all, she slapped her hands together and said out loud, 'Bapuji, please forgive me for marrying your son.'

This, according to Keisha, was her first compromise. I thought there had been a dozen even before that. But since this was Keisha's story, I let her continue uninterrupted.

There was no question of her moving into his house after the registered wedding. Her aunt wasn't going to be a pushover and insisted they had to have a church wedding before they could live as man and wife. Ashwin and Keisha began planning a semi-secret church wedding. Until then, they decided, he would live with his mother and she with her aunt. Around this time, Keisha started hearing stories about Ashwin's drinking problem.

She had been privy to whispers about it even earlier, actually, but hadn't thought too much of it. When they were dating, they met each other for a couple hours in the day and were both on their best behaviour. The stories she heard, she thought, were perhaps exaggerated. What was the harm in his drinking a beer once in a while? But after the wedding, the frequency with which she heard stories of him getting stone-drunk began to worry her.

The first Diwali after their wedding, all her friends told Keisha that she should wear a nice sari and go to her husband's home. Her aunt gifted her a beautiful silk sari and she went over with a box of sweets. Ashwin was at his store. As soon as her mother-in-law saw her, she asked her to change out of the sari and wear one of her housecoats. She was leaving for Delhi for a few of months the following day and needed some help, she said.

Keisha thought she might have to help packing. Turns out, she meant helping with spring-cleaning the house. 'She took down all the curtains, all the vessels, a ton of clothes and dumped them at my feet. Until 8 that night, I just washed and scraped and rinsed. She ate a couple of chapattis and pickle for lunch. It wasn't the kind of food I was used to, so I ate nothing,' she says. At some point in the evening, Ashwin came home to announce that he was going out to meet his friends.

'What about me?' Keisha asked.

'Just finish off and go home,' he said, 'just compromise for today, please.'

That was her second compromise.

While Keisha was talking, I had gone through her photographs. Ashwin was exactly the kind of ugly Indian that Kesavan described. Perhaps I was prejudiced but, mustached and vacant-eyed, he looked like a villain in a Hindi film. He had the surly countenance of a local dada and looked ready to roll up his sleeves and throw a few punches without provocation. I couldn't fathom what Keisha saw in him. 'Why did you marry him?' I couldn't help but ask again. 'The signs were so bad.'

'I thought things would change. And foolish as it now sounds, I was still hung up on my first boyfriend becoming my husband,' she says. At 8.30, she went home. Her aunt asked how her day had been and she lied again. They asked her where Ashwin was. She told them he was out with his friends.

'Why didn't you go?'

'I thought I should spend some time with you,' she lied.

She couldn't tell them that neither was she invited nor did she have the energy for an evening out.

Making the most of her mother-in-law's absence while she was away in Delhi, Keisha and Ashwin solemnized wedding #2—at the church, this time. The same friends were invited and this time her family was in full attendance. She wore a lovely white dress and looked gorgeous. After this, her aunt said she could live with her husband.

For some reason, Keisha did not want to move into the house she had helped clean up. She had a bad feeling about the place. And since Ashwin and she were to live on their own anyway, she saw no point in moving in there only to move out soon. So she kept making excuses. Eventually, Ashwin told his mother in Delhi that Keisha was coming to live with them. Mataji put her foot down and said no such thing would happen until wedding #3, the Hindu wedding, was solemnized. Keisha was secretly relieved.

It was after wedding #2 that Keisha began to really see Ashwin's dark side. First came the dress code. She was barred from wearing jeans, salwar kameezes without dupattas, and any make-up. She couldn't go to the club. She couldn't meet any friends—male or female. He would often come to her aunt's house roaring drunk and accuse her of all kinds of things. Why hadn't she thrown away her jeans? Whom was she showing herself off to? That was the first time Keisha asked herself why she had married him. But wedding #2 made the task of annulling a near impossibility. The church would never approve of it. So she clutched on to the hope that things would change.

The following month, her mother-in-law asked the two of them to join her in Delhi. Keisha went, even though she was uncertain about what she could expect. His uncles and cousins were all rather sweet to her. Mother- and sister-in-law were a whole other story, though. They constantly taunted her. They would sit Ashwin down and point her flaws out to him. Why wasn't she wearing a sindoor? Why were her salwar kurtas so tight? Why did she wear nail polish? Why was she so modern?

In retrospect, it was no surprise that Ashwin was so suspicious about her. This was the environment in which he had been raised. His mother was constantly feeding all his insecurities. Until then, Keisha had hoped that his mother would talk some sense into Ashwin, about his drinking as well as the way in which he abused her. 'I thought, now that the marriage was a reality, she would want her son to be happy. Even I wasn't foolish enough to think she would do anything for my sake, but I really did think she would advise him for his sake. On the contrary, I realized she was fuelling this whole thing,' she tells me.

The difference in their 'beauty quotients' had a lot to do with Ashwin's attitude to Keisha. When they first met, Ashwin's friends had teased him about how he had managed to land such a looker. Keisha herself is very aware of her beauty. She has thousands of photographs of herself. Even now, she uploads dozens of photographs on Facebook almost daily. She is stunning in all of them. This couldn't have gone down well with an already insecure Ashwin.

In Delhi, Keisha's mother-in-law told her she would be called Kamla from then on. Her name was too difficult and too Christian. For days, Keisha was yelled at for not responding to her new name. Things were dire by all accounts. She walked into the balcony one day to hear Mataji tell the neighbour all kinds of things about her. 'She was saying ". . . even though she looks so thin, you won't believe how much she eats! These Christians—you know how they are, don't you?" I couldn't believe it,' she tells me. One of Ashwin's cousins told Keisha quietly that she had made a mistake marrying into this family. But she didn't know how she could get out. The trip made her feel depressed and worried about what would come in the future.

When she went back to Kolkata, she gave a watered-down version of these events to her increasingly anxious aunt. Ashwin's mother had returned to Kolkata and the preparations for the Hindu wedding were on. The invitation cards were printed and Keisha was given a bunch that she could distribute. 'It said Ashwin—son of so-and-so, grandson of so-and-so, nephew of so-and-so—was marrying Kamla. There was no mention at all about who I was. This I couldn't take,' she says. She threw a fit and sent the cards back. She told them she would not attend the wedding unless her real name and those of her parents were on it. Grudgingly, they changed the card. This was the first time she put her foot down.

It was on the day of wedding #3 that her aunts saw Ashwin's house for the first time. Shocked, they pulled her aside to ask how she was going to live there. Ashwin's house was essentially one large room and a kitchen. Parts of it were not even plastered. The washroom was outside. They had put in a thin, wooden partition to split the room into two. Even that, her mother-in-law pointed to everyone, was done by Ashwin for Keisha, as evidence of the fact that Keisha was splitting the family.

Keisha and Ashwin were now man and wife under law, the church and the Hindu gods. She moved into Ashwin's house and despite the bitterness, was looking forward to starting her new life. The wedding night was a long-cherished fantasy, something both she and Ashwin had been building up to for more than a decade, since they first met at school.

The reality turned out to be as distant as it could possibly be from Keisha's fantasies. There was no bed covered with rose petals. In fact, there was no room even. Her sister-in-law and family slept on the big bed. In the other room, her mother-in-law and some aunts occupied the other bed. Ashwin slept on a single cot that was placed in a passage and Keisha slept on a thin mattress on the ground next to him. Blinking back tears, she held on to his hand until she fell asleep.

The next morning, her mother-in-law woke her up by yanking her toe. She barked at her to bathe, wear a sari and get into the kitchen, pronto. 'I don't know how I managed to wear a sari standing in that wet bathroom,' she says, 'but I did. In the kitchen, she asked me to pray to the "Hindu" god and then make tea. After tea, I made breakfast for the family. Then she made me wait in the kitchen, while everyone ate.'

When the whole extended family finished eating, the dirty dishes were heaped in front of her. There wasn't a proper kitchen sink. 'I had to sit on my haunches and scrub the dishes. When all the dishes were done, my mother-in-law served a small portion of breakfast and slid the plate towards me. I stood there in the kitchen and gobbled my breakfast down,' she says.

One of Ashwin's aunts who witnessed this was shocked. She asked his mother how she could make her daughter-in-law work in the kitchen like this the day after her wedding. 'There is no maid; she will have to work if she's living in this house,' her mother-in-law said. Keisha had imagined a honeymoon of some kind; this was certainly not what she had had in mind. When Ashwin woke up, it was to find her sitting and crying.

'I want to talk to you,' she said.

'I don't have the time,' he replied.

'It's twenty years now, he still hasn't found the time,' Keisha tells me.

This cook-wait-clean business went on the whole week the extended family was there and continued thereafter. Mother-in-law didn't use soap to wash the dishes, so Keisha had to scrub them with ash and the husk of a coconut. Her hands were chapped and often bled. When she complained about it, her mother-in-law asked her to wear surgical gloves and get on with it. After a month of this, when she could no longer bear it, she spoke to her aunt and for the first time told her a less watered-down version of her life in Ashwin's house. Her aunt immediately called Ashwin and reminded him of his promise that the two of them would live separately. He said he was low on funds and couldn't afford to buy an apartment immediately. He was planning to switch businesses and sell the shop. After that he would buy the apartment, he assured her.

Keisha should have left then. But she still had hope that things would turn around. By then she had stopped counting her compromises. Her cupboard arrived from her aunt's house and she arranged her things in it. On the inner side of the door, she stuck a photograph of Jesus. Every morning, she took half a minute of her time to open the door and pray. Mataji noticed this. The moment she heard the squawk of the cupboard door, she would yell at Keisha issuing an order. 'She wouldn't give me even thirty seconds to pray,' she says.

It is said of the modern woman that she has to straddle several roles. Keisha did too—that of the breadwinner as well as the maid. She had quit the airline by then and had moved to a better paying job in a travel company. Every day, she woke up at 5 a.m. to cook breakfast and lunch. Then she would sweep and swab the house, get ready and go to work. In the evening, she would come back, do the dishes that had accumulated, wash the clothes—hers, Ashwin's and mother-in-law's—and then cook dinner. On her lucky days, she would manage to grab dinner during the saas–bahu shows. That was her only entertainment.

For someone who was sufficiently agonized by her mother-in-law, I was surprised Keisha enjoyed watching these shows. Wasn't there enough abuse by your mother-in-law in real life, I ask her, why would you want to watch more of it on TV? 'They gave me hope,' she said, 'and certainly a sense of support. I felt like I wasn't alone in this, that everyone lived miserable lives. To be honest, I thought all marriages were just as bad as mine. That's what it seemed like on these shows and that helped me.'

Her friends and colleagues were constantly asking her when she was going to invite them to her new home. Keisha avoided it for as long as possible, but eventually ran out of excuses. She planned a small party after work one evening. She informed Ashwin about it and asked him to make sure he was home a little early. She left work by four, went to Gangaur Sweets—her favourite sweet shop—and bought snacks for the party. She ran home and spent the next two hours wiping and dusting until every inch of the house sparkled.

Her friends arrived at 6 p.m. Neither Ashwin nor her mother-in-law was there. She served the snacks and showed her wedding album around, dutifully pointing out each of her friends and relatives. Her colleagues complimented her on how well she'd maintained the house even though the building was old and falling apart. They waited for an hour to meet Ashwin and say hello to her mother-in-law. Since there was no sign of either, they decided to leave.

At the gate, they bumped into her mother-in-law. Some of them said hello and Keisha was trying to catch her eye so she could introduce them. But Mataji walked in without as much as a nod of her head. Keisha shrugged and made a face at her friends. They said it was OK and left. Five minutes after they had gone, Ashwin walked in. Keisha was mad at him for not being home when she had specifically told him that she was expecting some guests. But even before she could say a word, the mother-in-law jumped in. She was so angry and so loud that the entire neighbourhood could hear her.

'This is my house,' she roared at Keisha, 'nobody does these things in my house. No one brings food from outside. No one changes the bedspread without asking me. No one brings in strangers.' She went on and on. Ashwin said nothing. Keisha tried to say they were her friends and it was customary that they visit her after the wedding in her husband's house. But Mataji wasn't listening to anything. She ranted and raved and called her all kinds of names. She blamed her for killing Ashwin's father and bringing her Anglo-Indian body and its associated disrepute into their house. Ashwin didn't speak a word. When his mother was done, he left the house so he could go get drunk. Keisha rolled up her sleeves and washed their clothes.

After this incident, Keisha began pressurizing Ashwin to buy a house. She would constantly tell him that she wanted to leave this house. She was beginning to lose all hope for a happy married life. And she was right. Things only got worse. Ashwin was coming home drunk and spoiling for a fight every evening. Keisha was exhausted from being on her feet from 5 in the morning to 8 at night. In the beginning Ashwin would get home and provoke a fight. After a while, he didn't even bother with that.

He would just walk into the house and start beating her up. Slaps, blows, kicks—the whole deal. He would drag her around the room by her hair; he would jab a finger into her eye.

Her mother-in-law would sit right there, watching the fun. Sometimes, Keisha would even catch her smiling at what her son was doing to his wife. 'If it got really bad, like if he was going to break a bone or kill me, she would sit there and say, "Don't, Ashwin." Like in a really soft voice. So that she could claim that she had done her bit to stop it,' she says.

Now that Ashwin knew how much she earned, he saw no point in continuing to run the shop. He sold it, ostensibly to buy the apartment and fund a new business. But he did neither, choosing instead to just drink away the money. This made his temper even worse. He had all day to stay home and wonder about what his wife was up to. For the first time, Keisha took a realistic look at her life. It was a clean-cook-work-clean-laundry-whack routine. There was nothing more in her life. 'Sometimes I was shocked that this was my life. I could never have imagined it even a few years ago,' she says.

When Ashwin stopped working, her mother-in-law insisted that she hand over her salary to her. Keisha refused. She bought everything for the house, but she refused to give her salary away. And even though she was funding both mother and son, Mataji forbade her from buying anything that would help Keisha in any way. So Keisha couldn't buy a washing machine, for instance, because it would mean she wouldn't have to wash their clothes by hand. Nothing that helped ease Keisha's burden was allowed in the house. For years, she wasn't allowed even a mixer or a refrigerator.

By the first Christmas after she moved in with her mother-in-law, Keisha was near breaking point. She was desperate to go home. Every evening, she begged her mother-in-law to give her a week off. Literally beg. She would massage her legs and then hold her feet and plead with her. Mataji said she would think about it. As her anxiety built up, she got more and more desperate. At the time, a cousin of Ashwin's was staying with them. She too pleaded with her aunt that Keisha be allowed to go home. 'Who will do the work then?' Mataji asked. The cousin, a young teenager, said she would. And on that promise, Keisha was allowed to spend Christmas with her aunt and grandmother. On Boxing Day, she realized she was pregnant. Keisha was thrilled. She thought this was the trigger that would change her life. Things *had* to get better from there on.

When she came back after the week, she told her mother-in-law she was pregnant. Mataji was happy to hear the news, but the first thing she said was, 'Don't think this means you can stop doing the housework.' Through the nine months, Keisha's life continued on its pre-pregnancy trajectory. Including the whacks. So nothing changed really, except that she was more tired, more vulnerable and even more unhappy. After a heavy round of beating and kicks, Ashwin would threaten to kill her if anything happened to his baby. There was no logic to appeal to. Or any sanity to look forward to.

Mother-in-law would chip in with things that made Ashwin even angrier. 'Ashwin, this better be your baby. Ashwin, make sure when this child is born she doesn't take it to church. Ashwin, make sure it doesn't become a Catholic,' she would constantly tell him. 'Not once did she cook something special for me or do anything to help ease my burden,' Keisha is in tears by now. 'Even with a big stomach, I would squat and scour the dishes.'

In her third trimester, she went to her aunt's house for her confinement. She was eight months pregnant when her mother-in-law called one day and told her she had to come for an emergency. Her daughter was visiting, and she had been bitten by a dog. So when Keisha reached there, her mother-in-law told her to cook lunch for them all while she took her daughter to the doctor. Like on her first Diwali, she slogged all day.

By the time her mother-in-law returned, they had accumulated four more relatives. When everyone was fed, there was no food left. Ashwin gave her money for the tram fare and sent her home. (By this time my head was rhythmically pounding why-why-why-why.) Back at her aunt's she was so hungry, Keisha devoured a pack of biscuits. Her aunt, who knew that she hated biscuits, surmised that yet again she hadn't even been given a meal. There was nothing left to say or scold. They both just shook their heads and moved on.

When it was time, Keisha delivered a baby boy. She was relieved. A girl would certainly have meant more punches. Ashwin did not even come and visit his child for two days. Mataji had consulted an astrologer who informed her that it was best if the father saw the child after the second day; Ashwin blindly followed whatever his mother said. So he carried on drinking and hanging out with his friends, while his wife lay in bed with their newborn baby.

Keisha stayed at her aunt's for six months after the baby was born. Mataji called her incessantly, asking her to return. Keisha refused. When Ashwin came over, her aunt reminded him that he had promised if they had children, they would be baptized. But he said no, his mother would die if she even heard of it. Keisha stopped pushing for it. She didn't have the energy for that fight. If it has to happen it will, she told herself.

Unlike the last time—when she had returned to Ashwin's from her aunt's with the news that she was pregnant—this time around Keisha had no delusions; she knew nothing would change. Once there, she merely went back to her old routine. Now though, she was both mother and maid. She woke up at 5 to feed and bathe her child, then do the housework, wash everyone's clothes plus a bucket of the baby's diapers. It would be midday by the time she was done with most of the chores. She would make the baby fall asleep and take a short nap. Just then, mother-in-law would pick a steel plate and drop it from a great height. The baby would jolt awake at the clang and start crying again. 'She would do this every day. Sometimes she would do this while I was in the room, watching her. She would have a smile on her face and let the plate drop,' Keisha says.

She was breastfeeding the baby and was dizzy from exhaustion all the time. The baby didn't change anything about Ashwin either. He came home every evening and took up from where he had left the previous day. He hit her with cloth hangers, steel bars and even curtain rods. And then he added one more weapon to his arsenal—rape. He raped her every night for months. Mother-in-law would be in the next room and hear Keisha's screams of help. She would merely cluck and sometimes even ask her to keep it down. 'In the beginning I used to think that I was a glorified maid in that house. By this time, I knew I was worse than one,' she says.

The first few times, Keisha asked her mother-in-law how she could let her son beat her up and rape her like that. 'He is your husband, it's his right,' Mataji shrugged. Unsurprisingly, when her son was one, she was pregnant again. The second child was a girl. This time around, when she had to go back to Ashwin's house, her aunt insisted she hire a maid to help her. She didn't care how much it cost; she was willing to pay for her just so her niece would get some rest.

Mataji was most unhappy with this arrangement. This meant that Keisha would have less work to do and that wasn't a situation she considered favourable at all. Mataji initiated her games with the maid. She piled all kinds of work on her. Until the maid couldn't take it any more and told Keisha she would quit her job. She had been hired to look after Keisha and the babies, not clean her mother-in-law's house.

With two small children, Keisha was desperate and pleaded with Ashwin to talk some sense into his mother. For once he intervened. The maid would do the work related to the babies, he said, while Keisha would do the work around the house. Mataji wasn't losing out on anything, Ashwin pointed out.

Mother-in-law refused to be placated. She began to cry. 'Now that your family is complete, you don't need me,' she sobbed to Ashwin, 'your father always told me that the Christian girl would kick me out of this house.' Reminded of his dead father, Ashwin's heart melted. He turned around and beat Keisha up and accused her of driving a wedge between him and his mother.

The kids grew up in this milieu, witnessing the violence. Even if Keisha was ill, her mother-in-law wouldn't once ask her what was wrong; she would merely instruct her about what needed to be done in the house. 'But when she fell ill, despite all that she'd done to me, I just couldn't find the strength to ignore her. I would take her to the doctor, while Ashwin would roll in roaring drunk at midnight,' she says. With two kids now, Keisha was far too invested in the marriage to bother with the question of why she had married him. She resumed working, as an administrative officer in a small company, after a couple of years' break having the children. She also began to think about how she could make it better for herself.

By the time their fourth anniversary rolled around, Keisha made a rule. On Saturday mornings she would take the kids and go to her aunt's house. They spent the weekend there and returned on Sunday evening. This way she got some rest and also the chance to attend Mass. Around this time, two other positive things happened.

First, Ashwin took up a job again and has managed to stick with it. It's an office job, a regular semi-clerical, quasi-managerial one. It isn't a life-improving career decision, but at least he is earning some money and managing to keep his job down. Second, he told Keisha they should get the kids baptized. This way, he explained, it would be easier to get them admission in a good convent school. There was a condition, though. That his mother should never get even a whiff of this. Keisha's aunt told her to forget the motive and just get the baptism done with before he changed his mind.

The kids grew up seeing the demon in their dad and dadi. Yet, in the way only kids can be, they are incredibly fond of their father. They are very wary of their grandmother though. In 2009, fifteen years after she got married, Keisha decided she couldn't take it any more. She had to get away from her mother-in-law. Her aunts pooled their funds and rented a house for her.

One weekend, she left Ashwin's home and never returned. She moved into a small apartment with her two children. Ashwin visited every night, ostensibly to see the kids. He was always drunk. Once the children were asleep, he would begin to plead with Keisha that she come back home. In minutes the pleas would turn to threats and the threats to kicks and punches. After twenty minutes of this, he'd push her into her room and rape her. 'It was still better than living with his mother,' she tells me, 'although I do recognize that I was reduced to being my husband's mistress. He would have his way with me every night, then go home to his beloved mother.'

A year later, the landlady increased the rent. She couldn't afford to keep the place any more. Ashwin insisted that she move her stuff back to his house and live with his mother. But she refused. By this time, she had been broken, bashed and raped more times than she could count. She was popping anti-depressants, sometimes up to four a day. She moved the things that would fit into her aunt's house, sold the rest and went to live with her. Here too, Ashwin began to visit the children and then beat Keisha up. Within a week, the neighbours complained of the noisy quarrels. Keisha's aunt used that as an excuse to ban Ashwin from entering her home.

The children had grown up. In the photographs that I saw, the boy, who is now fourteen, is a strapping young lad with dreamy eyes. The girl, twelve, looks exactly like a teenage Keisha; she is supermodel ready. The photos were from the boy's thirteenth birthday party. The house seemed small and all of them crowded to fit around the cake and in the frame of the camera. Keisha, her ageing aunt, her frail grandmother and her two gorgeous children.

Ashwin stood in a corner, his body turned away from them, his expression a deep, simmering rage. It was a special day so he was allowed in the house, Keisha tells me. Her aunt has decided that if he wants to meet the kids, he should meet them outside her house. It has been a year since Keisha was last beaten up or raped.

'Why are you still married to him?' I ask.

'My son tells me clearly he doesn't want to be the child of a divorce,' she says. 'But when he is fifteen, I feel that I will finally have the courage to get a divorce.'

Even now, when Mataji is ill, Keisha is summoned. She takes her to the doctor, cooks meals for her and does what she can. But she refuses to stay the night in that house. Every once in a while, Mataji also calls her and asks her to fast on special days and do some pujas for her husband. She does. But her heart is not in it. 'I now know that she will never accept me,' Keisha says. And that has been the most liberating realization. Since she will never be accepted, she doesn't have to keep trying. Finally, Keisha has put her foot down. 'But sometimes I still think everything will work out. Ashwin will stop his violence, his mother will apologize and welcome me back and we will all live together like a normal family. In that sense, I still have hope,' she says.

'But why?' I am aghast and my voice is a surprised, loud squeak. Keisha sees my face and starts to laugh. In a while, I do too.

9

Occupational Hazard

Name	Age (in 2013)	Husband	Married
Nikita	43	Arun	2000

There are lots of things to be said against workplaces. They are stressful, they are often full of people who were put on this earth for the sole purpose of annoying you, the computer keyboards and washrooms are full of germs, and the coffee often tastes worse than muddy water. But to most middle-class Indian mothers-in-law, offices are simply breeding grounds for inappropriate sex. Deadlines, budgets and targets be damned, mothers-in-law seem to think that when people reach their office in the morning, all that they are looking for is indulging in random sexual acts with colleagues.

The resistance to a daughter-in-law who has a career is so high that an online matrimonial website has run a television ad campaign about it. If you type the words 'should wives' in Google India, it automatically generates an option that says 'should wives work outside the home'. Indian mothers-in-law, especially in the northern parts of the country, think of working daughters-in-law as an insult to the family. It is often a non-negotiable condition that the daughter-in-law should not pursue a career.

When Nikita came to Delhi from Kolkata and started looking for a job, she wasn't thinking about the possibility of rampant sex. She wasn't even thinking about the possibility of a romance. This was the height of the BPO boom and all she was thinking was where she could apply that would give her the best combination of relatively sane working hours and a reasonably good salary. She appeared for a couple of interviews and eventually decided to take up a job in a very well-established call centre in Gurgaon.

The pay was good; the company was the subsidiary of a Fortune 100 organization. It offered all the perks—like picking her up and dropping her home—and a decent canteen. She rented a small house and settled into her new life. It was 2000, a new millennium and, really, a new India. One where girls like her could very easily move across cities and simply plug and play into a new life.

At office, she noticed Arun right off the bat. She and a bunch of new recruits were in training the first ten days of joining and Arun—who worked as a quality control manager—popped in often to check on their progress. He was of average height, but his burly countenance made him seem bigger than he was. He was very confident about himself, quite cocky in fact, and initially she didn't like his guts.

'But he pursued me right from day one. He asked me for my number, I remember, and I refused to give it to him. By that night, he had tracked it down. We had a strange conversation, I was rather pissed that he called. But he spoke nicely and kept trying to persuade me to meet him for coffee. The next morning he called again to wish me good morning,' she says. Like in a true Bollywood movie, Arun half stalked and half charmed her. Being an ardent devotee of Hindi film romances, Nikita knew her moves and played them well. She resisted until the moment seemed right and then she agreed to meet him for coffee.

The coffee went well. There was an 'instant connection', and after just a few more coffees it began to feel like they had known each other for a long time. They shared similar interests and it just seemed natural to want to spend all their free time together. If their weekly days off matched, they spent them at the movie hall, followed by a meal. Arun rode a bike and he took her around the city, showing her the 'best place for a bread omelette, the best paratha man in the sea of paratha men, the best chhola kulcha in north campus'. He was very popular in office and he seemed to be friends with everyone. He helped jump-start her social life in the city.

After a year of dating, Arun told Nikita they should get engaged. He wanted her to call and tell her parents first. She wasn't sure. By nature, Nikita was sceptical of relationships and she wanted to be doubly sure of Arun before telling her parents about him. But he was very insistent. He knew his parents wouldn't come around so easily. And since 1995 it had become rather uncool to marry without the consent of the parents. Why 1995, you ask? I have four words for you: *Dilwale Dulhania Le Jayenge*. In the movie, Shah Rukh Khan's Raj is determined that no matter what the inconvenience, he would marry his sweetheart Simran only with the consent and blessings of the parents. Arun wanted to follow that example. From what he had heard, he thought that Nikita's parents were less strict and likely to say yes. Once they had their approval, he hoped it would be easier to get his own parents to agree.

Eventually, after months of his badgering, Nikita called her parents and told them. She was twenty-nine years old then, an age at which, for a regular Punjabi family, an unmarried girl is so over the hill that there is no possibility of her ever being happy. Predictably, when they heard the news, her parents were thrilled that she was at last settling down. Her mother was due to visit Delhi a couple of months later. She told Nikita she had her blessings to go ahead and commit to Arun and she couldn't wait to come to town and meet him in person. Arun bought her a ring, they called all their friends over for wine and Maggi, and in a true marriage of modern kitsch and traditional values, they were engaged.

After the engagement, Arun began to focus on getting his parents to come around. Nikita often asked him why they were so opposed to her and he told her that they were against the very idea of a love marriage. Arun has two older sisters. One of them married a man of her choice and the parents promptly excommunicated her from the family. Six years had passed and they were still unrelenting in their opposition. They had neither seen nor spoken to her in all this time. He had to play his cards right, he told her. While they might possibly cut him some slack since he was the much adored boy child, if he just sprang it upon them they were likely to refuse permission.

The first plan he devised was for her to meet his mother casually. They figured, Nikita and another friend could drop in at his home and say they were in the neighbourhood and were popping in to say hello. They roped in a friend and worked out the details. The idea was that this visit would help break the ice and, after an appropriate period of time, Arun could tell his mother that he was rather keen on that girl who had visited once.

On the appointed day, Nikita and the friend walked into his home. As planned, Arun had stepped out a moment ago. They sat down and talked to his mother for a while. It was a typical 'Hello Auntyji, how are you' kind of meeting. Nikita was focused on saying all the right things. Arun's mother was dressed simply, in a sari, and she seemed cordial but distant. 'I somehow did not get a good vibe from her. She looked homely and simple, but she also seemed really strong-headed and stubborn,' Nikita says. At one point, the friend mentioned that the two of them worked with Arun and his mother seemed quite put off by that. 'She seemed to freeze up immediately,' Nikita says. After twenty minutes or so, they thanked her for her hospitality and left.

As they walked out, her friend asked what she thought and

Nikita told her she felt quite odd and uncomfortable about her. They decided it was best not to mention that to Arun. They went straight to the café where he was waiting and, when he asked her, Nikita told him that it went well and his mother seemed really nice. Arun said he had revealed to his mother that he liked someone, but hadn't told her the name or any other details. Encouraged by the fact that the visit had gone well, he was determined to take things to the 'next level'.

In the course of the next month, he repeatedly brought up the topic of this girl he liked with his mother. Once she asked him what she did and he said she worked in his office. 'No,' his mother told him categorically, 'I don't want a working bahu. Your bride will be of our choice.' He pleaded with his mother to meet this girl, but she flatly refused. Eventually, he told her that the girl he liked was the one who had come home the other day, the one whose parents lived in Kolkata. 'You can be friends,' she told her son, 'but I'll never allow you to marry her.'

Even though Arun was not expecting any of this to be easy, he was surprised at how strongly his mother felt against his secret fiancée. He asked her why she disliked her so much. 'I told you I will not tolerate a working daughter-in-law. God knows what she gets up to. She lives here alone while her parents live in Kolkata. I find that inappropriate and wrong,' she told him.

Arun pointed out that both her daughters worked, even though they were married. 'That is the choice of their respective mothers-in-law. My choice is that my daughter-in-law will not be a working woman,' she told him. Despite this setback, Arun told Nikita he would keep trying to convince his mother. Nikita was getting increasingly worried. 'She is really nice once you get to know her,' Arun reassured her.

Soon it was the festival du jour of lovers—Karva Chauth. As the official festival promoted by romantic Bollywood films, it was especially significant for Nikita and Arun. Arun wanted his fiancée to fast for his good health and long life. Although Nikita loved what the day stood for, her body did not handle fasting well, and she was a bit reluctant to spend a whole day without eating or drinking anything. But Arun was insistent and she decided she would do it for his sake. That was love, after all, wasn't it? What's a little acidity when weighed against the long life of her soon-to-be husband?

Tradition demands that the evening before Karva Chauth, the mother-in-law gives the daughter-in-law a gift tray. Called a *sargi*, this tray usually includes a dress or sari, and some dried fruits and raisins that are used to make kheer the following day, the sweet dish that would be consumed once the fast was broken. Since there was no question of his mother gifting anything, Arun bought Nikita a red salwar kameez and gave her the sargi on his mother's behalf. Karva Chauth happened to fall on her day off, so Nikita stayed home and fought her hunger pangs.

Like a good, New Age boyfriend, Arun did not eat anything all day too, just to show solidarity with his fiancée. He told his mother he was working overtime and rushed over to Nikita's in the evening. Together, they waited to spot the rising moon and Nikita looked at it through a sieve and then at him. 'It was all very sweet and very romantic. He fed me first and then I fed him. We broke the fast together. I felt really happy and rather optimistic about the future,' she says.

Arun was feeling pretty upbeat too. He told Nikita that she should go over the next day and meet his mother with a box of sweets. 'Are you sure?' she asked him several times. He felt it was time. The following day, Nikita, like all prospective daughters-in-law, dressed in her nicest salwar kameez. She wore a bindi and bangles and other accessories that all Indian girls think is mandatory for their future mother-in-law to approve of them. She took a rickshaw and went over to Arun's house. His mother opened the door. Nikita went in, sat down and handed over the box of sweets.

'What is this?' Arun's mother asked.

'I had fasted on Karva Chauth for your son. And this is the prasad,' she said. Her voice was quaking, she was very nervous.

'But I didn't send you any sargi,' mother pointed out.

'I know you didn't. But your son gave it to me with this dress that I am wearing. And I fasted for his health and happiness,' she said.

Arun's mother picked up the box and opened it. She examined it for a long minute and, just when Nikita thought she was going to pop one into her mouth, she got up, walked to the door and flung the box right into the street. 'It fell with a plat,' Nikita tells me, 'I still remember the sound.'

At this, Arun who was hovering at the staircase came running down and asked his mother how she could do that. 'I told you no working bahu,' she told him sternly. Then she turned to Nikita and screamed at her. 'What kind of behaviour is this? Is this what your parents have taught you? What kind of parents allow their daughter to live on her own in a strange city? Who knows what you are up to and what kind of things you do after work with the men you meet in office?' she went on and on. It was the most humiliating two minutes of Nikita's life.

When the older lady stopped, Nikita calmly told Arun she was leaving, picked up her bag and started to leave. Arun said he'd drop her home. His mother forbade him from leaving the house. But he defied her and kicked his bike to life. Nikita cried all the way home. Arun was very apologetic. He said he had not imagined his mother would react like this. He thought, like in the movies, his mother's heart would melt on hearing about Nikita fasting for him. He imagined some tears and an embrace. Clearly, his mother wasn't watching his kind of movies.

A week later, completely oblivious to all these developments, Nikita's mother reached Delhi. Arun went with Nikita to pick her up from the railway station. As soon as they saw her, he bent down and touched her feet and sought her blessings. He took them both for lunch and engaged her mother in interesting conversation. When they reached home, her mother squeezed her tight and said, 'He seems really, really nice.' She had told Arun before he dropped them that she was keen on meeting his parents as soon as possible. A wedding meant a lot of work and she wanted enough notice. Nikita was her only child and, even though she hadn't wanted to pressure her into a marriage, truth was, she had been waiting for this for a long time.

Her mother was in Delhi for two weeks and every morning Arun fixed a time for the parents to meet and later cancelled it. He had one compelling excuse or another—his grandmother was unwell, an uncle had suddenly come from the village on a visit, things like that. Nikita was thoroughly irritated and her mother was beginning to get a bit anxious.

She complained to Nikita that she had come all the way from Kolkata and that it was extremely rude that his parents wouldn't even take an hour off to meet her, no matter how busy they were. The night before she was to leave for Punjab, Nikita told her mother that Arun's family hadn't yet approved of the wedding. She didn't play out the details of the sargi saga and didn't let on how much they were opposing it, but told her that Arun was confident that they would come around.

When she was done, her mother was evidently worried. 'You better be sure this is what you want and this guy will stand by you,' she told her daughter. 'If his mother was going to come around she would have done so by now. And the fact that Arun has been lying to us every day is also something to be worried about. I liked him at first, but now I am not so sure. Something doesn't seem right,' she told Nikita.

Another month passed and there was no change at all in Arun's mother. In the Bollywood movie equivalent, she was still before-the-interval while the two of them were ready for the last scene and the happily-ever-after that follows. It was time to face up to reality.

Nikita pointed out to Arun that it was never going to happen; his mother was never going to agree to the wedding.

So they picked a date—21 December—and decided they would get married, no matter who approved. If his parents didn't come around by then, he decided he would simply walk out on them. Although all her friends said they were happy for her, some did ask if she was sure it was going to work out well. 'The man was going to walk out on his parents to be with me. What more would you want?' she says. They went to the Arya Samaj on Hanuman Road, near Delhi's Connaught Place, and filled all the forms. It asked for the ages and dates of birth.

Nikita was thirty. It was only when she peeped into his form that she saw that Arun was only twenty-three. Nikita looks much younger than her age and Arun looks much older. They had both assumed that, like an ideal Indian couple, he was perhaps a couple of years older than her. She pointed out their age difference to him. He was also stunned but quickly recovered and dismissed age as a mere number.

It shook Nikita up though. She worried that there was so much about Arun she did not know. Maybe things were going too fast. But with Arun preparing to leave home, she didn't know how to apply the brakes. Now that the date was fixed, Arun worked on a final push to get his parents to agree. But he thought it would work to his disadvantage if he informed them that he was going to get married in December, whether or not they approved. So he pretended like no plans were afoot.

21 December that year was the coldest day in Delhi. One of her friends, who was also serving as a witness to the marriage, picked Nikita up from home. They hired a rickshaw to go to the Arya Samaj. Nikita nearly froze in her sari. Her mother had just had surgery and her parents were unable to make it for the wedding. Nikita spoke to them in the morning and they gave their blessings and said they were looking forward to throwing them a grand

reception in Kolkata. Arun and all their friends were waiting for her at the Samaj. After the ceremony, they all went to a restaurant for the wedding feast. Arun had told his parents he was going away for the weekend. When the party was over, the two of them returned to Nikita's home.

During that weekend, Nikita worried endlessly about her in-laws' reaction. She asked Arun if he was considering telling them about the secret wedding. He said his plan was to continue to work on them without springing this surprise. If he felt they were absolutely not going to come around, then he would tell them. If they wouldn't accept her even then, he was going to pack his bags and leave. It worried her, but she didn't want to push him to walk out on his parents. Despite this, they were happy together. All her friends remarked on her 'glow'.

On Monday, he went home. That was when it struck Nikita that this was not a normal way to live. They spoke on the phone all day and he said he was setting a deadline. Later, at night, he called her again. There had been a fiasco, he said. He had told his mother that if she didn't accept Nikita he was going to go ahead and marry her anyway. 'If you do that, please don't come back here,' his mother had told him. 'I don't like her and I will never accept her. She is a working woman.'

'She'll quit her job,' Arun said.

'Doesn't matter. She has been working all these years. She is a tainted woman in my eyes,' she said.

He tried again the next day. And the day after. Each time her name came up, there were fireworks in his house.

One Sunday, a few weeks later, he was over at Nikita's house. They were sitting down and watching something on TV when the doorbell rang. Nikita opened the door and nearly fainted when she saw Arun's mum and dad outside. His mother walked in and asked, 'Where is my son?' Arun heard her voice and came out of the room. His mother saw him, walked over and slapped him hard. Across his face. Right in front of Nikita. Then she started screaming. 'Is this what we have taught you? How dare you shack up with this horrible woman? Do you want her to work so she can prostitute herself while you enjoy the money?' All kinds of vile things were flying about the room.

Then his father stepped in and asked him how he could put his parents through this after he'd seen their disappointment when his sister chose her own husband. Arun said this wasn't a crime. He asked them why it was such a big deal whether he chose his own partner or they chose one for him. 'This is 2001,' he told them, 'the world outside has changed. You have to broaden your perspectives.' His mother simply said Nikita wasn't her choice and she would never accept her. While all of this slapping and arguing was going on, like a good hostess, Nikita went to the kitchen and came with a tray and two glasses of water for her 'guests'.

She served her father-in-law first, who took the glass and drank it. Then she went to her mother-in-law. She picked the glass and flung the water in Nikita's face. Nikita was shocked. She stood there, water dripping from her face, but didn't speak a word. Then she took the glass back from her mother-in-law and went to the kitchen. Her mother-in-law followed her there. First, in a triumphant gotcha tone, she explained that they had been noticing Arun's frequent absences from the house and they had hired someone to tail him for a week. That's how they found out that this was where Nikita lived and that he was visiting her every chance he got. She told her Nikita could never take her son away from her.

'You are too confident and too independent. I will never accept you. You are nothing but a *dandewali* (prostitute),' she told her. Nikita was horrified but remained polite. 'I said you are older than me but you are in my house. You can't talk to me like that here. Please leave. She was like, "Are you throwing me out?" I said no, I am requesting you to leave. Arun was having a conversation with his dad. She said, "You will never be happy. I curse you to a life of unhappiness." On their way out, though, his father put his hand on my head and said be happy, and they left. Obviously, he had no say in anything. The moment they left I held on to Arun and we started crying. It was traumatic,' she says.

I met Nikita in Kolkata. We had spoken a few times over the phone, mostly to figure out my travel schedule. Even though we had never met before, Nikita invited me to stay with her. When I declined and told her I'd book myself a hotel room, she went out of her way to make all the arrangements for me. When she came to meet me at the hotel, she brought a gift along—a small handcrafted purse inside which was a technicolour Ganpati. She was immediately friendly and within minutes we were chatting like old friends. As she told me the story of her marriage to Arun, she held nothing back.

Fair, cheerful and bird-like, she perched herself at the edge of the bed and talked away. At one point, she asked me to guess her age. I looked at her round face, bright eyes, her full cheeks and her glowing complexion. She looked twenty but for the dark circles etched around her eyes. I guessed her to be thirty-five. 'I am forty-two,' she said and laughed loudly at my expression of shock. Later, in the evening, she insisted we go to her club. There I met her father who demonstrated that same instant warmth. Theirs was an easy family. Nikita and her father laughed a lot. And going by the number of people who stopped at our table to chat with them, it was clear that they were popular members at the club.

It was then hard for me to understand what she saw in Arun and his traditional family. Why would she bother putting herself through this insane emotional trauma? She loved Arun, she tells me, and he made her happy. 'I'd say financially our families were on a par. Our fathers were both employed professionals. But in terms of value system, my family was far more evolved than his,' she says.

After his parents busted them at Nikita's home, even Arun saw no point in trying to get them to come around. They spoke to some friends and all of them advised the couple that it was best if the two of them just left the city. Arun asked if they could go to Kolkata and stay with her folks for a while. She spoke to her parents who were more than happy to have them over.

So, Nikita quit her job. Arun waited for a month since he was due to get a bonus. Nikita started packing the house up. Arun ferreted his clothes and other things out of his house, little by little. His parents were freezing him out. All conversations ended in much scolding and yelling. He systematically withdrew money from his account. Then true to their shared passion for Bollywood, at 2 a.m. one night, he threw his bags out his window to an empty plot of land next door and swung down a bedsheet from his first-floor room to the boundary wall.

On the other side, he picked up his bags and ran to the car in which his friends were waiting for him. Nikita had moved out of the house and he met her at the home of a friend. The next morning, they took the train to Kolkata. As the train pulled out of the platform, both of them strained to see if his parents were running in slow motion to reach them and bless them. Their story wasn't going to have that filmy ending, sadly.

In Kolkata, things were good initially. Nikita's parents were thrilled to have them around. They went to the club with her father. Arun was proudly introduced as the son-in-law. Her relatives came and met them and handed over belated wedding presents and blessings. Once, they heard from a friend in Delhi that Arun's mum had taken his elopement very badly and had become an emotional wreck. Nikita insisted that he call his mother. When he did, she screamed at him for a full quarter of an hour and told him he was dead to her. She forbade him from ever coming back, especially if she was dead. At least in that one aspect she played her role of the enraged mother well. Any director would have been impressed.

But finding a job was proving to be difficult. First, Kolkata was not a call centre or BPO destination, so there were hardly any companies where their kind of experience was valuable. Second, salaries in the city were so poor that both Arun and Nikita couldn't resign themselves to taking up the jobs coming their way. After a while, stressed and running out of funds, they began to bicker constantly. Tired of their frequent fights, her father put his foot down and said if the two of them couldn't work their issues out, they should just annul the marriage.

Fortunately, a month later, Nikita got a job in a multinational bank. Arun continued to look without any success. Again, it was a bit awkward that she was at work all day while he stayed home with her mother. Her boss in her new workplace was earnest and helpful. He noticed that Nikita wasn't happy and asked her why. She told him about her husband's lack of success in finding a job. He asked about his experience and background and told her to get him to come and meet him. The interview went well and Arun too ended up being hired by the bank. In a week, they found their own place and moved out to live by themselves. Finally, it seemed, Nikita and Arun got the life they'd always been dreaming of.

For nearly three years, Arun and Nikita lived happily in Kolkata. They worked together and at home they shared the chores. On weekends they threw parties for their friends, watched movies and went to Park Street's throbbing nightclubs. It was a good life. One evening, at a friend's party, someone told Nikita about a great job that was available in an optical company. Nikita thought it was too technical for her. But Arun loved all things technical and, when he heard about it, he expressed his interest in applying.

He went for the interview and aced it. In a month, he joined the new company. He was sent to the head office in Delhi for two months of training. His superiors in Delhi were very impressed by him and offered him a more promising position there. When Arun came back to Kolkata, he urged Nikita to quit her job and move with him to Delhi. It was 2005, jobs were plentiful and Nikita thought she would find something easily, so she moved. They rented a home and settled down.

Nikita started looking for work. She wasn't too keen on going back to a BPO because the hours were not family-friendly. Sometime after the move, Nikita told Arun he must call his parents. He wasn't too keen, but she was insistent; she felt bad about alienating him from his family. Eventually, he called and told them that he was in Delhi and they should all try and make things better. His mother answered the phone and told him he was welcome to come and visit her, but he couldn't bring his wife. Arun said he was unwilling to even consider that option, it was either both of them or neither of them. The following day, his mother called to say she could come too.

The first Sunday after they received the invitation, Nikita and Arun went over to his parents'. Her mother-in-law answered the door when they rang the bell. Following Arun's instructions, Nikita bowed down to touch her feet. Mama sharply moved away. His father blessed her and they went in to find that Arun's grandmother was there as well. 'Is *this* what you left home for?' she asked Arun dismissively, while running her eyes up and down Nikita.

Then she turned to Nikita and asked her if she knew how to cook. 'I hadn't even sat down and it had begun,' Nikita says. Arun pleaded with his grandmother to speak properly to his wife and he nudged Nikita to go and touch her feet. When she leaned down, Arun's grandmother gave her a hard whack on her head. 'I wanted to just run away from there,' she says. 'By this time, Arun's mother brought over a glass of water. My mouth was parched but I was seized by the fear that she had poisoned the water. I declined to eat or drink anything.' Mama carried on cursing her right through the day, reminding her that there was no place even in hell for women like her. Nikita felt drained by the time they left. Arun was annoyed too and yelled at her for forcing him to meet his parents.

The next time they visited was a fortnight later. This time too, in a mood of expansive forgiveness, Nikita had insisted that Arun call and the whole 'You are welcome but your wife isn't' scene was repeated. This time though, Nikita decided she would wear what she pleased and, instead of a salwar kameez, went in a pair of capri pants and a kurti.

Grandmother-in-law opened the door this time and asked her if she couldn't dress like a proper woman. Nikita said she was more comfortable in this and that she knew that Arun's sisters wore jeans. 'They are our daughters. Don't even think you are one of them,' grandmother said and allowed them in. This time though, Mama was easier. She got her to join her in the kitchen and help her cook. She made polite conversation and for the first time did not insult her. Until, that is, she asked what they usually ate for breakfast, and Nikita replied toast and butter. 'She took off on me. This is the problem with convent-educated girls. Can't you make my son some parathas? Do you know bread is made of maida? Your mother hasn't taught you anything and things like that. She ranted and raved for the next half hour,' Nikita tells me.

Over the course of the next couple of months, Nikita says, there were a lot of conflicting signals from her in-laws. On the one hand, they continued to berate her at any given opportunity. Yet, on the other, there was constant talk about how she should behave once they moved in. Mama told her things like when you live here, you have to keep your head covered when the men of the family are around and stuff like that. 'I was like, dude, are you fucking with me?!!' she laughs.

The contrast of how Arun's family seemed from the outside to how it actually was, was not lost on her. 'These are people who speak English. Their daughters live abroad—one in Singapore and the other in the US. Yet, when it came to their daughter-in-law, it was unbelievable how regressive they were. Cover your head! In Delhi! In 2005! Can you believe that?' she asks.

In the beginning, Arun was certain he didn't want to move in with his parents. Then, slowly, he started telling her that, in the long term, it didn't make sense for them to pay rent while his parents had a house in the same city. Nikita said she would find work soon and paying rent would not be a problem. At this, Arun really lost his temper. He said if she started to work now, it would lay waste all the work he had done in rebuilding bridges with his parents.

Nikita was beginning to grasp the enormity of the move to Delhi. She had no film references to draw from. She was on her own here. So for a while she allowed herself to stay home wondering what to cook for breakfast, lunch and dinner. Arun was visiting his parents a lot more now. Sometimes he went there straight after work and came home very late, having eaten dinner cooked by his mother. The two of them usually went on Sundays. Nikita sensed that Arun was drawing away from her. Yet, she didn't know what she could do about it.

One Sunday, at his parents' home, they were in the middle of lunch when the doorbell rang. Arun's mother went to answer it. Some relatives who were visiting Delhi had decided to turn up unannounced. She made them wait in the living room while she ran into the dining room where Arun and Nikita were. There, without a word, she pulled Arun and Nikita by their arms and in a crazy pantomime dragged them upstairs. She pushed them into the loft and locked them there.

Nikita was horrified. What the hell was this? For three hours they stayed there without access to a washroom or even sufficient air! At last, when the door opened, Mama explained that since the larger family did not know Arun was married, it would have been difficult to explain her presence. 'And these were people who were visiting for the first time; they would have wanted to see the house. So it was obviously not practical that we be allowed to stay in a bedroom. She explained all this with a shrug. Like it was no big deal,' Nikita says.

Nikita decided she had to take some measure of control over

her life. She applied for jobs and got one handling public relations for an aviation company. She did well at work, and when the company was expanding, she was made head of the department and given a raise. But in the evenings, she would come home to a huge row with Arun. His mother was calling him every day asking him questions about his wife's job and workplace. 'How many men work there? What clothes does she wear to work? Does she apply make-up?'

Arun yelled at Nikita, saying his mother was driving him crazy. When she got the raise, she began earning more money than him and that became a big issue. 'He would tell me he was stressed at work and his mother was harassing him about my job endlessly. Eventually he begged and pleaded. And I knew it was absolutely the worst possible decision I could take, but I succumbed to the pressure and decided to quit,' she says. As a consolation prize, his mother said he could drop her off at hers in the morning and she would teach her how to run a 'proper' house. Nikita refused. She didn't want to deal with the prospect of another stint in the loft.

Around this time, there was a wedding in the family. Mama said Arun and Nikita could go with them, but she should be properly dressed. Nikita wore a sari that her mother-in-law approved of and was quite excited by the prospect of finally being a part of his family, messed up as it was. Her in-laws picked them up from home and they drove straight to the venue. There, Mama told everyone that Arun was living in his company's guesthouse in Gurgaon. And when people inquired about Nikita, Mama introduced her as a 'distant relative'. When they came back, she got into a huge row with Arun. 'My parents treated him like a son-in-law. How long was it going to take for them to even introduce me as a daughter-in-law, forget treating me like one?' Nikita wondered. After all, it was four years since their wedding.

Nikita found the answer to that question the next time she went to her in-laws' house. After lunch, Arun's mother brought out a bunch of photographs and laid them on the table. 'What is this?' he asked.

'Choose the one you'd like to marry,' his mother told him.

Nikita jumped up with an 'Excuse me! He is already married to me.'

'That may be in your house. In this house, he will marry a proper girl we choose,' Mama replied. 'I told you I could never accept you.' Nikita left the house and never went back.

Arun's visits to his parents, however, only increased. Soon, he was there nearly four or five days a week, while Nikita waited for him at home. When he did come home, he was often drunk. Nikita was certain his mother was filling up his head with nonsense about her. They had been married for nearly five years then and the romance and the excitement that had kept them going in the early part of the marriage were beginning to fade. It was the perfect time for his mother to wear him down.

Arun began accusing her of exactly the same things his mother used to. That she was a working woman, that she was tainted, that she was a prostitute. At first, Nikita tried to reason with him. Then she began arguing with him. Around this time, a friend of theirs who had known them well in Kolkata visited them for a few days. Even the friend was shocked at how much Arun had changed. He was unsocial and abrasive. He did not come home most of the evenings he was there. The one evening he did, Ankit was drunk and ended up insulting him. Within a year, Arun was unrecognizable to everyone who knew him.

He had become a clone of his parents. He was mimicking everything his mother said about her. He would give Nikita a hundred rupees every day to run the house. And in the evenings, he would make her account for every paisa. His father used to do the same thing to his mother and he had hated him for it. Yet, that was exactly who he ended up being. Finally, Nikita had to face the fact that her mother-in-law was right: there was no happiness for her in this marriage. Five years after they were married, Nikita walked out on Arun and moved back to Kolkata. A year later, they divorced.

Arun remarried—a non-working woman of his mother's choice. When I looked him up on Facebook, he was posing with his sari-clad wife and their little daughter. Nikita figures the photograph was shot in his parents' home. 'Who knows, maybe his mother herself was behind the camera, since she finally got a daughter-in-law she chose: one who has never stepped inside an office,' she says.

Last year, Nikita began dating a man she met on the internet. It was seven years since the divorce, and she was living alone in Kolkata. Paul was Australian and they both shared a curiosity about and a belief in astrology and the occult. They met playing a game on Facebook and eventually ended up chatting all night on Skype and spending all day sending each other text messages on WhatsApp. Nikita had quit her job and was looking for a suitable position. Paul was recovering from an accident and was also not working.

After six months of internet-enabled romance, Paul decided he was coming to India to meet Nikita. He was talking about a proposal; he had even bought a ring. When I was first introduced to Nikita, I noticed that she and Paul were rather public about their relationship on Facebook. Each day had several 'I love you baby' and 'I miss you baby' messages on both their walls.

When I met Nikita in Kolkata, it was a month before Paul's visit to India. She was nervous about how she would feel meeting him in person. 'Now, look at the irony here. His mother is the warmest, gentlest person I have ever met,' she tells me. Paul had connected Nikita and his mother, and they had spoken and also become friends on Facebook. 'At Christmas in his mother's house, there was a stocking with my name on it,' Nikita told me. I got the sense that Nikita was excited about the relationship, although she had doubts about getting engaged to Paul.

Over the next few months, I noticed the 'I love you baby' messages had tapered off. I called Nikita to find out what had happened. She was ill and couldn't speak to me. It was a few weeks later that she finally called me back. Several things about Paul's background didn't add up, she told me. She suggested that he put off his visit to India for a few months and 'he just flipped out'. Nikita tried to talk him through it and they were virtually on Skype for a whole week. 'Then his mother wrote me a long mail explaining that Paul had a lot of mental issues and was on all kinds of medication. His condition had stabilized around the time he met me and his mother thought maybe I was the calming presence Paul needed. But when he flipped out, she figured it had been a temporary lull. She told me that she cared for me too much to see my life destroyed by her son. She advised me to get out of the relationship.'

I was terribly disappointed to hear that. I thought that Nikita's professional limbo was, in a way, also partly because she was planning to emigrate to Australia to be with Paul. She was, eventually, left with neither a good job nor a good husband.

'Look at the funny side,' she tells me, 'my first mother-in-law wanted to ruin my life because I married her son. And my second mother-in-law thinks I am so good, I shouldn't ruin my life by marrying her son. My mother-in-law karma has come full circle.'

Nikita is still single. Her life hasn't followed the romantic movie script she had always dreamt of. But, optimistic and positive, Nikita is counting her blessings that she isn't in a crime thriller, playing the victim. Locked up in a loft.

10

The Missing Link

Name	Age (in 2013)	Husband	Married
Arti	43	Vishal	1998

In an Indian marriage, the husband is Godot. He is the obvious, yet elusive, centre of it. The usual, often foolish, explanation for the mother-in-law–daughter-in-law tension is that they are both competing for the same person's affection. Truth is, the dispute is merely one of boundaries. If the man in the middle were to clearly draw the lines between his relationship with his mother and that with his wife, there would, in fact, be no dispute at all. In Samuel Beckett's play, *Waiting for Godot*, Godot who is the cause of much admiration, speculation and trouble eventually does not appear at all. Much like the husband, who never turns up to take charge of the situation between his mother and wife in a real or reformative way.

The reasons men stay out of this conflict—sometimes with disastrous results—are both physiological and sociological. In his research on married couples, John Gottman, who wrote *Why Marriages Succeed or Fail*, analysed heart rates, blood pressure and adrenaline levels of couples when they were fighting. He discovered that, when arguing with their partners, men become physiologically overwhelmed more quickly than women. Their pulse rate and blood pressure rise rapidly and remain higher for a much longer time. Men's bodies, Gottman reveals, are more vulnerable to stress and hence their natural instinct is to remove themselves from the confrontation. They 'stonewall'—shut down receptors—and hope the threat will go away.

Sociologically, too, men are trained early to stay out of this conflict. 'Oh you tell me you love me now. But I am sure as soon as you get a wife and have your own family, you will want to have nothing to do with your poor old mother,' is a statement that has been aired in every Indian household. (If you have ever wondered why the *mere paas ma hai* line has survived for years in our collective conscience, it's because mothers have worked very hard on setting the premise for it.)

Mummyjis prime their sons to get on their side from the time they are out of their diapers. They tell them repeatedly that they are expecting to be chosen against when the wife enters the picture. These boys grow up hearing about their mothers' sacrifices and the limitlessness of their love. So what's a man to do when the wife comes along and, much like his Mummyji always predicted, there arises trouble between her and the wife? He can't defend his wife and prove his mother's accusation of abandonment right. And if he is a remotely decent kind of guy, he cannot defend his mother either, because his wife is pointing out behaviour that seems obviously wrong. So he stonewalls. And hopes things will blow over.

It is ironic that most women consider their husbands to have played an active role in helping them with their mothers-in-law if they have done nothing at all. 'My husband is quite a nice guy, he does not tell me what his mother bitched to him,' is a line I heard so often, I began to believe it is the baseline for good husbands. Yet, as these women begin their stories, it is apparent that, had their husbands played a more active role in demarcating the territories between their wives and mothers, it would have solved pretty much most Mummyji issues even before they had arisen.

Arti, who has now been married for over fifteen years, is not in the group that claimed their husbands' non-interference was a blessing. She is firmly of the view that his failure to put his foot down is as much a cause of the unpleasantness in her life, as her mother-in-law's downright nastiness.

Arti was born and raised in Kashmir. But when she was nineteen, she had to leave her home with her mother and younger brother under rather traumatic circumstances. Militancy was at its bloodiest peak then and her father was a victim of it. When he was murdered, the family saw no reason in staying back in Kashmir.

Like thousands of Pandits before and after them, they came to Delhi and sought to build a new life here. Arti resumed her education and completed her master's degree. Since she was keen on a career in media, she followed this with a couple of diplomas in broadcasting. By the time she was twenty-four, she had found herself a steady job in broadcasting.

I met Arti on a humdrum Monday. We were nipping out to talk over lunch, and after a bit of back and forth about what we'd like to eat and where, I finally picked her up from outside her office. Fair, wiry and tall, I spotted her from afar. With her oversized spectacle frames and the severe drape of the dupatta, she looked more like a professor and less like a journalist. There was an air of melancholy about her. She smiled rather shyly and we shook hands in the self-conscious way when you don't know whether it is appropriate to lean in for an air kiss or not.

We walked back to my office—I'd offered her spicy biriyani from the canteen. Our conversation during the walk was guarded—where do you live, how do you commute, that kind of thing. Even though we were in the same profession, we did not know too many people in common. When we reached my office, I settled

Arti down and switched my recorder on. She laughed suddenly, slapping her palm over her mouth, like she was doing something wild and inappropriate. She was at the wrong end of a recorder for the first time in her life, she told me. But in a moment, her face reverted to its severe and sad look.

When she was twenty-five and settled in her job, Arti's mother asked her if she had anyone in mind whom she was keen on marrying. Because of the shock of her father's death—something she was yet to recover from—Arti had never thought of boyfriends or relationships. She had no one in mind, she told her mother, and she was open to an arranged marriage. In India, marriage is a mandatory marker of time, not emotions. She was twenty-five; it was time. Arti was educated enough and practical enough to know that.

Her mother began scanning Kashmiri publications right away. Soon enough, she spotted a matrimonial advertisement from a businessman. 'The ad said they were looking for someone who was fair, beautiful, educated, the usual things. They wanted everything, basically,' Arti says. Her mother showed her the ad and asked her what she thought of the guy. She was a bit sceptical about the fact that he ran his own business; she preferred someone who was employed. But that was hardly a reason for opposition and her mother went ahead and corresponded with the advertiser. The first step was matching the horoscopes. Two independent pandits looked at them. Both of them pronounced that the horoscopes matched perfectly and predicted a very happy union.

A matched horoscope is 40 per cent of the work done. The next step was to meet each other. Vishal—the prospective groom—suggested the coffee shop of a luxury hotel in the neighbourhood. Arti went there with her mother and brother. When they reached, Vishal was already there. He had come with his brother. This was a departure from the norm. Usually, the girl and the boy were accompanied by their parents as well as siblings. 'I took that as a sign that his parents were liberal. It is unusual that either the bride or the groom goes to a meeting without her or his parents,' she says.

Conversation, as it tends to be in these situations, was awkward. Vishal was a reserved sort, given to few words. And Arti herself was feeling too shy and uncomfortable to take the lead. They asked each other rather droll questions—what are your hobbies? (Hers, painting and music; his, driving and photography.) Then they both talked about their work and that was pretty much it. 'There was very little to go by. But my inner voice told me, he would be my life.' Arti laughs; the irony is not lost on her.

They left the hotel and walked out. The three of them were waiting to hire a rickshaw to go home when Vishal and his brother spotted them. They stopped the car and offered to drop them home. Arti's mother declined, but the boys insisted and they all piled in and went home together. 'That was another good sign. I thought they were kind and generous. When you have nothing concrete, everything becomes a sign,' she says.

At home, they discussed the boys. Her mother, brother and her inner voice were in favour of Vishal. So she said yes. Her mother informed Vishal's parents about their decision and the next thing they knew, a date was fixed for the engagement.

'Didn't you meet the family before that?' I ask.

'No, they said as long as Vishal was happy, they were OK. Later on, I realized why they didn't,' she says.

The engagement was at his house. Arti went with her family and a bunch of cousins, uncles and aunts. On Vishal's side were his parents, his two older brothers, their wives and kids, and his three older sisters. Arti's first recollection of her mother-in-law was how gorgeous she was. Green-eyed, fair-skinned and black-haired, she was the quintessential Kashmiri beauty. Although she wore a rather serious expression, she was very warm and affectionate towards Arti. She came over, hugged her new daughter-in-law and welcomed her into the family. 'I already have three daughters,' she

told her, 'now you are my fourth.' Arti was glad. Her mother-in-law
seemed nice. Vishal's sisters were very pleasant too. Each of them
welcomed her into the family. They were all thrilled their youngest
brother was 'settling down'.

The wedding was fixed for a year later. In the interim, Arti and
Vishal engaged in the arranged marriage version of courtship. They
went out every once in a while, for drives in his car, followed by a
meal. But they talked very little. It wasn't in his personality to be
boisterous and she was unsure about how to behave around men.
When they ate out, he often asked her what she liked to eat. He
ordered a variety of things for himself. But he told her that he wasn't
fussy about food at all, he ate whatever was placed in front of him.
Arti was relieved: she wasn't a good cook, nor was she interested
in picking up culinary skills. At home, she avoided the kitchen.

'Later, after I married, I realized that food was all my husband
ever thought of. He ate little, but he thought of eating all the time.
And if something wasn't cooked to his taste, he wouldn't eat it at
all. I don't know why he told me he wasn't fussy about his food,'
she says.

She also met his family during that year, but it was usually for
religious functions or special days. Each time she met his mother,
she was just as warm as on the engagement day. Except, Arti began
to notice, that she was often really rude to whoever was with her.
One day, she went to Vishal's house for a puja. Since her brother
had moved abroad by then, and as propriety demanded that she
not go alone, she asked a cousin of hers to accompany her.

When they reached, Vishal's mother, Maji, greeted her cheerily.
'This is my cousin,' Arti introduced. 'OK, whatever, just go sit
there,' his mother barked at her cousin. It was awfully rude. And
Arti didn't know what to do. But her mother-in-law turned to her
sweetly and asked her to accompany her to the kitchen.

Arti confesses she was a little scared of her mother-in-law
from the first time she met her. She had a very serious and stern

expression. She always looked angry. But she behaved with great warmth towards Arti, and so she stayed collected, yet cautious.

Vishal's family did not have many demands for the wedding. All they said was that the reception should be a grand affair. Among Kashmiris, Arti informed me, dowry is expected but not demanded. Her mother started the preparations for the wedding and Arti too got sucked into the shopping and grooming frenzy over the next few months. Before she knew it, the day of her wedding had arrived. Arti was quite excited. This was her big day and she had been waiting for it.

'The day went very fast with all the preparations, greeting the guests and then the actual ceremonies,' she says. By the time they took the pheras it was late at night. 'But the minute the seventh phera was over, I tell you, I could feel a 180 degree turn in my mother-in-law's attitude to me,' she says.

As soon as they were relieved from the rituals, Arti was called to the side of the venue where Vishal's family was. And Vishal went to Arti's side to meet and greet his new relatives. There, standing in the middle of all the guests, Maji screamed at Vishal. 'What are you doing there?' she yelled. 'They are outsiders.' Everyone was shocked. Arti's relatives tittered. Some of them asked her mother if Maji was mad. Arti and her mother were both shocked and scared, but they shrugged it off as being a result of the stresses of the big day.

Then her family bid her goodbye and Arti left for her husband's home. On the way, his adrenaline still pumping, Vishal told his mother, 'Look mama, I'm finally bringing Arti home.'

Maji threw him an icy glare. 'So what's the big deal? Park her in a corner somewhere,' she said.

And that was the welcome she got.

Among all the daughters-in-law I spoke to, Arti was the one who found the process of talking about her past the most painful. She had to stop several times. She clutched her forehead in her hands, she blinked away tears. While most women were happy to have a chance to vent, Arti's pain was a raw force. Even fifteen years after the wedding, she could barely think about the story, much less talk about it.

Her marital house was a two-storeyed, three-bedroom affair. Maji and Papaji occupied one room. The other two were on rotation. Since they were newly married, Vishal and Arti were allowed one of the bedrooms. The day after the wedding, Arti sat on the bed while sorting through her stuff. Maji came thundering in. 'Sit down,' she yelled. Arti looked around, confused. She didn't understand what this was about. 'Sit down, how dare you sit on the bed!' Maji screamed. Arti looked for a stool or a small chair. There was neither. 'Down where?' she asked, puzzled.

'On the ground,' Maji said. 'Are you a maharani that you will sit only on the bed?'

Arti was shocked. She ran to the kitchen and asked the elder daughter-in-law what this was about. 'We are not supposed to sit on the sofas or the bed,' she informed her.

Arti could not believe this. 'But why?' she asked.

The elder daughter-in-law shrugged. 'That's the rule. Only the family—that is Maji, Papaji, the three sons, the three daughters and the grandchildren—is allowed to sit on the sofas or the bed. Daughters-in-law have to sit down. Any concrete surface is fine. Don't worry, we can sit on the staircase,' she said.

When she noticed Arti's horrified expression, she shrugged and added, 'Anyway, it doesn't look nice, no? That she is sitting on the sofa and you are sitting at the same level on the next seat.'

'This daughter-in-law is a professor,' Arti tells me. 'She handles hundreds of teenagers and teaches them complicated scientific theories. And even she has been brainwashed to think it's OK if the mother-in-law tells her daughter-in-law that she isn't allowed to sit anywhere but on the floor. Can you imagine?'

Soon, Arti herself was inducted into the chores of the household. The three daughters-in-law were to rise at 5 and go straight to the kitchen. There they cooked breakfast and lunch. Arti was in charge of making the rotis. One day she counted that she had made sixty rotis. After that she stopped counting. By 8, the daughters-in-law were expected to serve breakfast, pack lunchboxes for the three men, their three sisters and four children.

Then they themselves went to work. Daughter-in-law #1 was the professor and daughter-in-law #2 held a senior position in a public sector bank. Arti worked in broadcast media where she helped expose society's injustices by being the voice of the marginalized and the impoverished. In the evening, she joined their ranks. Once home, it was straight to the kitchen for the banker, the professor and the journalist. They slaved over dinner, washed clothes and straightened out the house.

At Vishal's home, talking among the daughters-in-law was banned. Maji actively pursued a divide-and-rule policy. She did not want an uprising from the daughters-in-law. The three of them whispered to each other only if they were certain (500 per cent sure) that Maji was on the other floor. If she appeared suddenly, like errant students at the sight of the principal, the three of them scattered in different directions. 'Don't you have any work that you are all chatting to each other?' Maji would yell.

Other injustices abounded. While the family ate out of crystalware—one of the precious possessions they had managed to bring from Kashmir—the three daughters-in-law were given separate steel plates and glasses. After office, before resuming their dinner chores, they hid in the kitchen and drank a glass of tea. Usually, they weren't allowed tea or any other 'optionals'.

Maji would not touch them, even accidentally. All three daughters-in-law were expected to hand their full salaries over to her. When they went to her with the money, she would turn her face away and ask them to leave it on the table. After they left the room, mother-in-law would pick up the envelopes and count the cash.

'She virtually treated us like untouchables,' Arti says. Even though mother-in-law ate the food cooked by the 'untouchable' daughters-in-law, they were not allowed anywhere near the puja room. If they had to pray, they were to stand outside and peep in.

'It was about a month after the wedding that it became clear to me why my mother-in-law did not meet me before the engagement. It was because it was unimportant. She was only hiring a maid. She didn't care what I looked like or what my personality was,' Arti tells me.

This is where you, the reader, will ask: but what about the husband? Godot did nothing. At first, Vishal refused to believe that his mother wouldn't allow his wife to sit on the sofa. Maji got a whiff of the fact that the news of her rules was reaching the son. So when Vishal was around, she would make a huge production of adoring Arti.

'Come sit with me. You aren't eating well. You've become so thin,' she would tell her. How could Vishal believe his mother was cruel to Arti when he was seeing with his own eyes how lovingly she treated her? In two days Vishal would be comforted by this demonstration of his mother's humaneness. The next time Arti complained, he told her she was making up these stories.

Even so, Maji preferred to err on the side of caution. She knew that she would be outed only if Arti and Vishal actually spent time together. So her first strategy was to assign the rooms in a dynamic fashion. No one knew where he or she would be sleeping on any given night. Even if Arti and Vishal got a room, it would be one where at least four people stored their clothes, books and other stuff. So it was unlikely that they would get to whisper or even talk uninterrupted for more than five minutes. This was true for all three sons and their wives. Maji actively monitored intimacy.

Maji's rules extended to the outdoors too. None of the sons were allowed to go unchaperoned anywhere with their wives. If a son and his wife were going out—for shopping, a movie or just a walk—they had to be accompanied by at least one sister. Usually the whole family joined in. Further, she stipulated that the wife was not to be accommodated in the car if only the husband was in it. So, even though Arti and Vishal left for work at the same time, she had to walk to the bus stop, while he drove past her.

'In the early years, I would walk down the road, turn the corner and hop into the car my husband was waiting in. But one day, one of his sisters saw us and complained to her mother. She called both of us in and yelled so much that it was audible to the whole neighbourhood. She asked my husband if he was my driver, things like that,' Arti says. After this, Vishal was too scared to even offer her a lift secretively.

Since they weren't allowed any private time, it was hard for Arti and Vishal to forge a bond with each other. They only ever interacted with each other in the presence of the family and a mother who terrified both of them. 'Since we had had an arranged marriage, we hadn't known or loved each other before the wedding, either. It was impossible to get him to be my ally. In retrospect, I think this was a well-planned strategy by my mother-in-law. The only way her joint family would stay joint was if the wives didn't have any say or even a connection with their husbands,' she says.

Not being allowed in the car alone with her husband was not the worst of Arti's deprivations. The daughters-in-law weren't allowed anything. They couldn't enter the room if the air conditioner was on, even for chores. 'One evening I had finished washing clothes—their clothes—and had to go through the living room to the balcony to hang them out to dry. I opened the door and my mother-in-law literally shooed me away. Like she said shoo-shoo.'

'I told her I was just going to the balcony to dry the clothes. She said she knew I was using that as an excuse to enjoy the air conditioner while I walked to the balcony and back. She asked me to come back later,' she says. After that, in the summer months,

Arti had to wait till past 11 a.m. when the family had switched off the living room air conditioner to go to the balcony to hang the clothes to dry.

Another time, Arti was chopping fruit for the family. By then, she knew that she was not supposed to pop even a piece of it into her own mouth. She served them watermelons, and when Maji walked into the kitchen and saw their hard, green remains, she told Arti she was supposed to eat it. 'It's what you feed cattle. And she wanted me to eat that. She stood there hoping to enjoy the show of watching me eat it. I said I don't eat watermelons and threw them away,' she says.

Arti and the other two daughters-in-law were served a heap of rice in their steel plates. 'She wanted us to eat just as labourers do,' she says. If there was any leftover vegetable or dal, they could have that. Most days, it was just the rice. When Arti went to her mother's home one day and was served normal food, she was so overwhelmed, her whole body shook. She could barely eat. Her mother asked her what was wrong, but she didn't want to upset her with the reality of her life.

'What did your husband do about any of this?' I ask her.

'Nothing,' she says.

'Perhaps in the early years, he did want to stand up for his new wife but did not have the courage to do so. Then as the years went by and the marriage became invisible, there was no motivation for him to do anything either,' she says.

In India, modernity is like a new outfit, you wear it only when you go out. Once home, you can take it off and go back to living like it is 1813. The other daughters-in-law in the house were not the only ones who were educated and employed. Vishal's three sisters were also highly qualified and were employed in prestigious organizations. Yet, they saw no reason to challenge their mother's bigoted views. On the contrary, they fuelled it and were active participants in the physical and emotional violence. 'They are people whom you will love if you meet them. They are warm, friendly and normal. You wouldn't believe that this is how they are at home,' Arti says.

The first year of Arti's marriage to Vishal was torturous to say the least. It had fallen significantly short of even her modest expectations. And it was about to get worse.

A year after her wedding, Arti discovered she was pregnant. She was quite happy and eager to be a mother. When she announced it to her in-laws, it was received with characteristic indifference. Her mother-in-law never inquired about her health. On the contrary, she was quite upset at her for being pregnant. The source of Maji's biggest stress was that she had three unmarried daughters. To her, the fact that this chit of a girl was not just married but now also about to become a mother was a slap in her face. She didn't see it as a reason to celebrate at all, even though she was about to become a grandmother all over again.

Once during her second trimester, Arti was craving something cold and sweet. She mentioned this to Vishal and he brought home some rasgullas for her. 'These are for Arti,' he told the marauding nephews and nieces. His mother overheard this and came running in. 'Why are they for her?' she asked. 'She is pregnant no, Maji, she was craving something sweet and cold,' he told her. That was enough. His mother took off on him first, and then her. 'Are you her servant?' she asked and went on to chide him for running around trying to please his wife.

When Arti appeared, Maji turned to her. 'Are you the first female on earth to get pregnant? How dare you ask Vishal to bring you stuff? Aren't you getting food in this house? There will be nothing special for anyone just because they are pregnant,' Maji went on and on and on. Then she called the grandchildren and distributed the rasgullas to them. The last one she popped into her own mouth. Arti shrugged. Her craving had long vanished anyway.

I ask Arti if she did not feel let down by Vishal. 'I was surprised and disappointed initially,' she says. 'But think about it from his angle. This is what he has seen in his family. His mother bullies the daughters-in-law and his brothers have never stood up for their wives. What you see in your family is what's normal to you. This was normal to him.'

A few days after the rasgulla incident, Arti was in the kitchen making rotis when Vishal's older brother walked in. 'Your rotis are burning,' he said.

'I'll take care of it, bhaiyya, you go ahead and sit down. I'll bring them to the table,' she replied.

Brother-in-law #1 couldn't believe what he was hearing. 'Look Maji, this chit of a girl is answering me back,' he howled. At this, the mother and a sister ran in. Like a ten-year-old schoolboy, brother-in-law told them what had happened. Enraged, her mother-in-law came up to her, grabbed her by her shoulders and shook her. Hard.

Then the sister joined in. They pulled her out of the kitchen by her shoulders and her sister-in-law pushed her on to a bed. Arti was terrified by their anger and scared for her baby. She sat down and was shaking in fear and shock. After some time, she casually walked out of the house, hired a rickshaw and went to her mother's. There she broke down. Her mother asked what the matter was and, despite herself, Arti confided everything to her mother. Her mother was shocked and horrified by all of this. She told her she should stay and not go back to that house.

In the evening, Vishal came to try and coax her back home. Arti refused. She told him how terrified she was, how his family had no business behaving with her like that. He assured her he would counsel them about their behaviour. Arti's mother was livid too. Setting aside the respect she was expected to demonstrate to her son-in-law, she asked him how his family could treat her daughter that way. 'They are nice people,' he reassured her, 'they just lose their cool easily.' He spent an hour in her house talking to Arti and her mother. 'At the end of it, like a fool, I went back to his house,' she says.

I ask her how her mother-in-law reacted on seeing her come back. 'There was no reaction. She handed me a basket of vegetables and asked me to chop them up for dinner. Now, an issue becomes an issue only if you acknowledge it, right? If you pretend like nothing at all had happened, the issue doesn't exist. The general sense in the house was that I overreacted,' she says.

I ask her about her father-in-law. What was he like, did he also yell at the daughters-in-law?

'He was a good man,' Arti says, 'but he was so scared of his wife. As soon as my mother-in-law started shouting, he would run into his room and hide there. Then, when everything settled down, he would come out and ask me if I was all right.'

Arti considered getting out of the marriage several times. But she felt that her family had, after all these years, finally reached some kind of peace. Her mother was relieved that Arti was 'settled' and her brother was employed. Arti didn't want to shatter that illusion. She thought she should just try harder and stay with her husband instead of putting her mother through the stress of a separation or a divorce.

A few months after her attempted breakout, Arti gave birth to a baby girl. According to Kashmiri tradition, she went to her husband's home right from the hospital. The first few months were a blur of sleepless nights and tiring breastfeeding.

Once the baby was a bit older, Arti was told that she was to clean up after her, and then hand her over either to her mother-in-law or one of Vishal's sisters. Initially, she didn't understand why this was happening. Soon, she cottoned on to the fact that the baby was 'theirs' while she played the role of some kind of ayah. She wasn't allowed to hold her baby, sing or coo to her. Her job was merely to clean the baby up and 'prepare her'.

When the little girl turned one and old enough to assimilate information, they almost entirely took her over. 'She will call me Mummy,' her mother-in law announced.

'But I am her mother,' Arti pointed out.

'No, you are Arti,' she told her. 'There is only one mummy in this house and that is me.'

Arti didn't know what she could do. She told Vishal about it, who shrugged it off and assured her that mother only meant the baby belonged to the family now. But as the child grew older, Maji and the sisters began poisoning her mind against her mother.

'Arti is fair, but you are dark; how could she be your mother?' they would ask the eighteen-month-old. Or, 'Arti has brown hair, your hair is black. If she was your mother, your hair would also be brown,' they would point out. Eventually, the child caught on and began viewing Arti with suspicion.

One evening, when her daughter was about two, Arti was downstairs making tea. When she was done, Maji instructed that she bring it up and serve the family there. The baby, now a toddler, was playing in the room. After she had served everyone, Arti picked up her baby and hugged her. 'Come to mama,' she told her little one. At this, her mother-in-law flung her tea and lunged at her. 'You are not her mother, I am. How dare you talk like this in front of her and us?' she screamed.

Arti couldn't help herself. She said, 'This child is mine first. I gave birth to her.' This time, one of the brothers did the shaking and pushing. When she recovered, Arti grabbed the child and, once again, ran home to her mother. That evening, the older brother came to take her back. Arti refused. Her mother too was adamant that her daughter would not go back to that weird household.

He blamed Arti. 'She talks too much,' he told her mother. 'Every house has its rules and regulations. She doesn't live by our rules,' he complained. Arti was certain that there was nothing in that house for her. When he saw that there was no convincing them, he grabbed the child and left. 'I was running after him and trying to pull my daughter away from his hands. But he was big and strong. He just dumped her in the car and drove away,' she says.

By this time, Arti was crying intensely. We sat there as the silence in the room filled with her sobs. Eventually, she straightened up and wiped her face. I offered her a glass of water. 'Don't worry, I'm all right,' she said and carried on with the story.

After the baby was taken away, Vishal called her a few times. Arti was torn between claiming her child and returning to 'that hell'. Her daughter was on solids by then, but Arti was also still feeding her breast milk. The child hadn't yet taken to any other kind of milk. Two days of tears and confusion later, one of the other daughters-in-law called Arti and told her that she should come back since the child wasn't eating anything. She immediately took a rickshaw and went over. As soon as she stepped in, her mother-in-law handed over a bottle of milk to the child. She gulped it down, greedily. 'They had starved her all day and then made the daughter-in-law call me. I came home to see the sight of my child drinking from the bottle. It was the ultimate sign from Maji that the child did not need me any more,' Arti sobs.

Despite the stress, Arti couldn't get herself to live away from her child. So she stayed on. Every day, Maji and the sisters poisoned her daughter against her. They would tell her that Arti didn't love her. They pointed out that Arti left her in the house and went to work, while her grandmother was at home with her all day. When a child hears something a thousand times a day from five different people, it is inevitable that she will believe it. Slowly, but surely, Arti lost her daughter. She was just Arti to her daughter. Maji was Mummy.

I ask her if the older children—her husband's nieces and nephews—were also raised as their grandmother's kids. Arti says yes. When she married, the youngest of the kids were ten. She noticed that they referred to their grandmother as Mummy and called their mothers by their names. They were also incredibly rude to their mothers. At the time, Arti just assumed they were badly brought up children. She did not realize, nor was she warned by anyone, about this programme of handing over your children to your mother-in-law. Vishal, too, did nothing about his mother's appropriation of their child because it was the norm in his family.

When her daughter was three, Arti was pregnant again. This time she knew what she had to do. After she delivered the baby, she went straight from the hospital to her mother's home. She stayed there and refused to go back to her husband's house. She wasn't going to risk losing this daughter to them. Vishal began visiting her. Initially, he stayed the day. Then he began staying a couple of nights and so on. 'By then I had lost all hope of having a normal married life. But I also had two children. I just decided to make the most of what I had. I worked, I looked after my daughter and my mother. Vishal's choices were his own. Or his mother's,' she says.

All told, it was a good arrangement, but Arti missed her firstborn terribly. She kept trying to persuade him to bring the older child too. He was too scared of his mother to risk it. He'd promise her he would do so the next time and the time after and so on, but never managed it. Arti visited the house every week or ten days. 'One day, I went there and my older daughter was playing in the garden. I remember she looked up and saw me and there was this expression of utter terror on her face. Like she had seen a monster. She ran to her grandmother,' Arti recalls. They had told the child so many horror stories about Arti that her child was genuinely scared of her.

During these visits home, Maji did not ever make any conversation with her or ask her why she wasn't coming back. She just barked instructions. 'Fetch this, cook this, clean this,' were the only words she used.

Arti tried hard to get her child back. She went to the police station a couple of times. But they spun complicated procedures around her and refused to take any action. In the meantime, Vishal was feeling awkward about staying with Arti in her mother's home. It wasn't the done thing, society laughed at the 'ghar jamai', he told Arti. Slowly, he let on that he had an apartment in another part of Delhi. The three of them should move there, he suggested.

Arti insisted that he bring the older child there too. He promised her he would. The day after they moved into his apartment, Vishal went to fetch the older child. But he came back with one of the nephews instead. Maji had refused to let her go, he said, and had offered the boy instead. 'Basically, they planted their spy. The boy, who was sixteen or so, would relate everything that happened in the apartment to my mother-in-law,' Arti says.

Arti continued to try and get her daughter back. One day, when the child was about five or so, she managed to catch her alone for a few minutes. 'Why don't you love mama?' she asked.

'If I love you, then all these people (her father's family) will get angry with me. They will all stop loving me,' the little girl told her.

'I could see how torn she was. I thought then, for her sake, I should make the sacrifice. If she is happy with them, I thought, I shouldn't make her feel conflicted. So with a broken heart, I let her go. I hope she realizes one day that I did it out of my love for her. Maybe, when she becomes a mother herself, she'll figure it out,' Arti sobs.

Over the years, the older child became another one of the rude, abusive youngsters that Vishal's house seems to breed. She was always aggressive towards Arti, calling her names and saying things just to spite her. 'You are ugly, my aunts are beautiful,' she would tell Arti if she dressed up for a puja or a festival. They met every week or fortnight when Arti visited her in-laws. Despite the fact that Vishal had moved out to be with her, there still wasn't much intimacy or companionship in the marriage. They both knew they had been dealt a bad hand and they just resolved to live with it as best they could. Arti remembers how she felt he was her soulmate when she first saw him and can't stop thinking about how foolish she was.

When the younger child turned five, Arti began to worry that she was at the age where her mother-in-law would want to grab her. She never left her alone with Vishal's family when she was visiting. She didn't allow her any phone calls that were unmonitored. One morning, when she was getting ready to go office, one of the sisters barged into the house. She began pulling all of Arti's things from the cupboard and piling them on the floor. 'What are you doing?' Arti asked.

'This is our house,' she said and continued riffling through the stuff.

Arti wondered what this latest move meant, but she was getting late for work. She decided she would deal with it in the evening. But all morning, she had a sick feeling in her stomach. Then suddenly, she realized that it was her younger daughter's last day of school before the autumn break. She grabbed her bag and ran to her school. There, parked outside, was Vishal's family car. The driver was inside.

'What are you doing here?' she asked him.

'I've been told to bring baby home,' he replied.

Arti went to the school, grabbed her daughter and ran with her to her mother's house. She never went back to that apartment. All her things were still inside—her clothes, jewellery, everything— but she couldn't care less. None of that was worth losing another daughter.

Now the older child is fourteen and the younger one is eleven. The older girl is less rude to her. She talks to Arti about casual things, her favourite singer Adele, the movie she watched recently and things like that. But she still doesn't acknowledge that she is her mother. Her loyalties, which were firmly with her grandmother, are now shifting to one of her aunts. 'Last year, my dad-in-law passed away. I went there for a few days. My daughter had a note from school, which was to be signed by the mother. Loudly, in front of me, she told her aunt, "This says to be signed by the mother. You are my mother, you should sign it." I know she did it just to spite me, but what can I do?' Arti says.

At least she is now certain that the younger child is safe from them. Having moved out of the apartment, Arti and Vishal rented a house near her mother. They live there with their younger daughter.

Arti is forty-three now, and has been out of Maji's clutches for many years, but she has not recovered from the past. She has no sense of confidence, she says, and every time she feels happy about something, she finds herself thinking about the child who is lost to her. She can't laugh without feeling guilty. 'You may have heard many stories about mothers-in-law by now. But mine is unique.'

When he's with her, Vishal proclaims helplessness over his mother's ploys. When he goes to his mother, he proclaims helplessness over his wife's stubbornness. On both sides, he is the invisible force. Sometimes, he plays the victim. But often, he just sits there quietly, trying to keep his mother and his wife happy. He manages to do neither. It's been fifteen years since he married. So far, three lives—that of Arti's and their two kids'—have been compromised. But Maji continues to wreak havoc and Vishal still has no strategy other than stonewalling. Even Godot would have appeared by now.

11

A Full Circle

Name	Age (in 2013)	Husband	Married
Lalitha	60	Krishnan	1975

Among Malayali women of a certain age, telling stories of misery is a competitive sport. It often begins with a listing of illnesses—real and imagined. Then, depending on the kind of reaction they get from the listeners, the story moves on. To problems with the house help (who are always unreliable, often suspicious); their children (none of whom are living lives that match their potential); to their siblings who are alive (and not pulling their weight in selling the ancestral property) and siblings who are dead (and have left them to solve this problem all on their own); the neighbours (who wake up too late and bang doors in their rush to get to work); the traffic (which makes it impossible to walk on the streets they are too ill to walk on anyway); the price of sardines (which they remember buying at one rupee for a lot of hundred); and the government (which is not thinking about the long-term effect of their policies). If you still appear to be keen, they move on to the problems faced by their relatives and friends, starting with the sickest and moving slowly to the one worst affected by government policies.

I wasn't prepared for the 'full treatment' one morning when I dropped in to visit my aunt. I had an hour before I was to leave for the airport and was prepared for a breakfast of good dosas and a quick round-up about her health. As soon as I walked in, the airline sent a message saying my flight was cancelled. That left me with three hours and gave my aunt an unforeseen jackpot of a captive listener. I was digesting the half-dozen dosas by lying on the sofa and saying 'hmmm' every three minutes as my aunt droned on. She was done with her miseries and those of her family members. 'Poor Lalitha, she is back in Bangalore now. Her mother-in-law is so dominating. And her mother-in-law's mother also lives with them. And poor thing, last year, her only son got married. Forget finding a Tamil Brahmin wife, he selected a Christian one. Lalitha was so torn, she kept saying no, but last year she had to say yes . . .'

I sat up. 'Who is this Lalitha?' I asked.

'My friend, I told you, who lives in Bangalore. Her mother-in-law is so dominating. And poor thing last year . . .' Aunt stuck to her script.

'Could I speak with her?' I asked.

'Of course,' aunt said and, without wondering even for a second about why I would want to speak to her friend, put on her spectacles, peered at her phone and called her.

'Aunty was just telling me that you have a dominating mother-in-law,' I told Lalitha when she came on the line, 'and your son is recently married. I want to talk to you about having a mother-in-law and being one. Could I come to Bangalore and meet you?'

'Sure, why not?' said the enthusiastic voice at the other end. 'We could even Skype, you know.'

A couple of months later, I went to Bangalore. Lalitha picked a place close to her home where we could meet. I got lost and called her for directions. In a tone of practical impatience, she told me, 'Please give the phone to your driver.' Lalitha seemed efficient and used to taking charge. When I finally managed to find the place, I saw her standing outside.

She is dressed in a printed silk sari. Her hair is tied in a severe bun, no flyaways, no mess. Fair and big-toothed, she smiles easily and talks rapidly. We sit alfresco and the diamonds in her nose and ears glitter wildly in the evening sun. She is, I have to concede, the perfect icon of the Tam Brahm aunty of 2013. The sort who will wake up at 4 for the Satya Narayan puja and then Skype with the grandchildren in Sacramento. She has a gift for me, a little flashlight that I could fit into my jeans pocket—'Because you travel so much, it's sensible and safe,' she says while handing it over. I get the feeling that 'sensible' and 'safe' are perhaps Lalitha's life philosophies. Despite the fact that we are one generation apart and have never met before, she is instantly warm.

'I am very religious and conservative, a typical south Indian,' she tells me, 'and my mother-in-law is a very dominating lady.' The second of six children, Lalitha got married as soon as she finished her college. Her husband, an appropriate man from the same community whose horoscope matched hers, had a promising career in a multinational company. Lalitha moved to Bangalore, to live with her parents-in-law as well as Uma, her husband's younger sister. It was exactly the kind of life she knew she would lead.

In the early days, her mother-in-law was rather sweet to her, Lalitha tells me. She was the one who taught her the right way to do all the pujas. She even learned to cook from her. 'We were quite like friends then,' she says. In quick succession, Lalitha had two babies—first a girl and then a boy. A couple of years later, Uma got married and moved to Mumbai. She had a daughter too. Then tragedy struck. Uma's husband was killed in a road accident.

Frightened and depressed, Uma moved back to her parents' home with her daughter. The family was plunged into mourning. In the seventies and early eighties, young widowhood was a virtual life sentence. 'Everything changed when my brother-in-law passed away. More than twenty years later, we still haven't gone back to normal. My mother-in-law is still depressed about her daughter being a widow,' Lalitha says.

Lalitha's life too changed forever. At home, any expression of joy or celebration was banned. She wasn't allowed to dress up or go for a movie with her husband or even wear flowers in her hair. 'Because Uma couldn't do any of these things, I was told that I couldn't either,' she says. When she got married, Lalitha told herself that her mother-in-law was her new mother. At the time, she didn't think too much about being 'dominated'. But once Uma moved in, Lalitha found that her life was increasingly unlivable. She did feel sympathetic to Uma's plight, but she didn't see why that meant she too had to live a life of empathetic widowhood.

Uma and she never hit it off. While Lalitha is friendly and affable, Uma is a loner. In the beginning, when she had just got married, it didn't matter that she and Uma weren't close. Lalitha knew it was only a question of a couple of years until Uma got married and left home. Uma herself was looking forward to a future outside that home. But now they all had to realign their expectations.

Things changed. Her mother-in-law grew more protective and possessive about her daughter. The only person who mattered in the house was Uma. 'So much so that I couldn't even pamper my children, for fear that Uma would feel bad about her daughter,' Lalitha says. As the years progressed, the house became suffocating. Resentment built up. Unpleasant things were said. Even more remained unsaid. Lalitha felt that her mother-in-law and Uma were ganging up against her. Her husband, like most men of his generation, kept himself away from the goings-on in his house. His job was to provide for the family and he focused solely on it.

Since Uma's return to Bangalore, nothing Lalitha did was deemed right. Every meal she served was criticized, every puja she did was considered inadequate and ineffective. As her children grew up, Lalitha threw herself into other activities. She is an active member of the local bhajan circle. Being a trained classical singer, she led the bhajan recitals at several important ceremonies. Her mother-in-law neither complimented her, nor did she encourage her singing in any way.

Often, she pretended like Lalitha wasn't around. She and Uma criticized her in the third person in front of her. 'Oh, this one made that horrible vegetable today,' they would say or, 'Is this one going out again today?' Lalitha began to spend more and more time outside the house. She went to the temple every day. She joined devotional groups and spent time with them in the evenings. Her father-in-law, for as long as he was alive, was supportive of her. He encouraged her to get out of the house more, meet people, pray and travel.

Her children, too, were always a great source of solace to her. Accomplished, loving and devoted, they were her weapons against her mother-in-law. No matter what her mother-in-law said about her, she could always look at her children and know she had done a darned good job raising them. As a mother, she was an unqualified success. And when it was her time to be a mother-in-law, she promised herself that she would never behave so badly.

As the years passed and her children grew up, Lalitha learned to detach herself from her family. 'At one point, after my children left home, I realized that I wasn't going to get help from anyone. I told myself that no matter what the situation was I just had to handle it myself. It was quite liberating,' she says.

If she went to the market and bought brinjal, for instance, her mother-in-law would remark that those were the worst brinjals she had ever seen and that Lalitha wasn't even capable of shopping for vegetables. Uma would have bought much better brinjals had she gone, her mother-in-law would say.

When she was younger, this kind of hurtful remark would

prompt Lalitha to flee to her room upstairs in tears. Now that she had stopped caring, she would merely reply that she agreed with her mother-in-law and that henceforth Uma should be the one to go and buy things for the kitchen. Lalitha herself could use the time to go visit a friend or do something she enjoyed.

It isn't much, on the face of it, but it is a significant reflection of how empowered she feels now. 'Still, sometimes I feel like crying, I won't deny it. But then I push myself into other activities. I am sixty now, this is my time. If I don't live now, when will I?' she asks.

In the meantime, her children have built their own careers and lives. Lalitha's daughter, who is as pious and orthodox as Lalitha, got married and moved to the US. There she holds down a full-time job and looks after her two children. Her son Karthik, who is certainly the light of her life, was a brilliant student. He finished his engineering degree and then got admission in an elite MBA programme. Lalitha was waiting for Karthik to give her the nod, so she could find him a perfect wife

Karthik, though, had other plans. In business school, he met Michelle and decided she was the one for him. Michelle's parents are originally from Mangalore but she had grown up in Delhi. He knew it would break his mother's heart that she wasn't a Tamilian, a Brahmin or a Hindu. But he was certain that he would be able to wear his mother's objections down.

After two years in school, the young couple took up jobs in Mumbai. Lalitha was in the US then, helping her daughter with her new baby. Her husband called her one morning and said that Karthik was very ill. He had been admitted to the hospital and Uma and he were leaving for Mumbai to help look after him.

Until his dad and aunt came, Michelle was taking care of Karthik. She stayed with him all night and went to office straight from the hospital. When his family arrived, Michelle met them at the hospital, updated them and left for work. That night, delirious with fever, Karthik called out for Michelle several times. His father heard it. It wasn't hard to put two and two together; he gauged that Karthik and Michelle were in a serious relationship. When he spoke to Lalitha, he joked to her that she should prepare herself for some 'good news' from her son.

'What is it?' Lalitha asked him, anxious. She didn't have the patience to wait for Karthik to tell her.

'Your son is going to marry a Christian girl,' he told her.

Lalitha nearly had a heart attack when she heard it. 'No, no, you are just joking with me,' she told her husband. She was certain that it wasn't true. By the time she returned to India, she had worked herself into such a frenzy that she couldn't wait for Karthik to bring the topic up. One day, when he was visiting them in Bangalore, she asked, 'Appa was saying something about you the other day. Do you have a friend called Michelle from college?' She heard herself and thought she was sounding overtly breezy and casual, but she simply couldn't hold on to her anxiety any longer.

'Yes,' he said.

'Is she a good friend?'

'Of course, she is,' he said.

'I just knew then at the bottom of my heart that this was true. But I refused to believe it. I just lived in denial. I told myself if I didn't think about it, it would go away,' she tells me.

A few months later, Karthik came to Bangalore again. He was out all day. In the evening, he went for a quiz competition and came home the winner. He was really excited and buzzing with his victory. Lalitha had just finished her evening pujas. After she congratulated him, he told her to sit down. There was something he wanted to talk about. 'Amma, I have something to tell you and you must say yes,' he began. 'I want to marry Michelle. I know you aren't happy about the fact that she isn't a Brahmin girl, but she is perfect for me. There is no one else I'd rather be with. You have to agree to this, Amma.'

Lalitha started to cry. 'Think of me,' she said, 'how can I face all these people with this news?' She knew this would be another reason her mother-in-law would use for her taunts. Karthik told her she should not bother about other people. He begged her to just meet Michelle first, before she said no. Lalitha refused.

I ask Lalitha what her objections were. She reiterates that she was scared of society and the extended family. 'Karthik does not understand because he doesn't live here any more. I have to continue to live with these people. Obviously, I had issues with it.' Lalitha's friends, the people in her bhajan groups and the ones she went on pilgrimages with, were also extremely traditional and conservative. To them, finding a way to tune out their annoying mother-in-law was a good thing. But losing a son to a Christian girl was a scandal. Lalitha knew she wouldn't find support anywhere.

To me, it seemed like Lalitha was so involved in her culture and tradition that she simply did not see a possibility of a non-Brahmin daughter-in-law. Now that she was confronted by the possibility of having one, she did not know what to do. Nothing in the life she had led so far suggested that it was all right for her son to marry outside the community. She was an orthodox south Indian lady—all her life she had dealt with her problems through that prism, never defying her mother-in-law, devoting herself to her children, finding solace in religion. Suddenly the foundations were being uprooted.

Soon, she realized that Karthik was visiting home very often. Every couple of months, he came to Bangalore on some pretext or the other. And each time he would bring up the conversation about Michelle. Lalitha made sure she was never available for these discussions. She thought if she ignored it, it would go away.

A year later, she was in Mumbai visiting Karthik. She was set to go to the US from there and spend six months with her daughter. It was a trip she was looking forward to. In Bangalore, her mother-in-law and Uma were driving her crazy. She was happy to be out of there for seven months: one month with Karthik in Mumbai and the rest in the US.

During her stay in Mumbai, Karthik had asked her nearly every day if she would meet Michelle but Lalitha refused. She still didn't 'have the guts' to say yes to the marriage. Late one evening—Lalitha remembers she had even changed into her nightclothes—the doorbell rang. She opened the door and saw a girl standing outside. 'I am a friend of Karthik's,' she said. Somehow, Lalitha knew that this was no ordinary friend; this was *that* friend.

Lalitha's heart was racing. She had no idea what to say or do. Michelle had brought some fruits. Karthik took them from her and disappeared from the room under the pretext of leaving them in the kitchen. A most awkward few minutes went by. Lalitha was fraught. 'Oh my God, these two are a team and I am all alone,' she thought to herself. She doesn't remember what they talked about, or whether they talked about anything at all.

As soon as Michelle left, Lalitha reached for her phone. She did not have an international dialing facility. So she texted her daughter in the US and asked her to call back. As soon as the phone rang, she grabbed it and burst into tears. Her daughter was driving to work at the time, she tried to calm Lalitha down as much as she could. Then she called her husband, who was home, and asked him to please speak to her and get her to relax a little bit. Late that night, after she was spent from all that crying, Karthik asked her what she thought of Michelle. Lalitha said she was never going to say yes to this wedding. She felt it was all getting out of control and she was relieved to go to the US and hide for some time.

By the time she came back, the whole family was lining up against her. Her husband brought the topic of the wedding up, almost immediately upon her reaching Bangalore. He told her that had Michelle been a Brahmin, he would himself have gone over to her parents' with a proposal. The young couple had been nice enough to wait nearly four years for her permission. 'He told me not to delay it. That it was inevitable and I should just agree,' she says. 'I told him that I had done pujas and maintained fasts to get Karthik out of "the affair".'

'Well, Michelle must have done even more,' he laughed.

Grudgingly, she agreed to meet her. She went back to Mumbai and Karthik called Michelle over. When she arrived, Lalitha told her she should first speak to her daughter in the US. 'She knows my heart best.' They called her and for forty minutes Michelle chatted with her future sister-in-law.

She told Michelle that simply because she was petite, she shouldn't assume her mother-in-law was weak. Not even for a minute had she assumed her future mother-in-law was weak, Michelle told her honestly. She also told Michelle that even though Lalitha had come around to the possibility of Karthik's marrying her, it did not mean that she was happy about it. When she hung up, Michelle came over and told Lalitha, 'Amma, you can trust me. I'll listen to whatever you say.'

'I felt quite happy that she called me Amma,' Lalitha tells me.

Now that she had agreed to the wedding, Lalitha felt she should work on herself. Even though Michelle wasn't of her choice, it still didn't mean she could break her resolutions of not behaving with her daughter-in-law in the manner in which her mother-in-law had behaved with her. She told herself that she wouldn't be a dominating, arrogant, annoying mother-in-law. Lalitha was torn between her anger at this girl who had brought this complication into her life and the promises she had made herself when she was the victim of her mother-in-law's taunts.

In this battle between her two selves, her bad side won initially. First, she said she couldn't deal with the Anglicized and very Christian-sounding name, Michelle. 'We'll call you Meena,' she told Michelle. And second, she wasn't going to agree to a church wedding. 'Karthik is my son and I have so many dreams for his wedding. I wouldn't like to ruin it with a church wedding,' she told her. Surprisingly, Michelle agreed to both her conditions.

I felt this was an awkward juncture in our conversation. Daughters-in-law I met whose names had been changed by the families they married into, or had conflicts with their in-laws about the rituals around the wedding, spoke about these issues with a great deal of pain. Even though Lalitha told me that Michelle was fine with these demands, I thought they weren't appropriate conditions for Lalitha to insist on. I was wondering how to tell her this, without sounding offensive, when Lalitha said, 'I regret that. I shouldn't have behaved like that.' I was relieved to hear that. I could continue to like her.

When Lalitha went back to Bangalore, after having arranged the details with Michelle, she found that things had been moved around in the puja room. For three years she had kept a few special photos of gods. These were the anti-marriage gods she'd recruited for her anti-Michelle war. All those photos were now missing. When she turned around, she saw her mother-in-law standing behind her. 'You have failed,' she told Lalitha. 'And because of you, we now have a Christian daughter-in-law.' Lalitha knew her worst fears were now realized. The family would throw mud at her. She would never hear the last of her poor parenting skills.

Karthik married Michelle in Bangalore. The wedding was entirely Tamil Brahmin in its character. After this, everyone travelled to Delhi, where Michelle's parents lived. They hosted a big reception and a small church wedding. Only the two families were present in the church and a priest blessed the couple. 'Walking to the church was the saddest moment of my life,' Lalitha tells me. 'But the good part is that I adore Meena. She is a wonderful person. She knows I am orthodox and she forgives me my inability to accept everything about her.'

After the wedding Karthik and Michelle moved to New York. Lalitha has been on a long-distance project to make Michelle as

Brahminical as is possible. She insists that she wear a bindi and that she never remove her mangalsutra. 'But I tell her nicely, I don't order her,' she says. The last time Michelle sent her a photograph, Lalitha noticed that she wasn't wearing her mangalsutra. When they Skyped, she asked her about it. 'Oh, it's just hidden inside the neckline of the top,' she told her. Lalitha is suspicious about this reply, but shrugs and says, 'It is also possible that she was wearing it and it was hidden.' I try to look earnest when I agree with her.

Lalitha hopes Meena, which is the name she uses for Michelle even with me, will carry forward at least half the customs and traditions she observes. In this regard though, Karthik is an even greater source of worry. He was quite religious when he was living at home. 'Now just to impress Meena, he pretends like he doesn't care about religion,' she tells me. Last year, when Lalitha visited them in New York, they went to a temple at Flushing. The priest gave them a flower and some sindoor. Michelle left the flower behind and smeared the sindoor messily all over her forehead.

Right there, in front of the temple, Karthik wiped it off her. 'And it was a Friday to boot,' Lakshmi shudders as she recalls, 'it's a special day for married women. I was really upset. I didn't talk all the way back home. They kept asking me why I was upset. Meena, I can understand. Of course, Karthik knew what he had done wrong.' In the evening, Lalitha went for a long walk to clear her head. When she came back, she told Karthik what she thought of his action. 'He apologized. Said he hadn't thought all of that. Then Meena went in and wore a big bindi and walked around the house all evening with that on her forehead. She did that just to make me happy,' she says.

What makes Karthik's behaviour even starker for Lalitha is that her daughter manages to maintain all the Tamil Brahmin customs. Her grandkids, although born and raised in the US, chant their mantras every morning before school. She cannot understand where she went wrong with her beloved son.

Once Karthik and Meena decide to have kids, Lalitha knows there will be more issues. She hopes the children will be raised as Brahmins. But she doubts it will be so easy.

'You remind me a lot of Meena,' Lalitha tells me.

'It's possibly because I am not wearing a bindi or a mangalsutra,' I laugh.

It is apparent that these lapses of mine worry her. In the café, all around us, are young people—college students and smart executives—living the middle-class Indian dream. On this hot summer day, they are dressed in shorts and clothes with no sleeves, stepping out for a smoke and hugging and kissing their friends in the easy and casual manner of the young. Lalitha's cultural confusions are understandable. She was raised to live in a different world. Even as she adapts to this new one, she does find it difficult to shed the past. It cannot be easy for her. I empathize with her. Yet, I flinch each time she refers to Michelle as Meena.   ·

Back in Gurgaon, I meet Michelle. It's 5 p.m. on a Saturday, and as shoppers stroll around us, we find a quiet table in a near-empty café. I ask for a double shot of coffee to make up for a missed siesta. Michelle is certain that she'll have nothing. When I insist, she tells me she has just finished lunch with her family at TGIF, and it involved quite a few of their ultimate margaritas: drinks so big that you could nearly drown in them.

Young, enthusiastic and easy, she was wearing neither a bindi nor a mangalsutra. I notice the absence of these immediately. But I am more curious about how she is dealing with her new name. Wasn't she offended by this Hinduization of her identity? I ask, certain that she would tell me she was. I'm surprised when she shrugs. 'Nah, not really,' she says.

The change of name wasn't a big deal, she tells me, because her name had always been mauled out of shape. People call her all kinds of things from Mickey to Michael. 'So when Amma told me that they would call me Meena, I just thought of it as yet another name that I had. And really, some five or six people in the world call me Meena. I am still Michelle to me, so it doesn't matter,' she says. She thinks of it as their pet name for her. When I probe and pry, she eventually says that in the four years that it took to get Lalitha to agree to the wedding, she had imagined she would have to pay some price. This was a small one, a battle she was quite all right with losing.

I remember Keisha telling me that the only time she threw a fit was when she saw that, in the wedding cards, her name was printed as Kamla. I ask Michelle how her name was on the card. 'In all the cards I was Michelle, except in the one for the religious wedding. This was like one of the hundred ceremonies we had. In that card even Karthik's name was different—I don't know what the exact process is, but I think they all have a religious name which is different from their real name—so I didn't protest,' she says. Karthik, on the other hand, has a huge issue with his mother rechristening his wife. He insists that she call her Michelle. He always refers to her as Michelle and they have long arguments where he talks about Michelle and his mother talks about Meena.

In the four years that it took for Lalitha to agree, Michelle stayed largely cool and mostly out of the picture. Her own family was not the sort to rush her into a marriage. They had met Karthik and they quite liked him. They knew the two of them were serious about each other and they left them to find a way out of the situation. A couple of times, Karthik suggested that they should just go ahead and marry. 'If my mother attends the wedding, great. If not, it would be her loss,' he told her.

Michelle was tempted to agree a couple of times. But she decided it wouldn't be a wise choice. 'We were living in the same city, we hung around all the time. I wasn't pregnant or any such thing. Actually, there was no reason to chase a wedding date,' she says. Since there wasn't a reason to rush into a wedding, they may as well give his mother some time to come around, she decided.

The wait wasn't very stressful for her. It was Karthik's fight, really. Every couple of months, he had to bring this up with his mother and things would get very heated. And even though Karthik and his mum were close, Michelle tells me, during those four years, each time they spoke they ended up having a massive row.

I ask Michelle about ambushing Lalitha in that Mumbai apartment. What did she feel about that first meeting? At this, Michelle pauses for a bit. She has to think. After several starts, she shakes her head and begins. 'Sometimes Karthik processes things in a very guy sort of stupid way. We decided that we should meet his mother, who had by then been in town for a month or so. Karthik picked a date and asked me to come over at a certain time,' she says. Michelle assumed that Lalitha was expecting her. So she dressed appropriately, brought some fruits—not over the top and not too little—and went over. She assumed there would be things that Lalitha would want to talk to her about. She even did a dry run with her room-mate.

'"What would you say if she asked about the difference in your religions?"

'"Yes, I am aware there are differences. But I am ready to work on them. We could find a middle ground that we are both comfortable in."

'My room-mate and I ran through all possible questions and I prepared Miss Universe–type politically correct answers for them,' Michelle tells me.

Still, it was with trepidation that she rang the bell. 'It threw me that Karthik's mother just froze on seeing me. There was no conversation at all. It was very awkward. She sat there and looked out of the window. I didn't know where to look,' Michelle says. It was a bit of an anticlimax. Nothing of substance was discussed. And when Michelle left that evening, it was with the feeling that it had been a bad start.

The next time they met was after Lalitha had reluctantly agreed to the wedding. Then she spent most of the time talking on the phone to Karthik's sister in the US. The third time, Lalitha was arriving in Mumbai early one weekday morning. Michelle picked her up from the airport and dropped her home. That was the first time they had an actual conversation. 'Because she is such a warm person, I think, we sort of instantly connected. There was never any awkwardness,' she tells me.

Michelle tells her friends that the fact that they waited four years actually helped her relationship with her mother-in-law. Once Lalitha accepted the fact that Karthik was marrying Michelle, she was 100 per cent on board. 'It would have been very different if we had just gone ahead and registered our marriage in the court or some such. I think she is appreciative of the fact that her consent mattered so much to us, that we were ready to wait four years for it.'

Religion isn't a big deal for her. She is a believer but she isn't religious. Michelle equates Lalitha's demands of her with those made by her mother. When she is in Delhi with her parents, her mother will insist that they go to church for Christmas. So she does. Similarly, when she is in Bangalore, she participates in whatever Lalitha asks her to. 'She knows I am not religious. But she does want to teach me about their customs. That is . . .' she waits for the appropriate word '. . . that's a little weird.'

One of the difficulties Michelle has with this aspect of her marriage is that she had no idea Karthik's family was this religious. Karthik is not religious at all, she says, he never has been. I think back to Lalitha telling me that Karthik had begun to pretend that he wasn't religious in order to impress Michelle, but I don't bring it up. 'When you meet a person, you think they are a reflection of their family, right?' Michelle explains. 'So when I saw how blasé Karthik was about religion, I assumed his family was like that too.'

Some parts of what Lalitha asks of her, Michelle is happy to do. Some parts, not so much. For Lalitha, religion is a mix of gods and planets. So astrology plays as much a part in her religious life as pujas and gods do. 'Ever so often, she would bring out horoscopes and make predictions. She would tell me this period is going to be bad, and stuff like that. That bothers me. More than anything else, I don't understand why she would stress herself out with these things. Come on, man, astrology is just . . . crap.'

She suddenly remembers that I have a line of communication to her mother-in-law as well. It's apparent to me that Michelle thinks she had gone too far and Lalitha would not be happy if she heard of her scepticism. So she smiles and shrugs and says, 'Oh well, there is no other word for it.' And we laugh.

I get the sense that Michelle is an easy kid, the sort of person who doesn't sweat the small stuff. She is nearly thirty, she has a promising career in consulting, she is widely travelled and comfortable in any part of the world. She isn't the sort to waste time trying to read between her mother-in-law's lines.

When I ask her about Lalitha's opposition to the church wedding, Michelle raises her hands. 'See, the deal is everyone got what they wanted for the wedding. My parents wanted to invite some three hundred people to the Delhi reception and have just the family for the church ceremony. They got that. My mother-in-law wanted the whole two-day Tamil Brahmin wedding and a reception for eight hundred people. She got that. If these weren't enough, we even had a sangeet and a mehendi—which weren't really part of the customs on either side. So no one can complain,' she says. I ask her what she herself wanted. 'I just wanted to get the whole thing done with.'

Eventually, of course, because they had so many events in so many places, Michelle's dream of going for the Wimbledon championship for her honeymoon had to be shelved. With the four days they managed to allot to it, Karthik and she took a quick holiday in Thailand instead. 'That was a compromise,' she says. 'Now, a year and a half later, I have finally stopped bringing that up. I was super pissed off then.'

The young couple is soon moving to Singapore. That's a short flight from Bangalore and she is certain she will be seeing and living with Lalitha a lot more. Michelle is cool, but she isn't a fool. She knows that with proximity will come more issues. Her mother-in-law has already started talking about a grandson.

For one, Michelle is not sure if she is ready yet to have a baby. And more importantly, she is annoyed with this 'grandson' business. She corrects Lalitha—tells her it's grandchild—but it doesn't work. Lalitha apologizes but tells her, in her religion, it's important that it be a grandson. 'I know these conversations will gnaw at me. The baby thing might be an issue. In general, since she is very accepting of me now, it is easy for me to have these discussions with her. It's not a situation where she dictates things to me and threatens me with a breakdown of our relationship. Also, Karthik and I agree on most of these things. So it's not like I am speaking a language different from his. But you never know with these things. They could become a big deal.'

Once the baby arrives, the difference in their religion is likely to come bouncing back up. Now that they are closer—geographically—all of these issues are certain to be magnified. Also, when they have a child, Lalitha is going to be around them a lot more. What has worked for Michelle is her strategy of agreeing to everything her mother-in-law says but going ahead and doing exactly what she wants. The premise of that strategy demands that they don't see each other much. That might not be the case in the future.

Michelle and Karthik have talked about it a little. If he wants his children to be raised to be Tamil Brahmins, she told him, then he will have to play a prominent role in that. She cannot be expected to become a full-on champion of an alien culture. Going by how he has been so far, it's unlikely that Karthik will want his children to recite the shlokas before heading for school. But Michelle isn't the sort to bring things to the edge. She will wait and watch.

In the four years that Lalitha didn't agree to the wedding, the real damage was wrought in her relationship with Karthik. Even today, they cannot have a conversation that does not end in a fight. Often, then, Lalitha uses Michelle as the go-between. She is happy being the medium of communication. 'That's not asking a lot of me,' she says, 'I just pass the messages back and forth.'

Michelle is aware of Lalitha's problems with her mother-in-law. When she goes to Bangalore, she usually just stays upstairs. The fact that she doesn't understand Tamil means she doesn't get dragged into their arguments. But she knows there are many. And she knows that Lalitha is very clear that she doesn't want her relationship with Michelle to be troubled in a similar fashion. 'I see that she isn't being mean when she insists on some unreasonable things. She is just conditioned that way.'

After I leave, I consider—purely for the sake of making mischief—telling Lalitha that Michelle was wearing neither a bindi nor a mangalsutra. 'I looked and it wasn't hidden in the neckline of her shirt,' I would write. But I could almost hear my aunt droning, 'and my friend Lalitha, her daughter-in-law does not wear a bindi or a mangalsutra, you know . . .' and so I let it pass.

Lalitha calls me as soon as I reach home after my meeting. 'Was she positive about me?' she inquires eagerly. I tell her she was. She asks again. I assure her again. Then she asks the same thing in five other ways.

I could see how eager Lalitha was to find validation from her daughter-in-law. When I was talking to her, I thought Michelle's empathy for her mother-in-law was the only thing that made me optimistic about the future of Mummyji relationships. However, the anxiety in Lalitha's voice in finding out what her daughter-in-law thought of her was the real sign of change. Love demands reciprocation, and acceptance works best when it is mutual. In spite of all the gruesome stories I've been privy to, in Lalitha and Michelle I finally find hope.

Conclusion

All I wanted to do was listen to funny stories about mothers-in-law. Yes, I read the papers. I know how grim the situation could be. Certainly, there was nothing funny about the son murdering his mother because he was tired of coming home to the squabbles between her and his wife. Or the story of the Mumbai daughter-in-law who had to file a case against her mother-in-law just to claim her husband's dead body. But I thought they were the exceptions.

What I was expecting to hear was about the Mummyji who wouldn't move her cupboard out of the son's room so she could accidentally-purposely walk in on him and his wife. Or the mother-in-law who insisted on hand-feeding her thirty-five-year-old son his dinner or hand-washing his underwear. Or the one who not only insisted on accompanying her son on his honeymoon but also sharing the suite. What I didn't expect to discover was that actual mothers-in-law were as scheming and as cruel as those that appear on television. So it's fair to say that I'm pissed off. The world owes me an awesomely funny mother-in-law story.

Sadly, the reality is that we're stuck with the serious. If, like the *Kamasutra*, India can lay any claim to inventing any kind of mother-in-law–related literature, it wouldn't be a joke-book, it would be a torture manual. Not the pull-the-nails and twist-the-toes kind of torture (not always, at least) but the dripping-water kind of mental sadism. In the light of this, I have decided I am left with no choice but to turn activist. My campaign is to save you, the daughter-in-law. If you are one or if you intend to become one, you should know there is a lot you need to be saved from.

First, save yourself, daughter-in-law, from the fashion police. This was one of my most surprising revelations. I had no idea that attire was so important. In story after story, I encountered Mummyjis with an eye out for sartorial indiscretions. How the daughter-in-law dresses is so important that Mummyji lays down her conditions even before the engagement. The first to go are jeans—those symbols of westernization that stretch snugly around the ass and tight at the waist. Equally abhorred are tops that are tight (other men can see the contours of her breasts, gasp!) or sleeveless (because armpits are the most erogenous of body parts).

In my research and analysis, I realized that while these objections were anatomy-related, the real issue was about attitude. A salwar kameez (with dupatta, always with a dupatta) wearing daughter-in-law projects a certain stance. That she is a girl who is obedient. The kind who will keep her eyes firmly fixed on the ground. Who will not have an opinion of her own that is contrary to the family's. That she will serve first and eat later and she will not cheat even a little bit when she's fasting on Karva Chauth. Families want a doormat. The question, girls, is, is that what you want to be? If your answer is no, then I'd say don't agree to the dress code. Ever. Not on the day you meet Mummyji for the first time, not the day before the wedding and never after it.

Of the daughters-in-law I spoke to, Carla was the one who broke out of the dress code the quickest. It gives me hope that she will also quickly break herself out of her mother-in-law's two-storeyed west Delhi observation tower. She will manage to get Ankit and move out, to another home, perhaps another city or even another country. She has spunk and strategy. She will soon find a way out. The daughter-in-law who worries me is Rachna. Sure, her mother-in-law will dress her up in an LBD and make sure she is threaded, bleached, waxed and facial-ed to within an inch of her life, but she will never set her free. Rachna shocks me with her entirely laissez-faire attitude to life and Mummyji. The only reason she eventually married Gaurav was because she felt obliged to his mother. One day, in the not too distant future, Rachna will wake up and realize she has dug herself into a hole. And knowing her, she will stay there, feeling more miserable with every passing hour, and yet lacking the courage to climb out of it.

The second point in my activist agenda is to save women from spineless husbands. I don't particularly fancy being the Grinch who stole your delusions of happily ever after, but someone's got to do the job. So here's the truth—marriages are difficult, sometimes brutally so, and the reason most people stay in them is because they worry it will be harder to cope with being single and stuck with the tag of being a divorcee. That said, marriages do provide a kind of a security blanket, and whether they like it or not, family members are expected to look out for you. The only way to maintain a modicum of balance—between its obvious benefits and apparent threats—is to have a supportive spouse. Of those I met, women who were sure their husbands were on their side were far more likely to fight the battles they needed to in order to live a relatively happy life. Initially, Supriya went at this the wrong way. She first tried to convince her husband about his mother's goodness. When she found out that Mum was not who she thought she was, not only was she stuck with trying to figure out a way to solve this problem but was also forced to admit to Robert that she had been wrong all along. Eventually, after therapy and tragedy, Supriya realized her only option was to indulge in some straight talk with Mum. Of the women featured in this book, hers is the only story that comes full circle. She eventually manages to make peace with her mother-in-law, a significant reason for this being she knew Robert was on her side. Payal's mother-in-law is far more demonic than Supriya's and she is also one of the few daughters-in-law in this book who has managed to 'win' the battle. She is clear that she couldn't have done so without her husband Prayag's help. Seema too can laugh off her mother-in-law's wiles because her husband Srini does not succumb to his mother's emotional blackmail.

Anshika, on the other hand, has had to fight her own battles. Her husband, Rohit, loves her dearly and is on her side, but he doesn't have the courage to stand up to his parents. Had Rohit been strong enough to be vocal about his support to his wife, he would have saved all of them this constant re-airing of grievances his parents indulged in. Eventually, Anshika had to manipulate her way through her sister-in-law and find support and encouragement from her colleagues. Rohit only told her he was on her side; he left her to fight her battles alone. The couple, who are childhood sweethearts, remain close but it could have gone either way. In many of the stories, husbands who don't stand up for their wives often end up destroying their marriages.

The extreme other end of unsupportive spouses is, of course, Arti's. Her story was so startlingly cruel that even now, when I think about, I shudder. It is impossible to imagine that someone seemingly so normal, vocal and efficient was living under such unspeakable conditions. Vishal, her husband, never once stood up for her. Even when he agreed that his mother was wrong, the only action he could take was to move in with Arti for a few days in the week. It is possible that Vishal is conditioned to that existence. After all, neither of his two older brothers spoke out to their mother in support of their wives. So Vishal didn't think it was his place to do so, either. Unfortunately, this doesn't stand up as a legitimate defence. If Vishal's brothers chose to let their wives suffer, that shouldn't have been reason enough for Vishal. Many lives and many psyches have been irreparably damaged in that house. After years of therapy and medication, Arti is managing to hold on to her grief over losing her child. But she knows she will never be truly happy. Ever.

Save yourself, women, I say, from men like Vishal and his brothers. And marry Rohit and his ilk only if you find everything else about them endearing. If you are the kind of woman who knows how she wants to live her life, then you need someone like Robert or Srini. A wall to deflect life's curved balls. I always find myself rolling my eyes when I hear women say that their wedding is the most important day of their lives. It perhaps is. Certainly, *whom* you marry on that day determines how you live the rest of your life. So forget about what you'll wear and how you'll have your hair done, focus on finding a man who has your back.

Speaking of people who have your back, here's an eye-opener. That sister-in-law? She is what the word 'frenemy' was coined for. You are likely to think of her as your best friend and biggest ally. If you are the older daughter-in-law in the family, she will be the one coming in and making all the changes. Some of which you might adore her for. If you are the younger daughter-in-law, you might think that the older one will be keeping guard while you usher in some modernity. Alas, the Indian family has even more complex webs of connection than what diplomats in the external affairs ministry are familiar with. The sister-in-law is your friend, until, that is, she becomes your enemy. As long as your modernity campaign is helping her, she will be on your side. But the minute she thinks you are gaining favour with Mummyji, she will turn against you.

It doesn't take much for her to ruin your cosy comfort zone. Although Payal helped immensely in jump-starting her sister-in-law's social life, she is very wary of her. She constantly looks over her shoulder. She knows that anything she tells her sister-in-law in confidence has the potential of being used against her when things go wrong between them.

Seema, though, is thankful her younger sister-in-law has demonstrated what an indifferent daughter-in-law is like. After five years of going on and on about Seema's lapse in not wearing a nine-yard sari for the wedding, her mother-in-law has at last realized that it shouldn't have mattered so much. Seema did everything right, but she didn't wear the sari. Now the younger daughter-in-law seems to be doing everything wrong, yet she wore the sari. Faced with this paradox, Srini's mother is finally making her peace with Seema.

This might sound strange. But it's not. Save yourself from a mother-in-law who hands down her used bikinis. It could also be her barely worn Victoria's Secret that Daddyji brought back from his trip to the US in 1969. Or it might be something totally different. The thing is, save yourself from a mother-in-law who seems too cool and too 'out there'. Don't marry a man just because all his friends think his mother is chilled out. Do not judge a mother-in-law by the yuppie language she uses. She can ask people to bugger off and call her friends bastards, but that does not mean she will extend that liberty to you. In all probability, like Deepa's mother-in-law, this seemingly cool specimen is probably that way just to be at the centre of everyone's attention. (I would wager that Rachna's mother-in-law also occupies some real estate on this spectrum.)

Quiz your spouse-to-be on what he thinks of his parents. If he is also swirling, glassy-eyed, in a vortex of his mother's coolness, think again. Is this the person you want to marry? Do you want your mother-in-law to be a permanent third party in the marriage? I found it shocking that Deepa's marriage crumbled in the time I was viewing it. Despite their problems, it seemed to me that she was willing to focus on Sandeep's positive qualities and ignore the rest. But as she began to realize the seriousness of her medical condition, she was determined to make the best of the time she had left. No more compromises. No more stepping aside for Neeta Aunty. If Sandeep still came with strings attached firmly to his mother, she wasn't interested in wasting her years on him. I say more power to her!

Whether you have a terminal illness or not, this next one is a non-negotiable. Save yourself from the Mummyji who asks you to quit your job. If you're sitting with your mother-in-law and she says, 'After marriage you'll have to quit your job,' don't even bother asking her why. Just run. And don't stop until you reach office. Of all the demands that the Mummyji makes of you, this one is the most damaging. If you have had a career, being a housewife—against your will—is likely to leave you frustrated, angry and constantly grimacing. Stand up for yourself; stand up for your right to have a career. You've probably been worrying that if you put your career ahead of your marriage, you would end up looking like one of those feminists who come on television debates and shout impractical inanities. I've news for you, sister: strident feminism is in. So embrace it. As tightly as you would your pay cheque.

The reason Mummyji asks you to quit your job when you get married is not because she feels you should 'spend time' with the husband or cook gourmet meals for him every night. The reason she wants you out of the office is because then you have no place to run to. You will have no money, and after a couple of years of staying home, no confidence in yourself to get out there. So you'll stay on, flipping chapattis and listening to an endless litany of your shortcomings. I am not saying that everyone should necessarily choose a career over home. I'm saying that that choice should be yours, and yours alone. No one has the right to ask you to choose against your career. Especially not Mummyji.

That's how Nikita lost the battle and the war. When she came back to Delhi, in an attempt to make peace with her mother-in-law, she did not look for a job. Within months, her mother-in-law had used all her maternal powers of guilt-tripping her son and got him back into her fold. Then, even when Nikita found a job, Arun forced her to quit. Today, she has neither a marriage nor a career. There is no nice way to say this: the Mummyji who forces you to quit your job does not have your best interests in her heart.

So who has your best interests? The obvious answer is, of course, you. But sometimes, it's not that obvious. Which is why, I'd say, occasionally, save yourself from yourself. Seriously. The number of stories I heard in which women made choices because that was what was shown in their favourite Bollywood film, or because the pet dog seemed to approve of the prospective groom's family and such is unbelievable. You may not realize this, but there are quite a few fools out there. Make sure you are not one of them.

Keisha, for example, had no business marrying Ashwin. And while it is apparent to anyone who has heard even the more marginal details of the story, Keisha herself thought she had made the right choice for about ten years. She had a mantra that her first boyfriend should be her husband and she saw it through. What I fail to understand is how this philosophy helped her life. She is the survivor of a ghastly union. Her marriage gave her bruises, broken bones and the brutality of rape. Ashwin's mother had done not just a deplorable job of raising him, but was also an ally in his cruelty. She enjoyed seeing Keisha beaten and kicked; she thought it served her right for her audacity in luring Ashwin away. To me it seems like all the signs about Ashwin were always there. Keisha should have saved herself from her younger self—the one who only wanted to marry her first boyfriend.

Lalitha took a while but eventually managed to save herself from her own traditional and ultra-conservative values. I totally adore Lalitha for her ability to put Michelle's happiness over her sense of being wronged. She tries hard to be the Amma her own mother-in-law wasn't. I feel certain that if Karthik had married a Tamil Brahmin girl, Lalitha would have been the ideal mother-in-law. When that didn't happen, she had to put herself through the wringer. Eventually, she managed to bury her concerns and her sense of betrayal for the sake of her son's happiness. And she sees the folly of her resistance now. 'I couldn't have asked for a better daughter-in-law,' she told me several times.

I met her daughter-in-law Michelle, and I tend to agree with Lalitha. If you are Michelle, you need no saving at all from yourself. She has the intelligence to see past the small stuff and the charm to get her way. She does worry, though, that once they move to Singapore, she will see a lot more of Lalitha. And that proximity will come in the way of her ability to not rise to Lalitha's bait.

Michelle is right to be worried. Proximity is often the death knell of a warm relationship with Mummyji. Even though Payal has not moved far from her mother-in-law, just the fact that she doesn't have to share her kitchen has helped heal her marriage. The worst of Payal's life was spent at the dining table of her mother-in-law's home, struggling to swallow food that tasted of the bitterness of their mutual resentments.

These ill effects on the daughter-in-law of being huddled around the family dining table have been well documented on television. The saas–bahu genre of Indian soaps is now about fourteen years old (that's twice the seven-year itch, for those of you who are mathematically inclined; and one full life sentence for those of you who are legally inclined) and worth nearly 200 crore rupees. Right from the pioneer, *Kyunki Saas Bhi Kabhi Bahu Thi*, the kitchen has been the war room, where plans are made and schemes are thought up in the loudest of whispers and much eye-popping. And the actual execution of these is in the dining room. After months of brewing an anti–daughter-in-law conspiracy, when Mummyji executes it, it is with a freshly steaming roti in her hand. When the daughter-in-law pushes her chair back and leaves the table, you know the camera will zoom in thrice on Mummyji and declare her the winner of that round.

I have watched at least forty hours of saas–bahu shows in the name of research. I know everything there is to know about how to humiliate and eliminate unnecessary in-laws. What shocked me though is that among the daughters-in-law I spoke to, the ones who watched the shows most keenly were the ones suffering from having the worst Mummyjis. Keisha told me that if she managed to finish her chores and catch an hour of saas–bahu on TV, she counted that as a good day. I asked her why she needed to watch a horror story of terrible in-laws when she was living in one herself. 'It makes me feel better. It tells me everyone's lives are similar. I don't feel alone in my suffering,' she told me.

I take comfort in the fact that saas–bahu soaps are now one of our best exports. A report in the *Economic Times* in January 2013 says that it's not just neighbouring Pakistan and Bangladesh who are hooked on to our shows. Even in countries flung as far as Serbia and Kenya, audiences are gripped by the Indian Mummyji's strategies to decimate the daughter-in-law. If nothing, we can be certain that daughters-in-law in other countries can now expect the same fate as those here. The Mummyji is going global and we should all be happy for her.

Since we are talking about global Mummyjis, here are two pieces of interesting findings. In Italy, a study found that the odds of a marriage surviving went up for every hundred yards the married couple put between themselves and Mummyji. The farther you stayed from Mummyji, the better were your chances of having a healthy marriage. Italian mothers, much like our own Mummyji, cannot deal with the fact that their sons are grown up and capable of living their own lives. Taking note of this problem, the courts there have made 'meddling by mother-in-law' a valid reason for divorce. The only way to survive Mummyji, dear reader, is to get as far away from her as possible. The Italians have figured it out; it's high time we did too. Take my advice: Run!

And in Japan, a study of 91,000 women over a seven-year period threw up another startling fact. Women who lived with their mothers-in-law were three times as likely to have heart disease compared to women who didn't. Forget the desire to live, Mummyjis are obliterating even our ability to live. So dismiss my call to save yourselves at your own peril. Truth is, your Mummyji is killing you. Literally. Slowly. Steadily. Stealthily. True story!

Ten Ways to Survive the Mother-in-Law

(1) Only marry the man who is on your side in any battle.

(2) Approval is not worth aspiration. Do not, under any circumstance, agree to conditions that you aren't comfortable with. If you have always wanted a career, do not say you'll quit your job, just to be approved.

(3) Give the fashion police mother-in-law a wide berth. If you are stuck with one, learn to change in the car.

(4) Look for mutual respect, not friendship.

(5) A little deception goes a long way. You can either be happy or honest. Choose the former.

(6) Distance is everything.

(7) Start early. Take on issues early in the marriage and create a precedent of dissent. Do not let them pile up and bury you under their weight.

(8) Your kids are your kids. Your rules trump home rules.

(9) Hide the remote and the mobile. Drag the husband into the crossfire.

(10) Discuss issues. Calmly. Have a margarita. Or many.

Acknowledgements

Chiki Sarkar not only conceived and commissioned this book, she is also its greatest champion. I am grateful to her for several things—for asking me to write it, the immense editorial inputs she provided and the many lunches she bought me.

Thanks to Nipa Charagi, Manisha Nanda, Sandesh Advani and my adorable aunt, Narayani Gopalakrishnan, for introducing me to some of my subjects. To Kamalika Nandi and Jayant Bhadauria in Mumbai, and Manisha Bhattacharya in Bangalore for allowing me to shamelessly help myself to their spare bedroom and their refrigerators.

Thanks to Mukund Padmanabhan, my boss, and the *Hindu Business Line*, my employer, for permitting me the liberty to work on this book while holding down a full-time job.

To my parents, Vasantha and Venugopal, for everything; my mother-in-law Eshwari for not being like Arti's, Keisha's or Nikita's; and to my daughter Kiera, most precious, for all that she is.

Most of all, I am grateful to the twelve women featured in this book who, for no gain or glory, generously spared their time and shared their stories.